How Stereotypes Deceive Us

Mr. Alex Grant
Oct 2021

How Stereotypes Deceive Us

KATHERINE PUDDIFOOT

UNIVERSITY PRESS

OXFORD
UNIVERSITY PRESS

Great Clarendon Street, Oxford, OX2 6DP,
United Kingdom

Oxford University Press is a department of the University of Oxford.
It furthers the University's objective of excellence in research, scholarship,
and education by publishing worldwide. Oxford is a registered trade mark of
Oxford University Press in the UK and in certain other countries

© Katherine Puddifoot 2021

The moral rights of the author have been asserted

First Edition published in 2021
Impression: 1

Published in the United States of America by Oxford University Press
198 Madison Avenue, New York, NY 10016, United States of America

British Library Cataloguing in Publication Data
Data available

Library of Congress Control Number: 2021942426

ISBN 978-0-19-284555-9

DOI: 10.1093/oso/9780192845559.001.0001

Printed and bound in the UK by
TJ Books Limited

Links to third party websites are provided by Oxford in good faith and
for information only. Oxford disclaims any responsibility for the materials
contained in any third party website referenced in this work.

For my family

Contents

Contents

Acknowledgements

The material in this book was written during my time as a research fellow on the European Research Council-funded Project PERFECT (Grant Agreement 616358) at the University of Birmingham, and after my appointment as Assistant Professor at Durham University. I benefitted greatly from research time afforded to me by both Project PERFECT and research leave funded by Durham University.

Some parts of this book are developed from previously published articles. Chapter 3 is a development of 'Stereotyping: A Multifactorial View', *Philosophical Topics*, 45, 1 (2017): 137–156, reprinted with permission from University of Arkansas Press; the early sections of Chapter 4 are a development of 'Dissolving the Epistemic/Ethical Dilemma over Implicit Bias', *Philosophical Explorations*, 20: sup1 (2017): 73–93, reprinted with permission from Taylor and Francis Group (https://www.tandfonline.com/); Chapter 5 includes sections from 'Stereotyping Patients', *Journal of Social Philosophy*, 50, 1 (2019): 69–90, reprinted with permission from John Wiley and Sons; and most of the material from Chapter 6 is found in 'Disclosure of Mental Health: Philosophical and Psychological Perspectives', *Philosophy, Psychology and Psychiatry*, 26, 4 (2019): 333–348, reprinted with permission from Johns Hopkins Press. I thank the editors and reviewers of, and others who kindly provided feedback on, these articles.

My interest in implicit bias and stereotyping as objects of philosophical study arose from attending workshops in Sheffield on implicit bias during my postgraduate study. Since then I have had many detailed discussions of the ideas in this book with fellow former Sheffield philosophy postgraduates and great friends, Katie Harrington, Jules Holroyd, Cristina Roedevin, and Clara Sandelind. I thank them for their input. I also thank my colleagues at the University of Birmingham for their help in developing the ideas in this book. Thanks especially go to Lisa Bortolotti, the principal investigator on Project PERFECT. The combination of philosophical rigour and respect that Lisa fostered in the project team provided ideal conditions for this work to be written. Thanks also to my colleagues in Durham who have been especially helpful in ensuring that I have had time for research in the trying times of 2020.

In the process of writing the material in this book I have had many fruitful discussions and received helpful feedback from a number of other people. I would like to thank them all, although I cannot mention them each by name here. Special thanks goes to Cian O'Donnell and Clara Sandelind for comments on late drafts of this manuscript. I would also like to thank Peter Momtchiloff at Oxford University Press and two anonymous reviewers of this book—the manuscript benefitted greatly from their input.

Finally, thanks go to my family. I have a brilliant, supportive mother, Mary McHugh, whose use of the phrase 'I am not as green as I am cabbage-looking' I would credit as providing some of the inspiration for this book. I have benefitted from the constant support of my siblings, John, Louisa, Clare, and Bobby, my nephew Tomas, my siblings' partners, and my partner's family, who have accepted me as one of their own for two decades now. I must thank my older child Max, who for the last four years has kept me firmly focused on completing my work tasks efficiently, so that I have plenty of time to spend with him. My younger child Jack has been born while I have been in the later stages of writing this book, and I thank him for being such a joy. But most of all thanks go to Will, for all his love and support. There is no doubt, I would not have written this book without him.

1

Introduction

1. What Are We Talking About?

Rona Jaffe's book *The Best of Everything* depicts the life of young women working in publishing in New York in the early 1950s. At one stage in the book, one of the main protagonists, Caroline Bender, meets a stranger at a party.

'Let me analyse you,' Paul Landis said, stirring the Martini briskly. 'Now, none of this is from Kippie, I'm getting it from looking at you. You went to either Radcliffe or Wellesley.'

'Radcliffe,' said Caroline. 'And there's a great difference.'

'All you Radcliffe girls say that. You live on the East Side between Fiftieth and Eightieth.'

'A safe guess,' Caroline said.

'Am I right?'

'Yes, but I happen to live far enough East so it's no longer chic. Only inexpensive.'

'You have a roommate.'

Somehow it annoyed her that he was categorizing her so neatly, even though he happened to be correct. It's as if he's not really looking at me, Caroline thought, but just at what he wants me to look like. 'Right again,' she said. 'Gregg Adams.'   (Jaffe 1958, 151)

In the 2004 Paul Haggis film *Crash* an off-duty junior police officer picks up a hitchhiker in Los Angeles at night. The hitchhiker is a young Black man. The hitchhiker comments on the country music to which the police officer is listening. The comments are favourable but the police officer takes them to be sarcastic. The hitchhiker says that he has been ice-skating and wanted to be a goalkeeper when he was younger, and the police officer scoffs. Then the hitchhiker notices that the police officer has a statue of St Christopher

How Stereotypes Deceive Us. Katherine Puddifoot, Oxford University Press. © Katherine Puddifoot 2021.
DOI: 10.1093/oso/9780192845559.003.0001

on his dashboard and begins laughing. The police officer believes that the hitchhiker is laughing at him. To prove that this is not the case, the hitchhiker reaches into his pocket to bring out the St Christopher statue that he too carries with him. The police officer reaches for his gun and fatally shoots the young Black man.

A report undertaken by the African American Policy Forum as a part of the #*Say Her Name* campaign, which brings awareness to the names and stories of Black women and girls who have been subjected to racist violence by the police, provides the following account of the death of Michelle Cusseaux, a 50-year-old Black woman who was killed by police in Phoenix, Arizona in the United States on 13 August 2014:

> Police shot Michelle Cusseaux to death in her home while they were attempting to take her to a mental health facility. Cusseaux refused to let the police in her home, prompting Officer Percy Dupra to break through the screen door to gain entry. Dupra encountered Cusseaux holding a hammer and shot her in the heart. Dupra claimed that although Cusseaux said nothing to threaten him 'she had that anger in her face like she was going to hit someone with that hammer'. Cusseaux's mother, Frances Garrett wondered, 'What did the police officer see when he pried open the door? A Black woman? A lesbian?' Cusseaux's mother further explained that Cusseaux was changing the lock on the door when the police arrived, and that was why she had the tools out.   (Crenshaw et al. 2015)

In September 2020 Alexandra Wilson, a Black barrister and author, who specializes in criminal and family law, made the national news in the United Kingdom when she provided an account on twitter of being mistaken for a defendant three times in a single day (see, e.g. BBC News, 'Black barrister mistaken for defendant three times gets apology'). As she entered the court building, a security guard asked for her name so that he could try to find it on a list of defendants. Then, as she entered the courtroom, a lawyer said she needed to wait outside and an usher would let her in (the usher was in fact next to her). Then the clerk of the court said very loudly that she should leave the courtroom and the usher would be out shortly, asking if she had representation.

At the launch of his bid to be president in June 2015, Donald Trump made the following claims about people who emigrate from Mexico to the United States of America:

When Mexico sends its people, they're not sending their best. They're not sending you. They're not sending you. They're sending people that have lots of problems, and they're bringing those problems with us. They're bringing drugs. They're bringing crime. They're rapists.

On the definitions of stereotypes and stereotyping adopted in this book, these incidents all involve stereotypes and/or stereotyping. Here are the definitions:

Stereotype: a social attitude that associates members of some social group more strongly than others with certain trait(s).

Stereotyping: the application of a social attitude that associates members of some social group more strongly than others with certain traits to an individual or individuals who are perceived as a member of the relevant social group, leading that individual or those individuals to be associated with the trait.

The social attitudes described here are psychological states: beliefs or implicit attitudes. When stereotyping occurs these psychological states lead individuals who are stereotyped to be associated with a certain trait or traits.

In each of the cases just described, people are associated with certain characteristics due to their perceived membership of a social group. Caroline in *The Best of Everything* is perceived as a young career girl, and assumptions are made about her lifestyle, and, in particular, her education, opinions and living arrangements. In *Crash*, the hitchhiker is viewed as a Black male, and associated with violence, so when he reaches into his pocket, it is judged that he is reaching for a weapon. Michelle Cusseaux is viewed as a Black woman, someone with mental health issues, and perhaps also as a lesbian, and is consequently associated with threat and aggression while she is standing in her own home holding a household tool. Alexandra Wilson is viewed as a Black woman and associated with criminality rather than with being a professional lawyer. Donald Trump associated Mexican immigrants to the United States with drugs, crime, and being rapists.

The application of a stereotype can lead an individual to be assumed to have certain traits (as Caroline is assumed to have attended one of two colleges and as Wilson is assumed to be a criminal and not to be a barrister) or for them to be more strongly associated with certain traits than other people but not assumed to possess the traits. For example, the police officer in

Crash presumably did not initially assume that the person he was letting into his car was carrying a gun and likely to use it. However, the Black man was associated in the mind of the police officer with violence, leading the action of reaching into the pocket to get out the statue to be misinterpreted as reaching for a gun.

Reflection on these definitions and examples reveals that stereotyping can come in many forms. Anyone who is perceived as a member of a social group can be stereotyped. If you are perceived as male or female; homosexual, heterosexual, or bi-sexual; trans or cis; a member of a particular race, religion or ethnicity; being a particular age; disabled or able-bodied; having a particular job, being unemployed or a stay-at-home mother, then you are likely to be stereotyped. And these are only some of the social groups that you could, and are likely to be, a member of. You will also have intersecting identities: for example, you might be Black and a woman, Asian, homosexual and a man, Catholic and a woman, or a student and disabled. Unless another person or other people are completely unaware of all of the social groups to which you belong, and they have no suspicions about which groups you might belong to, you could be stereotyped by them.

Stereotyping can also have a variety of consequences. Most obviously, stereotyping can affect the way that people are treated, whether it is good or bad, fair or unfair. The scale of the consequences can differ depending on the case. Caroline might have felt some discomfort and annoyance at being so easily categorized, but the stereotyping does not have any major impact on her life or the lives of others. In stark contrast, in the fictional example in *Crash* and the real-life example of Michelle Cusseaux (and many others) a person is killed. Alexandra Wilson described being upset by her experiences of being mistaken for a defendant in court. It is difficult to quantify the effect of Trump's public stereotyping of Mexican immigrants. However, there is good reason to think that it was significant. For instance, the Los Angeles County Commission on Human Relations Hate Crime Report, published on 28 September 2016, reported that after seven years of decrease in hate crimes, they rose in 2015. Hate crimes against Latinos in particular increased by 69 per cent in 2015 (the year that Trump made his speech). Meanwhile, in at least one specific case Trump's claims about Mexicans seem to have directly motivated a violent crime. Steve and Scott Leader assaulted a 58-year-old Mexican man, beating and urinating on him. They then explained their reason for acting in this way as, "Trump was right" (Vasquez 2015). If we take these perpetrators of the crime at their word then

Trump's stereotyping seems to have had a motivating role on their violent behaviour. The statistics on hate crime suggest that their case was far from unique. The consequences of stereotyping can therefore be small or large, circumscribed or wide-ranging.

2. Focus of the Project

For the purposes of this book, it is especially crucial to notice that stereotyping can lead to errors of judgement and false perceptions of individuals and groups, but it does not always have this negative effect. The police officer in *Crash* falsely perceives the Black man in his car as posing a threat of violence when he reached into his pocket. Police Officer Dupra, if taken at his word, falsely perceived the 5 foot 5 inch, 50-year-old Michelle Cusseaux as a threat because she was holding a hammer. Alexandra Wilson was misjudged to be a defendant. However, the annoyance that Caroline feels is not due to being misjudged, it is due to being too easily judged correctly. In applying his stereotype of a New York career woman to Caroline, Paul makes an accurate assessment about her educational history, living arrangements and opinions.

Why is this point crucial to the current discussion? My aim in this book is to illuminate the various ways that stereotyping makes people susceptible to making errors in their perception and judgement. In doing so, I aim to develop conceptual tools that can be used to distinguish cases where stereotyping leads us astray—leading to false perceptions and misjudgements—from cases where stereotyping helps us to make correct judgements. The core questions addressed by the book are the following: we tend to think that stereotyping leads us to misperceive and misjudge people, but when and how exactly does it do this, and how can we be sure for any individual act of stereotyping whether the stereotyping is leading us astray or helping us to make a correct judgement?

The project of this book is, then, to evaluate stereotyping along its *epistemic dimension*: how it impacts the ability to make correct judgements and accurately perceive individuals; how it can impede our ability to gain true beliefs, knowledge and understanding about individuals to whom stereotypes are applied. If we can better understand when and how stereotypes lead people to make errors, this provides us with conceptual tools that can be used to criticize acts of stereotyping when they are likely to lead to errors.

3. A Note on Methodology

This book is a philosophical project. It addresses philosophical questions about, for example, the nature of human psychology and society; about how we can come to know or fail to know about other human beings; and about how other human beings can come to know or fail to know about us. It assesses existing epistemological frameworks (accounts of the nature of rationality and what it is to have justified belief) provided within the philosophical literature, considering how well they apply to cases in which people believe stereotypes. It develops a new framework that can be used to evaluate beliefs which captures the many flaws present when people believe stereotypes.

It is important to recognize, however, that many of the questions addressed in this book are empirical questions as well as philosophical ones. We will consider, for example, how human psychology operates to produce distorted judgements about individuals. We will consider how human society contributes to the biases found in human psychology. We will consider empirical findings showing how implicit forms of stereotyping influence healthcare professionals in their clinical judgement and decision-making. We will consider accounts developed within empirical cognitive psychology of how people tend to attribute other people with mental states, with the aim of establishing how stereotypes can impede this process, leading to misperceptions of people with mental health conditions.

Due to the empirical nature of these and other questions addressed in this work, the book is interdisciplinary in spirit, drawing on work from a diversity of fields, including social and cognitive psychology, sociology, and criminology. As the focus of this project is on how stereotypes, once they are believed, can lead us to make errors in our judgements and perceptions of others, psychological research is especially prominent in the discussion. Because of the vast variety of existing empirical work on stereotyping, the book necessarily omits discussion of many highly interesting and important works. Moreover, as the approach in this book is heavily influenced by psychological research using quantitative methods, some important contributions to the understanding of stereotyping that could be made from studies using qualitative methods or other methods of gathering testimony of lived experience of stereotyping are omitted (although qualitative studies are discussed in Chapters 5 and 6). However, in writing this book I intend to make a good start at highlighting how relevant literature from various disciplines speaks to philosophical questions about the epistemic standing of beliefs that reflect stereotypes. My hope is that the current book provides the foundation for future research, which will shed further light on how other empirical research, including qualitative research and research that has yet to be conducted,[1] can and should impact our understanding of the epistemic standing of stereotypes.

4. Goals of the Project

The goals of the current project are not modest, however. The current project highlights serious issues faced by (1) people who might engage in stereotyping but wish to avoid making errors, and (2) people who want to avoid being misperceived by others due to being members of a group or groups that are commonly stereotyped.

The book aims to tear apart existing preconceptions about stereotyping, such as the view that stereotyping will only increase and never decrease the chance of true beliefs being formed if the stereotype that is applied reflects social reality. By the end of this book the reader should have a better understanding of the various factors that determine whether an act of stereotyping increases or decreases the chance of an accurate judgement being made. The reader should also have a new set of conceptual tools that they can use to challenge acts of stereotyping. Meanwhile, this book challenges the assumption so often made in philosophy that false or inaccurate cognitions have no epistemic value by showing that social beliefs that are inaccurate but egalitarian can bring epistemic value because harbouring such beliefs can involve avoiding stereotyping and attendant errors.

By primarily focusing on the epistemic dimension of stereotyping this book distinguishes itself from work that primarily focuses on the ethical dimensions of stereotyping. I do not endorse recent arguments to the effect that moral considerations determine whether or not it is epistemically permissible to engage in stereotyping (cf. Basu 2019a, 2019b, 2020; Basu and Schroeder 2018; Bolinger 2020; Moss 2018a, 2018b) (see Chapters 4 and 5 for discussion). I maintain that questions about the epistemic standing of stereotypes and stereotyping can be answered without consideration of the

---

[1] For instance, empirical research on how stereotypes relating to different aspects of a person's social identity can interact to influence how the person is perceived is in its infancy. I discuss some of this research in Chapter 3 but I believe that as research on this topic develops there will be significantly more to be said.

morality of stereotyping. However, as we shall see in Chapter 4, there are various ways that my epistemology of stereotyping is relevant to existing accounts in the ethics of stereotyping. This book can therefore be understood as presenting a challenge to some, and suggesting modifications to other, existing accounts of the ethics of stereotyping.

In addition to this, the book shows how existing epistemological theories are inadequate when it comes to the goal of capturing the flaws found in a significant subset of our beliefs—those involving stereotyping. It then proposes a new way to evaluate beliefs that avoids this problem.

The next section provides a detailed overview of how each of these goals will be achieved.

5. Overview of the Book

Chapter 2 begins by introducing in more detail and defending the conception of stereotypes and stereotyping that is adopted throughout this book. Accounts of the nature of stereotypes and stereotyping can be divided into two types: *normative* and *non-normative* accounts of stereotyping. Normative accounts of stereotyping have at least one of the following features: they define stereotypes as inaccurate or they maintain that stereotyping always leads to distorted judgements about individuals. Defenders of non-normative accounts accept that stereotypes can be accurate or inaccurate and that they can distort judgements or increase the accuracy of the judgements that a person makes. Chapter 2 defends the adoption of the non-normative conception of stereotyping. It assesses a number of arguments previously presented for and against the non-normative conception before providing a pragmatic argument for adopting it. The conception of stereotypes adopted in this book also implies that stereotypes can be social attitudes other than beliefs, including implicit biases. Chapter 2 explains and defends this choice.

Chapter 3 begins the project of identifying the factors that determine whether a specific act of stereotyping increases or decreases the chance of an accurate judgement being made. It outlines and defends the *multifactorial view of stereotyping*, according to which there are multiple factors that determine whether any application of a stereotype will lead to the misperception or misjudgement of the individual to whom the stereotype is applied. The multifactorial view is developed in contrast to two positions that are articulated in discussions of stereotyping: the *single factor view* and the *dual factor view*. On the single factor view, only stereotypes that fail to reflect social reality tend to lead to misperceptions, and if a stereotype reflects reality its application will facilitate correct judgements. On the dual factor view, the accuracy of the stereotype and the quality of the information about the specific individual that might be stereotyped jointly determine whether the application of a stereotype improves or decreases the chance of a correct judgement being made. In Chapter 3 it is shown that there are factors other than those identified in these two views that determine whether the application of a stereotype leads to misperception of an individual. The chapter therefore provides a more thorough account of the conditions that are associated with stereotyping errors than is found in existing discussions. It outlines a set of questions that can be asked of any act of stereotyping to establish if it increases or decreases the chance of an accurate judgement being made about an individual or specific case. Finally, it provides a way to respond to a common defence of stereotyping: that as long as a stereotype reflects reality there is epistemic value in applying it. The argument in this chapter therefore provides conceptual tools that can be used to critique acts of stereotyping.

Chapter 4 sets out in some detail a challenge to the intuitive view that having thoughts that reflect reality always increases one's chance of achieving epistemic goals like knowledge and understanding. It is shown that some social attitudes or stereotypes reflect reality but nonetheless bring substantial epistemic costs. Then it is shown that having attitudes that fail to reflect these realities would avoid the epistemic costs. The notion of epistemic innocence is introduced to capture this phenomenon. An epistemically innocent cognition is one that has epistemic flaws but nonetheless brings significant epistemic benefits. It is argued that the epistemic benefits of the target social attitudes that fail to reflect reality can outweigh the epistemic costs, so there are contexts in which it is best from an epistemic perspective to have social attitudes that fail to reflect social realities. These claims are taken to provide a case for base-rate neglect in the social domain. That is, the arguments show that there can be distinct epistemic benefits associated with making judgements that do not reflect base-rate or background statistical information. Finally, it is shown that the observation that stereotypes that reflect social realities can be epistemically costly has implications for three accounts relating to the ethics as well as the epistemology of stereotyping: Lawrence Blum's (2004) moral analysis of stereotyping; Miranda Fricker's (2007) analysis of epistemic injustice; and the moral encroachment view (Basu 2019a, 2019b, 2020; Basu and Schroeder 2018; Bolinger 2020; Moss 2018a, 2018b).

Chapter 5 focuses on an idea that has gained traction in recent work on implicit stereotyping: that people face a dilemma when it comes to stereotypes that reflect something of social reality, such as the stereotype associating certain crimes more strongly with Black people than White people in the United States. The putative dilemma is the following: where stereotypes reflect social reality, people can either do what is best from an epistemic perspective, and allow the stereotypes to influence their judgements, or they can do what is best from an ethical perspective and avoid stereotyping. In Chapter 5 the multifactorial view is put to work to show that while we can face a dilemma of this type—epistemic and ethical demands can conflict— we also face an even more serious practical difficulty: discerning how to achieve either or both of our ethical and epistemic goals within a particular context. I begin by showing that we can often achieve both our epistemic and ethical goals in the same way. It is shown that sometimes stereotyping can lead to poor judgement and decision-making (producing epistemic costs), but at other times it can facilitate correct judgements and well-informed decision-making (bringing epistemic benefits). Meanwhile stereotyping sometimes brings substantial ethical costs—leading to unfair and unjust discrepant treatment, but at other times it increases the chance of fair and just treatment by improving the quality of judgement and decision-making. I show that although sometimes the epistemic and ethical goals are in conflict, at other times they converge, that is, sometimes stereotyping is best and at other times it is worse, from both an epistemic and ethical perspective. Then I show how this means that rather than facing a straightforward conflict between their epistemic and ethical goals, which we could solve by determining which of the goals to prioritize, people often face the serious practical difficulty of establishing whether, in a specific context, either or both their ethical and epistemic goals are more likely to be achieved by stereotyping or avoiding stereotyping. The points made in this chapter are applicable to stereotyping in various social domains but are illustrated primarily by considering the situation faced by healthcare professionals.

Chapter 6 switches perspective to focus on a dilemma that is faced not by those who might engage in stereotyping but instead by those who are susceptible to being stereotyped due to some aspect of their social identity that they might choose to hide. As in Chapter 5, a general point is made by focusing on a specific case study: the situation faced by people with mental health conditions who must choose whether to disclose information about their condition. In Chapter 6 we see how the multifactorial view of stereotyping vindicates the fear experienced by people with mental health conditions that they will be misperceived if they disclose information about their condition. However, we also see that people with mental health conditions face being misperceived if they do not disclose the same information. This is because, in some contexts, for a perceiver to properly understand what another person with a mental health condition is thinking, how they are disposed to behave, and any specific needs they might be displaying, it will be necessary for the perceiver to be aware of and factor in the perceived person's mental health condition. In developing this argument, various accounts of how mental states are ascribed are appealed to. It is argued that each of various dominant accounts currently endorsed in philosophy and psychology suggest that it will be necessary to factor in a person's mental health condition to properly ascribe mental states to them. It is also shown, however, that the argument generalizes beyond the case of people with mental health conditions. It is shown that wherever a person's mental states or other features of their personal situation will only properly be understood if information about their social identity is known, they can face a serious dilemma. This chapter contains a discussion of strategies or interventions that can be used to tackle the problems associated with stereotyping.

Next the book begins the project of developing a theoretical framework to apply to acts of stereotyping. Chapter 7 is largely critical. It shows that the theories that dominate contemporary analytic philosophy which attempt to provide an account of what it is to be rational or justified each fail to capture some of the epistemic faults present when people believe stereotypes. Existing theories are divided into three distinct types: upstream, downstream, and static accounts. Each of these types of account is found to capture some but not all epistemic faults associated with acts of believing stereotypes. Therefore, it is argued, none of the accounts on its own provides an adequate framework through which to evaluate acts of stereotyping. On the contrary, a pluralistic approach, integrating insights from each of the approaches, is defended.

Chapter 8 engages in the positive project of proposing an evaluative framework that, if applied to acts of believing stereotypes, would capture all of the faults associated with these acts. The framework is labelled *evaluative dispositionalism*. According to evaluative dispositionalism, those evaluating acts of stereotyping ought to focus on the dispositions that are associated with believing the target stereotype. They should consider whether a believer has displayed poor dispositions in coming to believe a stereotype, and whether, as a result of believing the stereotype, the believer is disposed to respond poorly to evidence that they encounter. Evaluative dispositionalism builds on recent discussions of dispositions in epistemology, some focusing on the importance of dispositions that are manifest in believing while others focus on the importance of dispositions that are possessed due to believing. The position defended here argues that both of these sets of dispositions should be considered when evaluating acts of believing stereotypes.

Evaluative dispositionalism is shown to have numerous advantages. It is pluralistic in the way emphasized to be important in Chapter 7, but also simple and unifying. The approach provides clear prescriptions about how to approach acts of believing stereotypes: check the dispositions associated with so believing. It allows us to distinguish satisfactorily between different acts of stereotyping, explaining, for example, how two people can believe the same stereotype, under the same circumstances, while deserving different levels of praise and criticism (clue: they can have different dispositions associated with believing the stereotype). It provides a framework through which to understand various epistemic wrongs and it provides a way to distinguish some stereotypes that are morally objectionable from others that are not. Most importantly for current purposes, the approach succeeds where other epistemological views fail: capturing the multiple ways that stereotypes deceive us.

2

Defining Stereotypes and Stereotyping

1. Introduction

Throughout this book stereotypes and stereotyping are going to be discussed. This chapter presents and defends the definition of stereotypes and stereotyping that are adopted here. The definitions are non-normative and allow that social attitudes other than beliefs, including implicit biases, can count as stereotypes.

2. Normative versus Non-Normative Accounts

Let us return, then, to the definitions of stereotypes and stereotyping that are adopted in this book. In Chapter 1 I introduced the target definitions of stereotypes and stereotyping. The following are the definitions:

> Stereotype: a social attitude that associates members of some social group more strongly than others with certain trait(s).

> Stereotyping: the application of a social attitude that associates members of some social group more strongly than others with certain traits to an individual or individuals who are perceived as a member of the relevant social group, leading that individual or those individuals to be associated with the trait.[1]

---

[1] Note here that on these definitions stereotypes apply specifically to social groups. My focus is on social stereotypes of this type rather than psychological states encoding generalizations about inanimate objects, locations or animals. Many of the claims made in this book about how stereotypes operate will apply to inanimate objects, locations and animals. However, I limit my definition to social stereotypes about social groups because these stereotypes operate in some distinctive ways, particularly with regards to how they deceive us. Therefore, when I make general claims about how stereotypes deceive us they are meant to apply to social stereotypes about humans but not stereotypes about to inanimate objects, locations or animals.

How Stereotypes Deceive Us. Katherine Puddifoot, Oxford University Press. © Katherine Puddifoot 2021.
DOI: 10.1093/oso/9780192845559.003.0002

The stereotypes considered in this book are psychological states: beliefs or implicit attitudes. When stereotyping occurs these psychological states lead individuals who are stereotyped to be associated with a certain trait or traits.

On these definitions, stereotypes are not always inaccurate, and stereotyping does not always have a distorting effect on judgements. The account adopted here can therefore be labelled *a non-normative conception of stereotyping*. The view differs significantly from other, *normative conceptions of stereotyping* (for other, non-normative definitions of stereotyping see Beeghly 2015; Fricker 2007; Jussim 2012; Kahneman 2011). On normative accounts, stereotypes are defined as inaccurate, distorting, or both accurate and distorting influences on cognition.

Early defenders of the normative account were Walter Lippman and Gordon Allport. Introducing the term 'stereotype' into discussions of human social behaviour, Lippmann's *Public Opinion* argued that stereotypes are cognitive structures that shape our perceptions of the world, making the vast array of information that we encounter manageable by enabling us to categorize it (*Public Opinion*, chapter 6).[2] For example, on meeting a particular career woman for the first time, if the stereotype of a career woman is triggered, this allows the person to be categorized according to their gender and occupation, and their personal characteristics to be understood along the same lines as others of the same category. However, Lippmann also argued that stereotypes serve to defend the social position of the person who is stereotyping (*Public Opinion*, chapter 7).

> A pattern of stereotypes is not neutral. It is not merely a way of substituting order for the great blooming, buzzing confusion of reality. It is not merely a short cut. It is all these things and something more. It is the guarantee of our self-respect; it is the projection upon the world of our own sense of our own value, our own position and our own rights. The stereotypes are, therefore, highly charged with the feelings that are attached to them. They are the fortress of our tradition, and behind its defenses we can continue to feel ourselves safe in the position we occupy.
>
> (Lippmann 1922, p. 96)

---

[2] 'Were there no practical uniformities in the environment, there would be no economy and only error in the human habit of accepting foresight for sight. But there are uniformities sufficiently accurate, and the need of economizing attention is so inevitable, that the abandonment of all stereotypes for a wholly innocent approach to experience would impoverish human life' (Lippman, 1922, p. 90).

Stereotypes serve to rationalize the position of the person engaging in stereotyping; for example, their superior social position over others. For example, if career women are viewed as having predictable educational backgrounds, opinions and lifestyle choices then they can be treated as unoriginal, lacking the unique and distinctive features that might warrant a position superior to that which they currently occupy. The subordinate position of women within a profession could be rationalized by their lack of the characteristics required to be a leader or innovator. As stereotypes have this rationalizing role, the interests of those stereotyping determine the nature of the stereotype and stereotyping judgement. The perception of individuals and groups that are stereotyped is distorted to fit these interests.[3]

In another classic study of stereotypes and stereotyping, *The Nature of Prejudice*, Gordon W. Allport also defended the normative view of stereotyping. According to Allport's view, stereotypes are inaccurate because they are oversimplified and rigid. Rigidity can be defined in terms of persistence over time (Gilbert 1951; Karlins, Coffman, and Walters 1969; Katz and Braly 1933), or persistence in the face of changes to the groups the stereotypes relate to (Fishman 1956). In each case, rigidity can be a source of inaccuracy as long as stereotypes are not responsive to evidence suggesting that they are inaccurate. Sandford, Adorno, Frenkel-Brunswick and Levinson adopted a similar position in *The Authoritarian Personality*. They argued that there is a specific personality type that leads people to see the world in rigid ways, fitting with black-and-white categories or stereotypes.

There was therefore agreement among many of the leading theorists of stereotyping in the early and mid-twentieth century that stereotypes are bad in the sense that they are inaccurate and distort people's perceptions of other people. In a more recent discussion, Lawrence Blum (2004, 2016) agrees. Blum's (2004) goal is to establish what is morally wrong about stereotyping (see Chapter 4, Section 10) but in the process he endorses the normative view of stereotyping. He argues that stereotypes are 'cognitive distortions' that 'lead to various forms of moral distortion' (Blum 2004, p. 251). He acknowledges that there can be generalizations about social groups that are not stereotypes—leaving open the possibility that there can be generalizations about social groups that are accurate rather than inaccurate—but insists that stereotypes are false and misleading and problematically rigid, failing to update in response to counterevidence (Blum 2004, 2016). Blum (2004)

---

[3] See Beeghly 2015 for an alternative interpretation of Lippman's work as an example of a non-normative account of stereotypes and stereotyping.

takes the normative view of stereotyping to capture the natural usage of the terms 'stereotype' and 'stereotyping', claiming that when someone is said to be stereotyping there is an accompanying implication that they are making an error.

On this normative conception of stereotyping, Paul Landis's assessment of Caroline Bender in *The Best of Everything* (see Chapter 1) would not count as a case of stereotyping as long as the stereotype that Paul applies in judging Caroline is not inaccurate or misleading. His stereotype of New York career girls in the 1950s is arguably accurate, and it leads to correct judgements about Caroline's education and living situation. If these things are correct, on a normative account of stereotyping, there is a strong case for saying that he does not engage in stereotyping.

On such an account, it does not make sense to ask the question: *under what conditions does stereotyping lead to misjudgement and misperception?* Stereotyping would simply be the application of stereotypes that are misleading. Instead, the correct question to ask would be *under what conditions do people engage in stereotyping rather than making accurate associations between traits and social groups, and applying these associations to individuals?* As there are competing characterizations of stereotypes and stereotyping, which have such important implications for how the current project should be framed, it is necessary to provide a justification of the definitions that are adopted. Section 3 provides this justification.

It is worth noting, however, that if the arguments of the current book were framed in a way that is consistent with the normative approach, they would still be important and interesting. I identify the conditions under which the application of a social attitude associating members of a social group with some trait leads to errors so, on a normative approach, I could be viewed as identifying the conditions under which the application of the social attitude amounts to stereotyping.

3. Why the Non-Normative Account of Stereotyping?

Why, then, do I adopt the neutral, i.e. non-normative, account of stereotyping, according to which stereotypes can be accurate or inaccurate, misleading or not? There are bad, better and genuinely good reasons for adopting this position. This section distinguishes between them and outlines my own reasons for adopting the position.

3.1 Bad Argument 1: Look at all the Accurate Stereotypes!

One strategy that can be used to argue for the non-normative approach to stereotypes and stereotyping is to critique the alternative, normative approach. Lee Jussim has adopted this approach in his *Social Perception and Social Reality: Why Accuracy Dominates Bias and Self-Fulfilling Prophecy.* Jussim argues that it is wrong to claim that stereotypes are inaccurate because (1) stereotypes are beliefs about social groups, (2) there are many accurate beliefs about social groups, therefore (3) there are accurate stereotypes. For instance, if you believe that men are more likely than women to commit homicide then you have an accurate stereotype (Jussim 2012). Or if you believe that a higher proportion of African Americans than Whites voted for Democrats in the 2000 and 2004 US elections then you have an accurate stereotype (Jussim 2012). Given that there are all these accurate stereotypes, it is wrong to claim that stereotypes are inaccurate.

The problem with this argument is that it begs the question against the defender of the normative view. They could reply that the beliefs that Jussim identifies, which are accurate social beliefs, are not stereotypes because stereotypes are, by definition, inaccurate.

3.2 Bad Argument 2: Logical Incoherence

A further argument presented by Jussim (2012) states that the normative approach is logically incoherent. It would imply that, for any belief about two groups, both:

1. The belief that the two groups differ is inaccurate,
and
2. The belief that the two groups do *not* differ is inaccurate.

Take any two groups in a society, say 13-year-old boys and 13-year-old girls. You might believe that *13-year-old boys and 13-year-old girls are the same in respect R* (say, their propensity for mood swings). Or you might believe that *13-year-old boys and 13-year-old girls are not the same in respect R*. Jussim suggests that the normative conception of stereotypes and stereotyping implies that both of these beliefs are inaccurate. They are both social beliefs, so if all social beliefs are inaccurate, then they would both be inaccurate. However, Jussim argues, it cannot be the case that the belief that two specific groups are the same in respect R is inaccurate at the same time that the belief that the same two groups are not the same in respect R is inaccurate. The groups must either be the same with respect to R or not.

The charge of logical incoherence is a serious one. However, it is clear that the charge, as levelled against defenders of the normative conception of stereotypes and stereotyping, does not succeed as long as advocates of the normative view accept that some beliefs about social groups are accurate. They can maintain that some social beliefs, like those identified by Jussim (2012), relating to the similarities or differences between social groups, are true. One can accurately believe that the two groups are or are not the same. This accurate belief would belong in the subset of social beliefs that are accurate, and therefore not stereotypes, while other social beliefs are inaccurate, and are stereotypes.

3.3 Bad Argument 3: A Challenge to Multiculturalism?

Jussim (2012) believes that a further problem with the normative view is that it is inconsistent with some of the goals of those who promote multiculturalism. He defines multiculturalism as 'understanding and respecting the beliefs, values, and practices of people from different groups and backgrounds than oneself' (p. 288). Those who argue that multiculturalism is valuable assume that there are distinctive features of members of different ethnic groups to be understood and that it is possible to understand these features. The promotion of multiculturalism therefore implies that there are correct social beliefs that can be obtained, increasing understanding between different social groups. If there were no correct social beliefs, then this putative benefit of multiculturalism would disappear. Some defenders of the normative view of stereotyping might bite the bullet and accept that multiculturalism does not bring the benefit of increased understanding of other ethnic groups. But this is a bullet many would be unwilling to bite.

Must the defender of the normative view therefore bite this unpalatable bullet or dispose of their commitment to stereotype inaccuracy? There is another option: accept that some social beliefs are accurate, that it is possible to have accurate beliefs about other ethnic groups, and that multiculturalism promotes this, but maintain that these accurate beliefs are not stereotypes. Instead, the accurate beliefs promoted by multiculturalism belong in a subset of social beliefs: those that are accurate and therefore not, on the normative account of stereotypes and stereotyping, stereotypes.

The arguments so far are bad arguments against the normative view of stereotyping, and therefore cannot be used to bolster the case for the non-normative view of stereotyping. It is easy for the defender of the normative view to respond to each of the arguments by accepting that some social beliefs are accurate and that stereotypes are a subset of social beliefs, all of which are inaccurate. However, Jussim (2012) provides some better arguments against the normative view. Let us now consider these.

3.4 Better Argument 1: Difficulty Establishing Stereotype-Status

Taking Allport (1954) as representative of his target, Jussim (2012) argues that those who defend the normative view set the standards for identifying stereotypes too high. In order to be in a position to describe someone as stereotyping, on the Allport-style view, it would be necessary to have reason to believe that the social belief that they display is inaccurate. As it is often difficult to establish the accuracy or otherwise of a social belief, it would often be difficult to establish that a person is stereotyping.

For Jussim (2012), there are important implications of the difficulty of identifying stereotypes for research in social psychology on stereotyping. He claims that for any piece of stereotyping research to be accepted as such on the Allport-style view, the researchers would have to begin by establishing that the beliefs were inaccurate. If it turns out that the beliefs are accurate then the research is not stereotyping research because stereotypes are not the object of evaluation. This means that many studies that are currently treated as examples of stereotype research should not count as such.

From the perspective of a social psychologist these concerns might be extremely pressing. However, from the perspective of a neutral party, there seems to be little reason to define stereotypes in a certain way in order to ensure that what is currently labelled stereotype research can continue to be properly labelled in this way. But even if the definition of stereotyping were to be decided on the basis of the retaining the status quo within social psychology research, it is consistent with defining stereotypes as inaccurate that current research could continue to be labelled as stereotyping research even if the authors did not establish the inaccuracy of the object of their study. Stereotyping research could simply be research that aims to establish whether a set of social attitudes should count as stereotypes, for example, asking the question: should the beliefs found within population P about gender differences in attainment in mathematics be considered to be stereotypes?

It seems clear, then, that Jussim's specific claims about social psychology provide little reason for rejecting the normative definition of stereotypes and stereotyping. However, there is a serious concern in the ballpark, which can be understood by taking a step back from his discussion of social psychology and considering the situation faced by ordinary people in their everyday interactions.

It is commonplace to hear or read something and to identify it as an act of stereotyping. For instance, there is little reason to doubt that many people responded to Donald Trump's comments about Mexican immigrants (see Chapter 1) by thinking *Trump is stereotyping*. Ordinary people seem to be able to make this type of identification judgement, correctly judging that what they hear or read is stereotyping, without first being required to establish that what they hear or read is inaccurate or distorting.

Let us consider this point further. It does seem right that people are and should be able to criticize Trump on the basis that he is stereotyping without, for example, having to bring out statistics about rates of involvement in drug crime and rape to establish the inaccuracy of his claims.[4] However, it could reasonably be argued that the example of Trump's claim about Mexican immigrants in fact provides support for the normative conception of stereotyping. The accusation that Trump is stereotyping has normative force, implying that his claims about Mexican immigrants are inaccurate and likely to lead to distorted judgements about individuals (Blum 2004). It therefore might seem fitting to the defender of the normative conception of stereotyping, in light of this example, that the terms 'stereotypes' and 'stereotyping' should be reserved for inaccurate social attitudes, or those that lead to distorted judgements about individuals. It could be argued that *if* people imply that others are doing something wrong when they identify them as stereotyping, it is appropriate rather than overly demanding to expect people to have reason to believe that a social attitude is inaccurate or distorting before they identify it as a stereotype.

There is some intuitive pull, then, to the idea that it is overly demanding to expect a person to know that a social attitude is inaccurate or distorting before they identify it as a stereotype. However, the claim that a person is

---

[4] In Chapter 3 we can see how this can be done.

stereotyping often seems to imply that the person labelled as stereotyping is applying a social attitude that is inaccurate or distorting (Blum 2004). Therefore, there is also reason to think that it is reasonable to expect a person to know that a social attitude is inaccurate or distorting before labelling the attitude a stereotype.

3.5 Why We Should Adopt a Non-Normative Approach: A Pragmatic Position

So far we are yet to discover a decisive argument against the normative approach to stereotypes and stereotyping. I will now proceed to outline two positive arguments for the alternative, non-normative approach that justify my adoption of the approach in this book. The arguments originate in the work of Ashmore and Del Boca (1981, see also Jussim 2012). Ashmore and Del Boca adopt an extremely broad definition of stereotypes according to which a stereotype is 'A set of beliefs about the personal attributes of a group of people' (p. 16). The definition does not stipulate that stereotypes are inaccurate or distorting. Ashmore and Del Boca's reasons are pragmatic.

First, they argue that the act of defining stereotypes as inaccurate leads them to be treated as 'deviant, bizarre and pathological' (Ashmore and Del Boca 1981, p. 16). Research on stereotyping is thereby isolated from research on cognitive structures that are not deviant, bizarre or pathological—i.e. the cognitive structures responsible for the ordinary perception of individuals and groups. But it cannot justifiably be assumed that these cognitive structures are distinct. As Ashmore and Del Boca put the point, 'There may well be something "special" or "different" about beliefs regarding social groups; however, this is best regarded as an empirical not a conceptual issue' (1981, p. 17). It is possible that important lessons can be learnt about the nature and operation of stereotypes through research on non-deviant cognitive structures. Second, Ashmore and Del Boca argue that by defining stereotypes as bad, researchers assume rather than study the way that stereotypes operate to distort perception and judgements.

For these pragmatic reasons, the non-normative account of stereotyping is adopted for the sake of the current project. My aim is to illuminate the various ways that stereotyping makes people susceptible to making errors in their perception and judgement. I do not assume that stereotypes are inaccurate and distorting but study the conditions under which they can be (see Beeghly 2015 for a similar view).

I draw on a wide-ranging literature to identify the conditions under which stereotyping leads to errors. This literature includes the psychological, sociological, and philosophical literature on how perception and judgement can be positively and negatively influenced by associations that are made with individuals due to their perceived social group membership. As a result it will not be stipulated from the start that the focus of discussion is on inaccurate cognitions, or those that lead to distortion. Instead I leave open the possibility that there is a significant continuity between accurate and inaccurate, and distorting and non-distorting cognitions, that they might belong to the same psychological class, and that they might have many of the same ways of operating. I will be guided by the empirical research when identifying continuities and discontinuities between the inaccurate and accurate, and distorting and non-distorting social attitudes that are discussed.

It might be objected that this pragmatic approach presents too much of a deviation from everyday conceptions of stereotyping, and that philosophical investigations should be guided by everyday conceptions rather than pragmatic considerations. It might be argued that the ordinary everyday conception of stereotypes is that they are inaccurate and distorting, and this everyday conception should guide my philosophical inquiry. There is one serious problem with this objection. There does not seem to be a single, unambiguous everyday conception to use for guidance. As we have found in the discussion of Trump's stereotyping in Section 3.4 of this chapter, the claim that a person is stereotyping often has an accusatory tone, implying that they have done something wrong. However, we have already also seen that it is intuitive that a person can identify a social attitude as a stereotype prior to knowing if it is inaccurate. In addition to this, it is not uncommon to hear people saying things like 'humans need to stereotype to understand the world', and 'stereotyping is only a problem if the stereotype that is applied is inaccurate'. These statements suggest that people do not consistently think that stereotyping is always bad from the perspective of understanding the world. Sometimes ordinary people are quite willing to accept that something can be a stereotype without being inaccurate and distorting. Appeal to common usage does not therefore justify the adoption of the normative view of stereotyping and the rejection of the proposed non-normative view.

As the everyday conception of stereotyping is ambiguous, I am allowing myself to be guided by pragmatic considerations in selecting the non-normative approach to stereotyping.

4. The 'Concept' Conception of Stereotypes

Erin Beeghly (2015) also endorses a non-normative account of stereotypes: the *concept conception of stereotypes*. Beeghly's primary aim, like Blum's, is to identify the moral wrongs of stereotypes and stereotyping. Her explicit aim is to remain neutral with respect to the psychological underpinnings of stereotypes and stereotyping, as she claims when discussing competing psychological accounts of stereotypes and stereotyping that 'Though it seems that we may have to choose from among these views, for the purposes of most ethical and political theory, we actually don't' (p. 680). However, she does endorse the claim that stereotypes are concepts or the psychological items required for the formation and use of concepts:

> The view at which I have arrived is this: stereotypes play a special role in categorizing individuals and forming expectations about them. We can think of them either as concepts of social groups or as psychological items necessary for the formation and use of such concepts.
>
> (Beeghly 2015, p. 680)

I am in broad agreement with Beeghly in endorsing a minimal, non-normative conception of stereotypes. However, rather than defining stereotypes as concepts or the psychological items required for their formation and use, I define stereotypes as *social attitudes* that associate members of some social group *more strongly than others* with a certain trait or traits. This section outlines two reasons for this difference.

First, I believe that the definition of stereotypes needs to be narrower and more specific than *social concepts or their prerequisites* to capture how stereotypes differentiate between social groups. It seems to be central to both the everyday conception and the function of stereotypes that they involve differentiating between social groups: saying of some specific social group or groups that members of those groups possess traits that others do not, or that group members possess traits at a higher or lower rate than others. Here I agree with Lawrence Blum (2004, p. 247) who claims that stereotypes identify characteristics distinctive to specific social groups. The definition of stereotypes as social concepts or their prerequisites does not capture this feature. A person might have a minimal social concept of a particular social group x that associates all members of the social group with being people, e.g. *Christians are people*. They might possess a similar concept for each and every social group of which they are aware, i.e. a minimal concept that associates members of the social group with being people. These concepts would be social concepts, but they do not fit the everyday conception nor perform one of the main functional roles, perhaps the primary functional role, of stereotypes: to differentiate between social groups. In contrast, by building into my definition of stereotypes that they associate members of some *more strongly than others* with certain traits, I ensure that my definition captures this functional role.

Second, I am not satisfied that Beeghly's definition is sufficiently neutral with regards to the psychological underpinnings of stereotypes, in spite of her attempt at neutrality. One of the main motivations for Beeghly adopting the 'concept' conception of stereotypes is that it seems to fit with a selection of psychological accounts of stereotypes. Beeghly points, for example, towards Susan Fiske and Shelley Taylor's (1991) *schema view of stereotypes*, according to which they are informational structures that contain information about a concept, including its attributes and the relations among its attributes. On a view of this type, a stereotype is either a concept or closely tied to a concept. However, there are many competing conceptions of the cognitive underpinnings of stereotypes, as we shall explore further in Section 2.9 of Chapter 4, and this leaves open the possibility that stereotypes and concepts have divergent psychological underpinnings.

Take, for example, the view that stereotypes are networks of associations, which link together attributes (Manis, Nelson, and Shedler 1988; Carlston 1992). Men might be linked to good leadership, for example, as a part of a larger web of associations. These associations can be strengthened or weakened through exposure to items either co-occurring or failing to co-occur (e.g. men perceived to demonstrate good or bad at leadership). Beeghly takes this account to be consistent with stereotypes being defined as social concepts or the prerequisites for their formation and use. And it *is* possible that social concepts tend to take the form of associative links. It is also possible that associative links are prerequisites for the formation and/ or use of social concepts. However, it is also possible that social concepts tend to take some other form, and that associative links are not prerequisites for their formation and use. Social concepts might tend to take the form of prototypes, that is, abstract representations of typical features of members of a group, as is suggested by other psychological accounts of concepts (Cantor and Mischel 1979), and these prototypes might not require associative links for their formation or to be applied. Under such conditions, stipulating that what underpins stereotypes are social concepts or what is required for the formation and use of social concepts would obscure the true nature of stereotypes, suggesting that they tend to have one set of characteristics (being prototypes or being the prerequisites for prototype formation and use) when they tend to have another (being associative links and not prerequisites for prototype formation and use). In the absence of strong arguments in favour of thinking that stereotypes and social concepts or their prerequisites have the same psychological underpinnings, more neutrality than is found in Beeghly's account is required when defining stereotypes.

Defining stereotypes as I do, as social attitudes that associate members of some social group *more strongly than others* with a certain trait or traits, captures the way that stereotypes differentiate between social groups—seemingly properly a defining feature of stereotypes—while remaining neutral on the psychological underpinnings of stereotypes, and thereby avoiding the risk of presenting a distorted picture of stereotypes and their relation to social concepts.

5. Implicit and Explicit Stereotypes

In the pragmatic view of stereotypes and stereotyping on which the current discussion is based, Ashmore and Del Boca (1981) define stereotypes as *beliefs* about the personal attributes of a group, which are accurate or inaccurate, but I define them even more neutrally as *social attitudes* that associate members of some social group more strongly than others with certain trait(s). By adopting this more inclusive definition of stereotypes, my account implies that social attitudes other than beliefs can count as stereotypes. It means that the claims made in this book about how stereotypes deceive us can be taken to apply to mental attitudes other than beliefs, including implicit attitudes. This section argues that this is the correct result by making the case that implicit attitudes should be counted as stereotypes even if they are not beliefs but are other forms of social attitude instead.

There is now broad consensus that stereotypes can operate through implicit attitudes, which are also known as implicit biases, as well as explicit attitudes. For example, implicit racial attitudes are thought to explain a large quantity of the racist thought and behaviour in societies in which it is generally socially unacceptable to engage in explicit stereotyping (Dovidio and Gaertner 2004). Within these societies, many people explicitly endorse egalitarian principles, but nonetheless respond differentially to individual members of different racial groups due to their racial group membership.

As one result of implicit racial attitudes, Black men have been found to be associated with crime (see, e.g. Correll et al. 2002) and negative affective responses (Greenwald, McGhee, and Schwartz 1998)—as individuals and as a social group as a whole. The differential responses are explained in terms of people automatically and unintentionally making associations between members of particular racial groups and characteristics or affective responses.

There are now a number of competing accounts of the nature of implicit bias. In the psychological literature, two definitions of implicit attitudes have dominated (Payne and Gawronski 2010; Brownstein 2019). One definition focuses on the automaticity of some prejudicial responses, defining implicit biases as automatic associations between concepts relating to social groups (e.g. Black, old, female) and other concepts (e.g. lazy, weak) or affective responses (e.g. aversion or attraction) (e.g. Amodio and Devine 2008). The other definition identifies implicit biases with influences on thought or action directed towards members of social groups in virtue of their social group membership that are not accessible via introspection (Greenwald and Banaji 1995).

But more important for current purposes is the fact that there is disagreement about whether implicit biases are beliefs, belief-like states, or features of human psychology that are significantly different to beliefs. Implicit biases have been argued to be unconscious beliefs (Mandelbaum 2016; cf. Madva 2016a); *in-between beliefs*, i.e. to have a limited number of the stereotypical features associated with beliefs (Schwitzgebel 2010); and *patchy endorsements*, i.e. to have propositional structure but be poorly inferentially integrated with a wide range of other attitudes of the agent (Levy 2015). On each of these views, implicit attitudes are beliefs or belief-like. But they have also been argued by various authors to be significantly different to a belief: *aliefs*, i.e. associative, automatic, affect-laden, arational, action-generating states that are shared with animals and conceptually antecedent to other mental states (Gendler 2008a, 2008b, 2011); traits that are not detected accurately (Machery 2016); 'causally related, or co-activated representational contents, or affective and behavioural responses' (Holroyd 2016, p. 175); and *unconscious imaginings* (Sullivan-Bissett 2018). Those who argue that implicit attitudes are not beliefs often appeal to their lack of propositional structure, claiming that beliefs have propositional structure but implicit attitudes are associative rather than propositional attitudes (e.g. Gendler 2011). However, this point has been disputed in response to recent psychological research suggesting that implicit attitudes are propositional because they are inferentially promiscuous and responsive to argumentation

(De Houwer 2014; Levy 2015; Mandelbaum 2013, 2016). The question of whether implicit attitudes are beliefs has therefore not been settled. This means that a definition of stereotypes that specified that they were beliefs could imply that implicit biases do not count as stereotypes, and when implicit biases influence thought and action the result is not stereotyping.

Nonetheless, there is very good reason for treating many occasions in which people are influenced by implicit biases in their thoughts and action as cases in which they are stereotyping. The natural response to someone who associates Black people with violence is that they are stereotyping. If they intend to make the association, are consciously aware that they are doing so, allowing the association to influence their thoughts and actions in a way that suggests that they would endorse the association, then they seem to be explicitly stereotyping. Meanwhile, if they automatically and unintentionally associate Black people with violence, perhaps they are not consciously aware of making the association and they do not wish the association to influence their thought and action, then they are implicitly stereotyping. An association can operate implicitly without it following that the association is not a stereotype.

This strength of the claim that we should not restrict the application of the term 'stereotype' to beliefs is especially clear if we focus on the features taken to show that implicit attitudes are not beliefs. Implicit biases have been argued to (1) have associative rather than propositional structure, (2) be less responsive to evidence than beliefs, and (3) be less inferentially promiscuous. There is dispute about whether implicit attitudes really have these features but what is important for current purposes is that even if they do have these features, taken to distinguish them from beliefs, they should nonetheless be counted as stereotypes.

Let us begin by considering the possibility that implicit attitudes are associative rather than having propositional structure. Imagine that a person comes to associate members of a social group (e.g. Black people) with some traits (e.g. violence) through the process of associative learning. They have the concepts *black person* and *dangerous* repeatedly co-activated. For instance, media depictions lead the person to have the concept *black person* triggered alongside the concept *dangerous*. The association that is formed is an extremely strong candidate for being a stereotype. Meanwhile, it would be the result of associative learning and therefore an associative social attitude. This suggests that stereotypes can be associative. In fact, associative learning provides an excellent vehicle through which social structures like the media can lead members of social groups to become associated with traits (see Chapter 3 for more on the media influence on stereotyping). On this basis it seems right to say that associative learning is one source of stereotyping even if it is not a source of belief.

How about the possibility that implicit attitudes are less responsive to evidence than explicit stereotyping beliefs? Would this mean that they should not be counted as stereotypes? It would not. Recall that one of the earliest definitions of stereotypes, provided by Allport, stipulated that they are rigid, where rigidity can involve persistence in the face of changes to the groups the stereotypes relate to. Under this conception of stereotypes, they are defined in terms of being unresponsive to evidence. We might not agree with this definition. For current purposes, we aim to study stereotypes to discover whether they are all rigid rather than stipulating from the start that, by definition, stereotypes are rigid. However, it is highly plausible that stereotypes can be highly resistant to evidence even if they are not defined as such. This suggests that implicit attitudes should not be denied the status of stereotypes due to their putative unresponsiveness to evidence.

What if implicit attitudes are less inferentially promiscuous than beliefs, that is, what if they are less capable of interacting in a way that is sensitive to content with numerous other representational states (see, e.g. Levy 2015)? This would not indicate that they were not stereotypes either. It is not difficult to imagine a person who is so firmly committed to the content of a stereotype that they would not change other mental representations that they possess, including other beliefs, which are inconsistent with the content of the stereotype. Imagine too that the possession of the stereotype does not lead to any changes in other mental representations that the person possesses. For example, a person thinks that Irish people are drunks. They are so firmly committed to this stereotype that they do not change their stance even if the content of their other beliefs is inconsistent with the belief (e.g. their commitment to egalitarian principles, their understanding that statistics suggests that Irish people consume alcohol at a similar level to people from other groups, etc.). But the stereotype does not influence any of their thoughts or actions, e.g. about individual Irish people. Do they possess a stereotype? It seems clear that they do. Is the stereotype inferentially promiscuous? It is not. This means that a person can possess a stereotype even if it does not interact with other mental representations due to sensitivity to their content. The extent to which a social attitude is inferentially promiscuous does not therefore determine whether the state is a stereotype.

It should be noted that a person does not engage in stereotyping as defined in this book if a stereotype does not influence his thought and w/AE

action, so if implicit attitudes had no influence on thought and action they could not result in implicit stereotyping. A person may make an association, having a concept (e.g. *dangerous*) triggered in response to members of a social group (e.g. Black people) without the triggering of the thought influencing other thoughts and actions. Then they would not be stereotyping. However, implicit attitudes can influence thoughts and actions (for more on this point see Chapter 6, Section 2.1). As long as stereotypes are operational in the production of thoughts or actions, which could be said to 'express' the stereotypes (Blum 2004, pp. 269–270), stereotyping can occur, even if the person stereotyping does not believe the content of the stereotype.[5]

In summary, then, there is good reason to accept that stereotypes can operate via implicit attitudes, leading people to automatically associate individuals with characteristics in virtue of their membership of a social group. Even if the implicit attitudes are not beliefs there is a strong case for saying that they are stereotypes. When they influence thought and action, stereotyping occurs. For this reason, it is most fitting to define stereotypes as social attitudes that associate members of some social group more strongly than others with certain trait(s) rather than specifying that they are beliefs. It is appropriate to take claims about how stereotypes deceive us to apply to social attitudes other than beliefs.

6. Conclusion

This chapter has defended the adoption of a non-normative conception of stereotypes and stereotyping. According to this view stereotypes are social attitudes that associate members of some social group more strongly than others with a certain trait or traits. Meanwhile stereotyping is the application of such a social attitude to an individual or individuals perceived to be a member or members of the relevant group, leading that individual or individuals to be associated with the trait. Numerous arguments in support of the non-normative account have been considered but ultimately the case for adopting the account that is defended here is a pragmatic one. Treating stereotypes as deviant, bizarre or pathological isolates them from ordinary cognitive structures that they could be continuous with and we cannot assume that stereotypes are distinct from these structures. In fact, assuming

---

[5] Blum (2016) rejects the idea that implicit biases are sufficiently robust to count as stereotypes, however, for the reasons outlined in this section, I disagree.

that stereotypes are deviant, bizarre or pathological would be likely to obscure similarities between these social attitudes and other psychological states and processes. By adopting the neutral definition of stereotypes, I, like many researchers within social psychology, study the various ways that stereotypes can obscure our perceptions or judgements of individuals rather than assuming that they always operate to distort perception and judgement.

In addition to this, this chapter has defended an inclusive view of stereotypes according to which they can be social attitudes other than beliefs. It has been argued that implicit biases, which are taken by a number of prominent thinkers not to be beliefs, should be considered to be stereotypes whether or not they are beliefs. The features that suggest to some that they are not beliefs do not indicate that they are not stereotypes. Therefore, it is appropriate to define stereotypes as social attitudes rather than beliefs.

3

The Multiple Ways Stereotypes Deceive Us

1. Introduction

When we engage in stereotyping, does this increase or decrease the chance that we make a correct judgement about the individual(s) or case(s) to which the stereotype is applied? According to the conception of stereotypes and stereotyping adopted in this book there is no single answer to this question. Stereotypes do not by definition lead to distorted judgements or misperceptions. Some stereotypes reflect reality and have the potential to facilitate correct judgements about individual cases. However, there is very good reason to think that stereotypes often have the negative and distorting effect of producing poor judgements and misperceptions. It is worrying that when we apply generalizations about social groups to individual group members we are consequently susceptible to forming false judgements about them. Those of us who are acutely aware that we are members of stereotyped social groups are likely to be concerned that other people are likely to misjudge or misperceive us when they apply stereotypes to us. Many of us would like to be able to take a principled approach to criticizing acts of stereotyping, identifying precisely why the application of a stereotype in a particular case is likely to lead to misjudgements and misperceptions.

As part of the first major project of this book, this chapter develops a principled approach of this type. It identifies numerous factors that determine, for any act of stereotyping, whether the application of the stereotype increases or decreases the chance of an accurate judgement being made about the individual(s) or case(s) to which the stereotype is applied. It identifies various questions to consider when ascertaining whether an act of stereotyping is likely to lead to accurate judgements or misperceptions of individuals and cases, and various ways to criticize an act of stereotyping on the basis that it is likely to lead to such misperceptions.

How Stereotypes Deceive Us. Katherine Puddifoot, Oxford University Press. © Katherine Puddifoot 2021.
DOI: 10.1093/oso/9780192845559.003.0003

In the process of achieving these goals, this chapter defends the *multifactorial view of stereotyping*. According to this view, there are multiple factors that combine to determine whether an act of stereotyping leads to the misperception or misjudgement of an individual or event. The multifactorial view contrasts with two views that find support in existing discussions of stereotyping: *the single factor* and *dual factor views*. On the single factor view, the only factor that determines whether a stereotype leads to misperception or misjudgement rather than being neutral or facilitating correct judgement is the extent to which the stereotype reflects social reality. On the dual factor view, the accuracy of the stereotype and the nature of the available evidence about the individual—whether or not it is high quality and unambiguous—jointly determine this. In this chapter a more complex picture is developed according to which there are multiple factors that combine to determine whether stereotyping has a positive or negative impact on judgement or perception. It is in developing this picture of the factors that determine whether an act of stereotyping has a positive or negative impact that we shall see how to identify whether any particular act of stereotyping is likely to increase or decrease the chance of an accurate judgement or perception about those stereotyped.

2. Single Factor View

Let us begin, then, by considering one of the views in contrast to which the multifactorial view of stereotyping is developed: *the single factor view*. According to the single factor view of stereotyping, there is only one feature of any act of stereotyping that determines whether the application of the stereotype is neutral, increases or decreases the chance of an accurate judgement being made: whether or not the stereotype that is applied reflects some aspect of reality. As long as a stereotype reflects an aspect of social reality that relates to the judgement being made, the application of the stereotype increases the likelihood of a correct judgement. Moreover, a judgement that involves the application of a stereotype is more likely to be false than an alternative judgement that would have been made in the absence of stereotyping only if the stereotype fails to reflect an aspect of social reality that relates to the judgement being made. A stereotype reflects some aspect of social reality as long as there is a regularity found within society and the stereotype leads a person to respond in a way that reflects the regularity.

The following example illustrates the intuitiveness of the single factor view. Jones harbours a stereotype associating men more strongly than women with an interest in football. This stereotype reflects the reality that in Jones's society significantly more men than women have an interest in football. She meets a heterosexual couple, applies the stereotype, and consequently judges that the man is more likely than the woman to have an interest in football. Intuitively, the application of the stereotype will increase the chance of an accurate judgement being made about who will have an interest in football because it will lead to a judgement that is informed by information that is relevant to the judgement being made: information about the distribution of a particular trait (e.g., interest in football) across a society.

The appeal of the single factor view can be understood in terms of the notion of *statistical discrimination* (Schauer 2017). When statistical discrimination occurs, membership of a particular group is taken to be 'statistically indicative' of the possession of certain traits or characteristics (Alexander and Cole 1997). For example, membership of the group of people under the age of 17 is taken in the United Kingdom to be a proxy for being likely to be an irresponsible driver (Schauer 2017). People under the age of 17 are denied the opportunity to drive because they are part of a group of people taken to be irresponsible with respect to the specific activity of driving. The age of a person is taken to reliably indicate something relevant about them, i.e. whether they are responsible enough to be legally permitted to drive. Statistical discrimination is an everyday occurrence. Only members of some age groups are allowed to drive, fly airplanes, or vote, and the insurance premium paid on one's car can be determined by one's gender. Many of these forms of discrimination seem to be both inevitable and acceptable reflections of the reality of living in society. Few would want children to be allowed to drive cars and drink alcohol. Legal restrictions that reduce the chance of these things happening can be viewed positively even by those who rally against other forms of statistical discrimination based on social group membership, such as racial profiling.

What is the difference between the acceptable and unacceptable forms of statistical discrimination? One intuitive response is that statistical discrimination is acceptable as long as there is a genuine correlation between the target group (e.g. under seventeens) and the characteristic that the group membership is taken to be proxy for (e.g. irresponsibility). Where there is only a spurious relationship between group membership and the possession of the characteristic, rather than a reliable correlation, statistical discrimination is unacceptable (Schauer 2017). But where there is a genuine correlation, statistical discrimination increases the chance that correct judgements are made about individual cases, for example, that those people who are genuinely irresponsible are not allowed to drive.

It is tempting to apply this thinking when analysing acts of stereotyping; concluding that the application of a stereotype increases the chance of a correct judgement being made if the target property that is taken to be indicative of the presence of some characteristic(s)—the membership of a particular social group—reliably correlates with the presence of the characteristic(s). If being a young person reliably correlates with being irresponsible then intuitively the application of a stereotype associating young people with irresponsibility to an individual young person will increase the chance of a correct judgement being made about how responsible the person is.

An idea of this type is articulated and endorsed by Louise Antony (2016) in her discussion of the implicit stereotyping involved with implicit bias. Antony claims that we should consider the following questions when attempting to identify whether an implicit bias is good or bad from an epistemic perspective:

A) Markers and targets: what properties are we aiming to track (targets), and what properties are we using as markers of the target properties? B) Indication relations: do the markers in fact correlate with the target properties?

The markers that Antony identifies are indicators of social group membership and the properties that we are aiming to track are properties that might be possessed by members of a target social group (e.g. reliability, aggression, intelligence). Anthony suggests that if indicators of social group membership reliably correlate with the presence of certain properties then an implicit bias that associates the social group and the target property is epistemically good.

On such a view, stereotyping that is acceptable involves the reflection in a judgement of base-rate information, that is, background statistical information about the presence of some property among members of a social group. The neglect of base-rates is widely accepted to be a judgement error. The error can be understood by considering experimental work conducted by Daniel Kahneman and Amos Tversky (1973) in the lawyer-engineer experiment. In the experiment, participants were told that 30 engineers and 70 lawyers had been interviewed and that short descriptions had been written about them based on the interviews. The participants were then given a description designed to be either more fitting of an engineer stereotype; more fitting of a lawyer stereotype; or to be neutral, that is, no more fitting of either stereotype. Participants were told that they had been randomly assigned one of these descriptions and were asked to rate the probability (on a scale of 0–100) that the description is of one of the engineers or one of the lawyers. When asked this question, participants should take the base-rate or background statistical information into account, i.e. the information about how many engineers and lawyers were interviewed. However, among participants who were given a neutral description, the median response was that the probability that the description was of one of the engineers or one of the lawyers was 50–50, suggesting that they did not take the base-rate information into account, instead judging each outcome to be equally likely because the description was neutral.

Base-rate neglect can be viewed as a serious error because it involves ignoring important and relevant statistical information when making a judgement, and can lead people to form drastically inaccurate beliefs. As the neglect of base-rates can lead to error, it might be thought that where stereotypes operate as base-rates the application of the stereotype increases the chance of a true belief being formed. This idea can be unpacked as follows. Stereotypes that reflect aspects of social reality are, or encode, base-rates. Neglect of base-rates is likely to lead to error. Use of base-rates is likely to avoid the error associated with base-rate neglect. The application of stereotypes that reflect social realities is use of base-rates. Therefore, stereotypes should be applied whenever they reflect aspects of social reality because applying the stereotypes maximizes the chance of a true belief being formed.

The single factor view is therefore both highly intuitive and seemingly supported by work aiming to distinguish between different types (acceptable/unacceptable, useful/not useful) of statistical discrimination as well as research on base-rate neglect. The view can be characterized in the following way that captures its appeal:

Single factor view: judgements produced as a result of acts of stereotyping are more likely to be accurate than alternative judgements that might have been made in the absence of the stereotyping, because the stereotyping leads to a judgement that is informed by information that is important and relevant relative to the judgement, if and only if the stereotype reflects an aspect of social reality.

On this view, as long as a stereotype reflects some aspect of social reality the application of the stereotype increases the chance of an accurate judgement being made about an individual. This is because once the judgement is influenced by the stereotype it reflects important and relevant information.

3. Dual Factor View

On the other view to be critiqued in this chapter, the *dual factor view*, there is not one but two features of any act of stereotyping that jointly determine whether the application of the stereotype increases the chance of a correct or an erroneous judgement being made. We can find support for the view in the work of the social psychologist Lee Jussim and his colleagues (2009; Jussim 2012).

In their controversial work on social perception, Jussim and colleagues (2009; Jussim 2012) aim to show that stereotyping is generally not as bad as people tend to assume. Their defence of stereotyping focuses on establishing that two features are commonly found in acts of stereotyping: (i) the stereotypes that are applied are accurate; (ii) the stereotypes are applied when there is only ambiguous evidence available about a specific case. They take the presence of (i) and (ii) to indicate that an act of stereotyping is a positive thing. They therefore develop a position that strongly implies that two features—(i) and (ii)—are required for any act of stereotyping to increase the chance of an accurate judgement being made.[1]

The stipulation that a stereotype must be accurate is more demanding than the stipulation that a stereotype must reflect some aspect of social reality. A stereotype might reflect some aspect of reality, some regularity found within society, while also being properly called inaccurate. For example, a person might associate having an interest in football more strongly with men than women, this might reflect the reality that within a society more men than women are interested in football, but the stereotype might be inaccurate because it underestimates or overestimates the differing degree

---

[1] Note, here, that Jussim and colleagues' aim is not the same as mine: i.e. to identify various features of acts of stereotyping that determine whether they facilitate correct judgement or perception, or, alternatively, misperception or misjudgement. Instead, their aim is to analyse data on stereotype accuracy and the conditions under which stereotypes are applied, to show that (in their view) stereotypes tend to be accurate and they tend to be applied only when appropriate. However, the implication is clear: if one stereotypes and (i) the stereotype is accurate, and (ii) there is a lack of umambiguous case-specific information, then this is taken to indicate that the stereotyping is a positive thing.

of interest in football across the genders. Nonetheless the claim that the accuracy of a stereotype determines (in part) whether or not the application of the stereotype increases or decreases the chance of an accurate judgement is supported by the literature on statistical discrimination and base-rates. This is because an accurate stereotype is even more likely than one that merely loosely reflects social reality to reflect the statistical distribution of traits across different populations and encode base-rate information.

Second of all, according to the dual factor view, the quality of the information that is available about the specific case to which the stereotype is applied (e.g. the specific person who is stereotyped, the specific crime that is committed) can determine whether or not an act of stereotyping is more likely to produce an accurate judgement than an alternative that would have been made in the absence of the stereotyping. The application of the stereotype will increase the chance of an accurate judgement being made only if the available information about the specific case is ambiguous.

The following example is presented in support of this view. Jane is a life-long occupant of Alaska and Jan is a lifelong occupant of New York. Both say that it is cold where they are today. Jussim and colleagues (2009) claim that because the information about the temperature is ambiguous, one should be influenced in one's judgement about which place is colder by background information about the average temperatures in Alaska and New York. Similarly, they claim, when one only has ambiguous information about a specific member of a social group, one should be informed by the distribution of traits across social groups when making judgements about the individual. In their view, accurate stereotypes encode this information, so they should be applied. If, on the other hand, unambiguous information about the specific case is available, one should not engage in stereotyping. For example, imagine once again that you are trying to ascertain which of two people—a man and a woman in a heterosexual relationship—is interested in football. Someone mentions that the woman is a football pundit; a professional paid by a lucrative media outlet to discuss football. In this case you have unambiguous evidence that the woman is the one who is interested in football. You should not engage in stereotyping, applying the stereotype associating men more strongly than women with an interest in football.

Following the guidance to only apply a stereotype in the absence of unambiguous evidence will not always be easy. There will be some border-line cases, where it is unclear whether evidence is truly unambiguous. For example, you might meet a heterosexual couple, knowing that only one is interested in football, and notice that the woman is wearing a football scarf. Is this unambiguous evidence that the woman is the one interested in football? It might seem obvious that the person wearing the football scarf is the fan of the sport, but she could be borrowing her partner's scarf. It is therefore not obvious whether the evidence that the woman is wearing the scarf is unambiguous evidence in support of the belief that she is the football fan. But what Jussim and colleagues (2009) would emphasize is that establishing whether the evidence is ambiguous or unambiguous is crucial (alongside the accuracy of the stereotype) to determining whether it is appropriate to stereotype.

Jussim and colleagues (2009) therefore provide an argument that supports what shall here be called the dual factor view:

> *Dual factor view of stereotyping*: judgements produced as a result of acts of stereotyping are more likely to be accurate than alternative judgements that might have been made in the absence of the stereotyping if and only if (a) the stereotype that is applied is accurate and (b) only ambiguous information is available about the case to which the stereotype is applied.

4. Challenging the Single and Dual Factor Views

The single and dual factor views could be challenged by showing that the factors that are identified are irrelevant to whether or not an act of stereotyping leads to misperception. However, it is clear that each of the features identified in these views *can* determine whether or not an act of stereotyping leads to misperception.

Let us begin with the extent to which the stereotype reflects reality. The extent to which a stereotype reflects reality clearly can determine whether or not the application of the stereotype increases or decreases the chance of accurate judgement and perception. If a stereotype does not reflect any aspect of reality then its application is unlikely to increase, and likely to decrease, the chance of an accurate judgement being made about a case to which the stereotype is applied. If a stereotype that does not reflect any aspect of reality does increase the chance of a person being perceived correctly it will often only do so accidentally. Say, for example, that women are wrongly associated with a lack of intelligence, due to a widely shared stereotype. The stereotype is applied to an individual woman who is consequently judged not to know about the topic she is fluently and articulately discussing. If the stereotype had not been applied then it would have been assumed that the woman must be knowledgeable otherwise she would not be speaking so well. As it happens, the judgement is correct because this specific woman happens to be engaging in discussion about a topic about which she is ignorant. The stereotype is false and leads to a correct judgement, but only accidentally. Cases like these are the exception to the general rule that the extent to which a stereotype reflects reality tends to determine whether or not the application of the stereotype leads to misperception. In Chapter 4 we shall consider some interesting cases of egalitarian stereotypes that improve the chance of a correct judgement being made due to their failing to reflect reality. In very many cases, however, a stereotype reflecting reality increases the chance of it facilitating correct judgements and perceptions. Meanwhile, in very many cases a stereotype failing to reflect reality increases the chance that its application will lead to a person being misperceived. For instance, if a woman who is speaking fluently and articulately is judged not to be knowledgeable because of a culturally shared stereotype that women lack intelligence, then in most cases the judgement will be incorrect.

In addition to this, the quality of the available evidence about the individual who is stereotyped clearly can determine whether or not an act of stereotyping increases or decreases the probability that the individual will be perceived correctly. If there is high-quality, unambiguous information that is relevant to a judgement that is being made about an individual then the act of stereotyping is less likely to lead to accurate perception of the individual than if there is a lack of evidence of this quality. At one extreme, the evidence about the individual might be conclusive so the application of the stereotype could only hinder and not help to ensure that a correct judgement is made. But where evidence is strong but not conclusive there will often be little to gain and much to lose from stereotyping because the evidence will strongly support one conclusion and, as we shall see further as this chapter progresses, the application of a stereotype can lead to a distorted response to the evidence.

The strategy adopted in this chapter, then, is to challenge the single and dual factor views of stereotyping not by showing that the factors identified in these views are unimportant but by showing instead that there are more factors that determine whether or not the application of a stereotype leads to misperception than these accounts suggest.

5. Factor 1: Stereotype Accuracy

This section begins by providing a challenge to the single factor view of stereotyping only, providing a reason for preferring the dual factor view to the single factor view. Recall a seemingly subtle difference between the single and dual factor views: the former stipulates that stereotyping increases the chance of an accurate judgement being made as long as the stereotype that is applied reflects some aspect of social reality. In contrast, the dual factor view stipulates that a stereotype must be accurate for the application of the stereotype to increase the chance of an accurate judgement being made. A stereotype can be deemed to be accurate if it leads a person to respond in a way that is fitting with accurate statistical information, about the distribution of traits across groups. But a stereotype can reflect some aspect of social reality without leading a person to respond in a way that is fitting with accurate statistical information. For example, the stereotype can dispose a person to respond as if a trait is far more prevalent in one group than another when there is a smaller difference in the prevalence of the trait. This section shows how this subtle, and seemingly innocuous, difference between reflecting some aspect of social reality and being accurate can be of crucial importance to determining whether or not the application of a stereotype increases or decreases the chance of an accurate judgement being made.

To understand how the fittingness of people's responses to accurate statistical information can determine whether or not stereotyping leads to an accurate judgement or misperception, it is useful to consider the explanation of how stereotyping can increase the chance of an accurate judgement being made. The application of a stereotype can have this positive effect because stereotyping can produce judgements that are informed by important and relevant information. As stereotypes associate members of social groups with attributes in virtue of social group membership, the important and relevant information that they can supply is statistical information about the distribution of traits across a social group. For an act of stereotyping to increase the chance of an accurate judgement, it should therefore lead a person to respond in a way that is fitting with accurate statistical information about the distribution of traits across a social group. If an act of stereotyping produces a judgement that is not fitting with accurate statistical information, for instance, leading a person to respond in a way that overestimates or underestimates the prevalence of an attribute in some social groups, then there is good reason to doubt that the resulting judgement will be accurate.

The literature on stereotyping about the connection between race and crime in the United States illustrates how stereotypes can lead people to form judgements that are not fitting with accurate statistical information. In this literature, research has been undertaken to measure people's judgements about rates of criminal involvement and compare these judgements to crime statistics. A number of studies have found that people tend to overestimate the percentage of violent crimes committed by Black people (Chiricos, Welch, and Gertz 2004; Pickett et al. 2012). People also tend to misjudge the types of crimes that Black people engage in: overestimating the extent to which Black individuals engage in motor vehicle theft, rape, and criminal homicide (Gordon, Michels, and Nelson 1996). People have also been found to automatically associate drug crime with Black people—when asked to close their eyes and picture a drug user, 95 per cent of survey respondents replied that they imagined a Black person (Burston, Jones, and Roberson-Saunders 1995, cited in Alexander 2011). However, the reality is that White and Black people engage in drug use at roughly the same rate in the United States (Substance Abuse and Mental Health Services Administration 2004), and the use of some drugs such as heroin, cocaine, stimulants, or methamphetamine is higher among the White population than the African American population (Office of Applied Studies, Substance Abuse and Mental Health Services Administration, 2007). Moreover, people tend to significantly overestimate the risk of crime in areas with a high Black population (Quillian and Pager 2010), suggesting that they associate the Black population with crime substantially more than they would if their stereotypes accurately reflected the statistical reality. Each of these studies shows how the phenomenon that is the focus of the current section can occur: a stereotype is applied that associates Black people with criminal activity, but the stereotype overestimates the rates of criminal involvement among the Black population, and, as a result, an act of stereotyping fails to increase the chance of an accurate judgement, instead increasing the chance of an inaccurate judgement.

The psychological and the sociological literature provide some plausible explanations of why people who engage in stereotyping can fail to make judgements that are fitting with statistical realities. Two features of human psychology that seem to contribute to the explanation are that (1) humans tend to remember extreme members of a group better than less extreme members (Rothbart et al. 1978), and (2) what we remember determines how we stereotype a group (Rothbart et al. 1978). We are therefore predisposed to reflect people who possess extreme characteristics more heavily in our stereotypes than people who possess less extreme characteristics (Rothbart et al. 1978). For instance, as criminals, all else being equal, possess more extreme characteristics than law-abiding people, we are disposed to reflect actions of the former more than those of the latter in our stereotypes of any group containing both (Rothbart et al. 1978). This means that if we are exposed to descriptions of actions of members of a racial group, and some members of that group have engaged in crimes, the criminal activities are more heavily represented in the stereotypes formed about the group than the law-abiding activities. The likelihood that any member of the group will commit a crime will consequently be overestimated.

This phenomenon seems to be combined with a number of social phenomena meaning that people are especially likely to develop and apply stereotypes that reflect a distorted picture of the characteristics of some social groups. The media is one important social factor that can contribute to the development of stereotypes that overestimate or underestimate the prevalence of attributes in social groups. The media serves as an important 'cultural parent', heavily influencing how members of social groups are viewed (Weisbuch, Pauker, and Ambady 2009), and the general population of a society is sometimes exposed by the media to a disproportionately negative picture of members of a social group. For example, the US population is exposed to a disproportionately negative picture of Black involvement in crime via the media (see, for example, Dorfman and Schiraldi 2001). With regard to crime in general, although the proportion of Black and White suspects depicted in the news media has been found to fairly accurately reflect the proportion of crimes committed by members of the two racial groups, there are far fewer positive Black role models (e.g., police officers, news reporters) depicted in the news media than there are positive White role models (Entman 1992). For instance, a study of local news media in Orlando, Florida, found that only 1 in 20 White people portrayed in the news were crime suspects while 1 in 8 Black people portrayed in the news were suspects (Chiricos and Escholz 2002). This means that Black people are more heavily associated than White people with the negative rather than the positive aspects of crime. In addition to this, Black suspects are often depicted in a non-individualized way; they are more likely to be unnamed, and they are less likely to have an opportunity to speak or have a spokesperson speak for them in the media (Chiricos and Escholz 2002). The media thereby fails to reflect the variation between individual members of the racial category, leading to homogenization of Black people.[2] There is also reason to think that news reports of some actions of Black people rely on stereotypes of criminality while reports of the same actions, when they are conducted by White people, do not. For example, the action of taking some drinks from a shop in the aftermath of Hurricane Katrina was described in media depictions as 'looting' when undertaken by a Black person and 'finding' when undertaken by a White person (Shalby 2017).[3]

The media influence seems to combine with the psychological disposition to overestimate extreme examples in stereotypes, producing stereotypes that exaggerate the proportion of Black people who are involved in negative criminal activities. There is little reason to hope that this phenomenon is restricted to stereotypes about race and crime, so that the damage is limited and only race-crime stereotypes are consequently likely to lead to judgements that fail to accurately reflect the statistical reality. Wherever a disproportionately negative (or positive) media depiction is found, this can combine with the psychological disposition to overestimate extreme examples, leading to stereotypes that significantly exaggerate the proportion of a social group who have negative (or positive) characteristics.

This discussion of the influence of media on the formation of stereotypes is intended to be illustrative of a wider phenomenon: social factors interacting with psychological tendencies and thereby leading people to form stereotypes that overestimate or underestimate the presence of attributes among a social group. It is important to recognize that the social source of stereotypes can take many different forms. Some stereotypes might be newly introduced into a society, by, for example, a distorting media or a self-serving politician. Some stereotypes are deeply entrenched due to being introduced and sustained as a part of historical, and continuing, social injustices. In each of these types of cases, there is very good reason to think that the stereotypes will be inaccurate. For example, the stereotype of the African American family as matriarchal, and as lacking a father, arose from the oppressive conditions of slavery (see, e.g., Davis 1971; Le Rue 1970;

---

[2] For those interested in this issue, there is a wide range of literature to consult. For instance, for further discussion of how the media produces a misleading characterization of rates of criminal involvement see Anderson 2010; for the empirical literature see, e.g., Dixon and Linz 2000; Entman 1992; Gilliam and Iyengar 2000.

[3] Another example is the differing media responses to these two separates cases of seven-year-old boys, one White and one Black, who each took a relative's car for a joyride (Wade 2013).

Spillers 1987). Under conditions of slavery, children were often born to slave-owners who did not take on the role and responsibilities of father-hood, and African American males were often prevented from occupying the roles and responsibilities of fatherhood, leaving women to fulfil the responsibilities of both mother and father. Hortense Spillers (1987) argues that the idea of the matriarchal African American family provides a false impression that a woman who was a slave had the ability to 'claim her child' (p. 80) or that motherhood was taken to be 'a legitimate procedure of cul-tural inheritance' (p. 80). Meanwhile, Wahneema Lubiano (1992) describes how the stereotype of Black Women as 'Welfare Queens' was developed in order to scapegoat Black women for policies enacted by the Reagan Administration that cut crucial social support for American families. Given the explanations of the existence of these stereotypes, as arising from condi-tions of oppression and often continuing to be powerful tools to justify con-tinued poor treatment (Collins 2000, pp. 80–81), there is very little reason to think that they will accurately reflect social realities. Instead, there is very good reason to think that the stereotypes will lead people to overestimate or underestimate the prevalence of certain characteristics (absenteeism among Black fathers, dependency on welfare among Black mothers) among the social groups targeted by the stereotypes. Given how the stereotypes emerged it would be far more surprising if the stereotypes accurately reflected the relevant social realities, leading people to make judgements that accurately reflected current statistical realities, than if they did not.

The discussion in this section has identified some very good reasons for thinking that stereotyping can reduce the chance of an accurate judgement being made, producing misperceptions and misjudgements, because the stereotyping produces a perception or judgement that is not fitting with accurate statistical information about the distribution of attributes across social groups. When an act of stereotyping leads to a judgement that is not fitting with accurate statistical information, it is inappropriate to describe it as leading to judgements that are informed by important and relevant infor-mation. As we have reason to think that some beliefs produced as a result of stereotyping are likely to be accurate because they reflect important and relevant information, evidence that a certain type of stereotyping does not lead to judgements that reflect this type of information constitutes evidence that it will not tend to produce accurate judgements. Therefore, acts of stereotyping that lead to judgements that are not fitting with accurate statis-tical information are unlikely to produce accurate judgements.

It is clear that stereotypes can have the negative effects just described while reflecting some aspect of social reality. Take, for example, the stereotype associating Black people more strongly than White people with drug crimes. The stereotype could reflect an aspect of social reality, i.e. high *arrest* rates among the Black population for drug use, while also leading to judgements that fail to fit accurate statistical information about actual rates of *drug use*, which are similar across the Black and non-Black populations (Alexander 2011). In applying the stereotype associating Black people more strongly than White people with drug use, a person might therefore form a judgement reflecting an aspect of social reality. But they could nonetheless fail to accurately reflect the statistical reality of rates of drug use across different social groups.

We have now identified a feature of an act of stereotyping that can determine whether or not it increases the chance of an accurate judgement being made that is not captured by the single factor view of stereotyping: whether or not the act of stereotyping leads to judgements fitting with accurate statistical information. An act of stereotyping might involve the application of a stereotype that reflects some aspect of social reality, which would mean that on the single factor view it should increase the chance of an accurate judgement being made. However, because the stereotype does not dispose the person who engages in the stereotyping to respond in a way that reflects the statistical reality, the stereotyping could reduce rather than enhance the chance of an accurate judgement being made. This discussion gives us reason to prefer the dual factor view to the single factor view: the dual factor view captures an additional factor, omitted by the single factor view, that can determine whether an act of stereotyping leads to misjudgement or misperception.

6. Factor 2: Stereotype Relevance

While Section 5 provides reason for preferring the dual factor view to the single factor view, this section highlights the inadequacy of the dual factor view. It identifies a further feature of acts of stereotyping, omitted from the dual factor view as well as the single factor view, that can determine whether or not the application of a stereotype increases the chance of an accurate judgement being made or increases the chance of misperception: the relevance of the stereotype that is applied.[4]

---

[4] For further philosophical discussion of how stereotypes can be irrelevant but nonetheless influence judgements see Saul 2013.

Research from social psychology provides strong support for the claim that individuals are not appropriately sensitive to contexts in which any statistical information that might be encoded in a stereotype is relevant to a judgement. They do not only apply a stereotype when it is relevant. For example, two triggers for stereotyping identified by psychologists are a wounded ego and the desire to justify the current social system (see, e.g., Fiske, Cuddy, and Glick 2007; Uhlmann, Brescoll, and Machery 2010), and there is good reason to doubt that either of these factors correlates with stereotypes being relevant to a judgement. This section shows how, as a consequence of these facts about human psychology, a belief produced as a result of an act of stereotyping can fail to be accurate, and an act of stereotyping can fail to increase the chance of an accurate judgement, because a stereotype is applied when irrelevant.

Consider first the fact that stereotypes are often triggered as a result of an individual suffering a wounded ego (Spencer et al. 1998). Steven Fein and Steven Spencer (1997) found that people who were given poor feedback on an intelligence test were subsequently more likely to stereotype a gay man. Lisa Sinclair and Ziva Kunda (1999) found that if a Black doctor criticized a person they were subsequently more likely to engage in negative racial stereotyping. These and similar findings suggest that an individual's stereotypes are often activated as a result of a threat to his or her ego. Even if there are times when particular social stereotypes are relevant, they are extremely unlikely to be precisely those times when an evaluator has a wounded ego. It is very difficult to imagine what would explain this correlation. On the contrary, it is not difficult to imagine a situation in which an evaluator has his ego wounded, a stereotype is activated, but the stereotype is irrelevant. Take the following example. A police officer approaches the car of a Black male, which has been pulled over for a minor traffic violation, e.g. one of his headlights is not working. The police officer asks the man to step out of the vehicle but he responds slowly and cautiously to the command. The police officer is offended at what he takes to be a threat to his authority. This triggers a stereotype associating the innocent man with crime; the police officer evaluates the man as a criminal and treats him with hostility; and this leads to an escalation of tension and hostility between the two individuals. The stereotype associating Black people with crime is triggered although the Black man has not committed a crime, only a minor traffic violation. Examples like this illustrate that people's stereotypes, including but not exclusively their stereotypes relating to race and crime, can be triggered when irrelevant.

A similar point can be made concerning the second factor thought to trigger the activation of stereotypes. Social psychologists believe that people's stereotypes are activated when they feel a threat to the current social system and are motivated to defend it. This hypothesis is taken to explain, for example, why stereotypes differ over time in a way that is consistent with defending the current system. For instance, it is taken to explain why while slavery was legal in the United States, stereotypes of Black people were that they were happy, childlike, and affectionate, but with the fight to abolish slavery the stereotypes changed to represent Black people as threatening (Alexander 2011; Uhlmann et al. 2010). If stereotypes are activated by challenges to the status quo, and challenges to the status quo were correlated with the relevance of race-crime stereotypes, then there would be reason to think that the stereotypes are activated when relevant. However, just as in the case of the wounded ego, there is good reason to doubt that such a correlation exists. It is once again difficult to imagine why a correlation would exist but easy to imagine examples in which a stereotype is triggered, in this case due to a challenge to the current social system, but the stereotype is not relevant.

Let us once again consider race-crime stereotyping to see this point. Even if there were times when stereotypes associating Black people and crime are relevant, there is little reason to think that these are the same times when people feel a threat to the current social order and are motivated to defend it. On the contrary, it is not difficult to imagine a situation in which people are inclined to defend the current social order, negative stereotypes associating Black people with crime are consequently activated, and the activation of the stereotype is wholly inappropriate. Consider, for instance, a discussion between two individuals regarding changes to the US criminal justice system made under the Fair Sentencing Act of 2010 (Public Law 111–220). The bill reduced the difference in the sentences attached to the possession of crack and powder cocaine. The change to the law reduced discrimination against Black people in the legal system because Black people are statistically more likely than White people to be in possession of crack rather than powder cocaine, so were previously substantially more likely to receive the harsher sentence. Research suggests that when the issue was initially discussed, because the discussion would have involved scrutiny of the current social order, the judgements made by at least some of the discussants would have been heavily influenced by stereotypes that vindicate the status quo. The stereotype strongly associating Black people with crime is likely to have been triggered, meaning that some participants in the discussion were inclined to defend the current high rates of incarceration among Black people. However, the stereotype is not relevant to this discussion, which should focus on whether specific sentences are appropriate for particular crimes. Here we therefore find reason to think that stereotypes relating to crime are triggered, due to the desire to defend the social order, where they are irrelevant.

What this discussion shows is that human psychology predisposes us to apply stereotypes when they are not relevant to the judgements we are making. If a stereotype is irrelevant then any information that is encoded in the stereotype will be irrelevant (Saul 2013). The application of the stereotype will not lead to a judgement that is well informed by important and relevant information. It will therefore not increase the chance of an accurate judgement being made about an individual case. On the contrary, the act of stereotyping is likely to decrease the chance of an accurate judgement being made, increasing the chance of misperception. We have therefore identified a factor that can determine whether an act of stereotyping produces an accurate judgement or leads to misperception that is not captured by either the single or dual factor view: whether the stereotype that is applied is triggered where relevant.

7. Factor 3: Response to Case-Specific Information

Let us now turn to a further factor that can determine whether or not an act of stereotyping produces an accurate or inaccurate judgement about specific individual(s) or case(s): whether or not the application of the stereotype leads diagnostic case-specific information to become inaccessible or distorted. This feature is captured by neither the single nor the dual factor view. There are various ways that the application of a stereotype can prevent important and relevant case-specific information from being properly accessed and processed. This section outlines various psychological findings that show how stereotypes can have these effects.

First, when a stereotype is activated, ambiguous behaviour can consequently be interpreted in a distorted way that is fitting with the stereotype rather than, as it should be viewed: i.e. as ambiguous (Duncan 1976). When a piece of behaviour could be interpreted as properly belonging to various different categories (e.g. aggressive or playful), the activation of a stereotype sets expectancies, leading the ambiguous action to be interpreted in a way that is consistent with the stereotype (Duncan 1976; Sagar and Schofield 1980).

For example, in a study undertaken by Duncan (1976) participants were shown a clip of one person shoving another. When the protagonist was Black and the victim was White the majority of participants (75%) judged the shove to be an act of violence. When the protagonist was White and the victim was Black only a small minority of participants (17%) judged the shove to be an act of violence. The best explanation of the participant's interpretations of the shoving incident is that their judgements were determined by the stereotype associating Black people and not White people with violence. The same action was interpreted differently depending on the stereotype that was applied. Devine (1989) found a similar effect following from implicit stereotyping. She found that individuals unconsciously primed with words associated with the stereotype of Black people viewed ambiguous behaviour to be more aggressive than those who were not primed in this way. When the automatically activated stereotype associating Black people with violence was applied, an inaccurate judgement was made: ambiguous evidence was interpreted in a way that led people to think that the act was violent rather than ambiguous.[5]

Second, when stereotypes are in operation only some relevant information is likely to be remembered. There is a robust psychological literature examining how people's memories can become distorted as a result of the activation of stereotypes. Human memory systems have been found to be biased in two main ways as a result of stereotyping: either information that is consistent with a stereotype is better remembered than information that is inconsistent with the stereotype (Bodenhausen 1988; Cohen 1981; Signorella and Liben 1984; Stangor 1988; Levinson 2007), or vice versa (Dijksterhuis and van Knippenberg 1995; Hastie 1981; Hastie and Kumar 1979; Srull 1981; Srull and Wyer 1989). In each type of case, information that relates to a stereotype is more likely to be remembered than information that is unrelated to a stereotype. In one example of the former type of case, Cohen (1981) undertook a study in which participants were shown a clip in which a woman and a man were having a discussion. Some participants were led to believe that the woman was a waitress and others were led to believe that she was a librarian. Although they were shown identical tapes, participants who believed that the woman was a librarian were more likely to remember that she was wearing glasses, and participants who believed that she was a waitress were more likely to remember that she was

---

[5] For further evidence of the influence of implicit associations on the interpretation of ambiguous behaviour see Gawronski, Geschke, and Banse 2003.

drinking beer (she was both wearing glasses and drinking beer). In other words, participants were more likely to remember the woman as possessing features that fit the stereotype associated with her job than features that do not. In an example of the latter type of case, participants were told that either members of a group or an individual had a particular trait (e.g. friendly and sociable or unfriendly and unsociable). The participants were later found to recall behaviours that were inconsistent with the description of the group or individual at a higher rate than behaviours that were consistent (Srull 1981). Numerous studies have been conducted aiming to identify the factors that determine whether a bias in favour of stereotype-consistent or stereotype-inconsistent information is found. Factors including whether or not the stereotype is well established (Fyock and Stangor 1994; Stangor and McMillan 1992), competing cognitive demands (Hastie 1981; Hastie and Kumar 1979; Srull 1981) and time constraints (Dijksterhuis and van Knippenberg 1995; Rojahn and Pettigrew 1992; Stangor and McMillan 1992) have been found to influence whether stereotype-consistent or stereotype-inconsistent information is better remembered. (For a systematic meta-analysis see Rojahn and Pettigrew 1992 and Stangor and McMillan 1992.) For current purposes, what is important is that biased recall influenced by stereotyping, in either direction, will prevent certain information from being accessed and properly utilized. Either information that is consistent or information that is inconsistent with a stereotype is unlikely to be given appropriate weight due to the operation of a stereotype.

Third, when people are categorized together due to their traits (e.g. skin colour, gender, financial situation) because a stereotype is activated they become viewed as group members. The group may be a minority or a majority group. Members of minority groups are seen as less diverse, and more likely to share characteristics (Bartsch and Judd 1993). For example, male nurses, who are a minority group, are viewed as more similar to each other than female nurses (Hewstone, Crisp, and Turner 2011). Members of minority groups are assumed to share characteristics with other members of their group who have been previously encountered. Differences between members of minority groups are less readily noticed than differences between members of majority groups.

Where a person is a member of multiple subordinate groups, e.g. Black and a woman, they are especially likely to be treated as indistinguishable from, and interchangeable with, others who share the relevant aspects of their social identity. For example, it has been found that experimental participants are poorer at recognizing the faces of previously seen Black women than they are at recognizing previously seen White women, Black men, and White men (Sesko and Biernat 2010). Moreover, participants were more likely to misattribute the contributions made by Black women to others than they were to misattribute contributions of members of the other groups (Sesko and Biernat 2010). These effects have been explained in the following way: there are default stereotypes for social groups that reflect what are taken to be more prototypical group members. For example, the White woman stereotype is the default stereotype for women and Black man is the default stereotype for Black people. Information about individuals who do not fit these default stereotypes—such as information about Black women—is not as easily categorized and remembered as information about people who do fit them. There is good reason to think that stereotypes are responsible for this effect because the effect disappears when people are encouraged to focus on individuating information about specific Black women (Sesko and Biernat 2018).

Data suggesting that Black women are rendered invisible in these ways demonstrates how race and gender categories can intersect to produce psychological biases that mimic structural biases that have been emphasized by feminist intersectional theorists (e.g. Beale 1970; Cooper 1892; Crenshaw 1989, 1991; Davis 1981; hooks 1982; King 1988). Take, for example, Kimberlé Crenshaw's (1991) discussion of how Black women's experiences of domestic violence are not properly addressed by feminist movements that focus on the experiences of White women, or anti-racist movements whose members are reluctant to publicize data that implicates Black men as perpetrators of the violence. Where organizations are designed to cater for the needs of women, they focus on the needs of White women, and where they are designed to cater for the needs of Black people, they focus on the needs of Black men. The needs of Black women, including those who are at significant risk due to domestic violence, are not recognized or addressed by the organizations. The data on how people applying stereotypes can fail to recognize Black women or their contributions shows that once stereotypes are internalized human psychology produces a similar effect to the workings of these social organizations.

Fourth, in a related phenomenon, where individuals are viewed as forming distinct groups due to the characteristics that they possess, in other words, as a result of the activation of a stereotype, differences between the groups are magnified (e.g. Tajfel 1981). A stereotype associating one set of individuals with a characteristic can highlight differences between that set of individuals and others, preventing similarities between members of the different groups from being noticed.

Fifth, when people engage in stereotyping they can fail to develop explanations of other people's behaviour that are well-grounded in evidence or likely to track the truth about the behaviour's cause or motivation. People who rely on stereotypes tend to explain actions in terms of the dispositions of the actor if the actions fit the stereotype of the actor's social group, but explain the action in terms of the situation of the actor rather than the disposition if the action fails to fit the stereotype. For example, if a Black person shoves a White person, their action is attributed to their dispositions, but if a White person shoves a White person, the action is explained in terms of features of the situation (Duncan 1976). The same action, produced by the same cause in an extremely similar situation, is explained in different ways depending on the social group membership of the individual being assessed. In addition to this, stereotypes are often taken to provide sufficient explanations of individuals' behaviours so further explanations are not sought where they should be (Sanbonmatsu, Akimoto, and Gibson 1994).

Sixth, where multiple intersecting social identities are salient, stereotypes associated with one or more of those intersecting identities can function to obscure other aspects of a person's social identity. A person's racial identity can, for example, obscure perception of their gender identity. Recent work in psychology aims to explain how this occurs. It does so in the following way. Stereotypes associated with various aspects of a person's social identity— their gender and race, for example—can either overlap or conflict. For example, both men and Black people are associated with being aggressive, dominant, athletic, and competitive while women and Asians tend to be associated with being shy, family-oriented, and soft-spoken (Galinski, Hall, and Cuddy 2013; Goff, Thomas, and Jackson 2008; Johnson, Freeman, and Pauker 2012). Meanwhile, information about race biases categorization by gender. Where race and gender stereotypes align, information about the gender of the person is relatively easily categorized because of its consistency with the racial stereotype, and people are able to avoid making mistakes in ascribing people with a gender. However, when race and gender stereotypes conflict—for example, in the case of a Black woman—people are more susceptible to making errors in ascribing gender (Goff et al., 2008). There can be errors too, however, when the stereotypes about a person's racial and gender identities overlap. People have been found to be more likely to make mistakes in determining a target person's sexual orientation if the racial and gender stereotypes associated with the target are overlapping, for example, if the target is a Black man or Asian woman (Johnson and Ghavami 2011).

Finally, when stereotyping occurs, the testimony of people who are stereotyped can be silenced and they can be denied the credibility that they deserve. Kristie Dotson (2011) describes how *testimonial silencing* can occur through either *testimonial quieting* or *testimonial smothering*. Testimonial quieting occurs when an audience fails to recognize that a speaker possesses knowledge that they can convey through their testimony. If, for example, Black women are stereotyped as not being knowers, then information that they attempt to convey can consequently be ignored (Collins 2000). Testimonial smothering occurs when a person chooses not to speak out, smothering their testimony, because the testimony is risky and they believe that if they do speak they will be misinterpreted (Dotson 2011). Dotson provides the example of Black women in the United States who have undergone domestic violence from a Black male partner. They might choose not to speak out about their experiences because they fear that their testimony will be interpreted as supporting the stereotype that Black males are violent (for further discussion see, e.g. Crenshaw 1991; Richie 1985; Walker 1988). The existence and application of the stereotype of Black males as violent leads Black women to smother their testimony because they realize that the possession of the stereotype can lead to misinterpretation of some evidence, of a specific domestic abuser, as supporting a general stereotype.

Where people do speak out they can be denied the credibility that they deserve as the result of the operation of stereotypes about their social group, in what has become known as testimonial injustice (Fricker 2007). For example, a woman's testimony might be dismissed on the basis that it is based on mere 'female intuition' (Fricker 2007, p. 9), or the testimony of a person with a mental health issue might be dismissed on the basis that they are 'crazy' or 'irrational' (Crichton, Carel, and Kidd 2017). When evaluating testimony humans have a tendency to assess the reliability and trustworthiness of the testifier. If a stereotype associates a social group with being unreliable or untrustworthy then members of that group can be given less credibility than they deserve.

In one example of how testimonial silencing or testimonial injustice can operate, Lisa Cooper and colleagues (2012) found that where physicians scored highly on measures of stereotyping of Black people as noncompliant, their Black patients were less likely to be given the opportunity to speak and explain their symptoms. This finding could be explained in terms of

WPAE Cite Troubling Tohchin (Susan Yong & expron

testimonial quieting as a physician refusing to give uptake to the testimony of their patients, or as patients smothering their testimony in response to indications from their physicians that the testimony would be misinterpreted. Alternatively, it could be explained in terms of testimonial injustice, as the physician giving the patient less credibility than they deserve as a source of information about their condition. In each case, the finding seems to be the result of the operation of a stereotype. Information that people might supply, including information about their specific case that might otherwise be balanced against information encoded in the stereotype, is inaccessible as a result of stereotyping.

These effects of stereotyping can be either amplified or suppressed by the presence of multiple salient social identities (Hall et al. 2019). One stereotype can counterbalance the effect of another stereotype, leading to suppression of the impact of the first. For example, Kang and Chasteen (2009) found that anger was recognized less readily on elderly Black men's faces than on young Black men's faces. This suggests that the stereotype of Black men as angry is counterbalanced by the stereotype of an elderly man. But stereotypes do not always counterbalance each other, even when people have two salient social identities that seem to have conflicting stereotypes associated with them. For example, studies conducted by Todd, Thiem, and Neel (2016) suggest that even at the age of five years old Black children are more strongly associated with threat than White children. When people were primed with the faces of young Black children, they found it easier to identify threatening stimuli (e.g. guns) and more difficult to identify non-threatening stimuli (e.g. toys or tools) than when they were primed with faces of young White children. The fact that a five-year-old Black boy is a young child, and young children presumably tend not to be associated with threat, does not mean that the stereotype of the young child mitigates the impact of the stereotype of the Black man. Moreover, the co-existence of certain social identities can heighten or amplify the effects of stereotyping. For example, Asian women are especially susceptible to being misperceived in ways associated with being feminine because both the stereotype of Asians and the stereotype of women associate people with being feminine, and both of these overlapping stereotypes are applied to Asian women (Hall et al. 2019).

Let us now consider how each of the distorting effects of stereotyping considered in this section might play out in a specific case. If a judgement is made about the guilt or innocence of a Black male suspect of a crime (a) ambiguous behaviours of the suspect can be interpreted as consistent with criminality; (b) features of the suspect that fit the criminal stereotype (or which are inconsistent with the criminal stereotype) can be noticed, attended to, and remembered while others are ignored; (c) differences between the suspect and other previously encountered Black males can be missed; (d) similarities between the Black suspect and non-black individuals who have positive features that suggest that they are not criminals can also be missed; (e) the Black suspect can be given less opportunity to explain his situation than if the stereotype were not applied. Where these phenomena occur, only distorted case-specific information will be available to be balanced against the stereotype.

On many occasions, case-specific information will be more diagnostic than any background statistical information that might be encoded in a stereotype. Under such circumstances, being influenced in one's judgement by a stereotype can reduce rather than enhance one's chance of making an accurate judgement that is well informed by important and relevant information. This is because important and relevant case-specific information is not properly accessed and processed. The findings cited and theoretical positions outlined in this section show that there are many ways that the application of a stereotype can impede the information-gathering process.

8. Rejecting the Single and Dual Factor Views

Let us now return to the targets of the discussion so far in this chapter: the single and dual factor views of stereotyping. We can now see that these positions are oversimplified. They identify factors that determine whether an act of stereotyping increases or decreases the chance of a correct judgement or accurate perception. Whether or not a stereotype reflects reality, whether it does so accurately, and whether or not there is good-quality, unambiguous information about a specific case, can determine whether or not the application of a stereotype increases or decreases the chance of an accurate judgement being made. But there are numerous other factors that also come into play. We have seen that the relevance of a stereotype within a particular context and the extent to which a stereotype distorts case-specific information can also be decisive.

9. Presenting the Multifactorial View

There are, then, multiple features of any act of stereotyping that determine whether it is likely to lead to misperception, and numerous things to consider when evaluating an act of stereotyping.

WPAE

- Does the stereotype reflect some aspect of social reality?
- Does the stereotype dispose the person who applies it to respond in a way that is fitting with accurate statistical information?
- Is the stereotype that is applied relevant to the judgement in which it is applied?
- Does the application of the stereotype lead information about the specific case to be distorted or ignored? For instance does the application of the stereotype lead to:
  - distorted remembering,
  - the misinterpretation of ambiguous evidence,
  - false assumptions about similarities/dissimilarities among groups and group members,
  - aspects of the social identity of the person who is stereotyped being missed, — *Link to Leonas*
  - testimonial silencing,
  - testimonial injustice? — *Link to Fricker*

Hence, in the place of the single and dual factor views I propose the multifactorial view of stereotyping:

Multifactorial view: multiple factors determine whether judgements produced as a result of acts of stereotyping are more or less likely to be accurate than alternative judgements that might have been made in the absence of the stereotyping.

10. Making Use of the Multifactorial View

The multifactorial view thus presents a principled way to identify whether, for any act of stereotyping, the application of the stereotype increases the chance of an accurate judgement or misperception: consider the questions outlined in Section 9. The multifactorial view also shows that there are more ways that one can criticize an act of stereotyping than on the single and dual factor views. An act of stereotyping can be criticized as not increasing but decreasing the chance of an accurate judgement being made, leading to misperception of individual cases, on the basis that it has any one of many features.

The multifactorial view provides the beginning of a useful response to a defence of stereotyping that might be tempting to some: that where a stereotype accurately reflects some aspect of reality, it is good to apply it, because applying the stereotype increases the chance of an accurate judgement being made. What the discussion in this chapter shows is that there are multiple factors that need to be considered other than simply the extent to which the stereotype reflects reality. There are also multiple ways that an act of stereotyping can be criticized even if it involves the application of a stereotype that reflects some aspect of social reality. It can be argued, for instance, that the act of stereotyping is bad because the stereotype is applied in a context in which it is irrelevant, or because the application of the stereotype leads to one of the specific types of distortion of diagnostic case-specific information described in Section 7. (We shall see this response to defences of acts of stereotyping developed further in Chapter 4.)

11. Conclusion

The reader should now occupy a much better position with regards to discerning, for any act of stereotyping, whether the application of the stereotype increases the chance of an accurate judgement being made or increases the chance of misperception and misjudgement. Advocates of the single and dual factor views of stereotyping identify some factors that can determine whether stereotyping has the positive or negative outcome, but the multi-factorial view of stereotyping highlights factors that are missed by these views. It shows that in order to ascertain whether the application of a stereotype increases or decreases the chance of an accurate judgement being made about an individual case we need not only consider whether the stereotype reflects reality or is accurate, or whether there is unambiguous case-specific information. We need to also consider whether the stereotype is applied when it is irrelevant and whether it is likely to have one of the many distorting effects on case-specific information described in Section 7 of this chapter. This means that we should consider a larger set of questions when identifying whether any stereotyping in which we might engage is likely to lead us to error. And we have a wider range of ways to criticize other people's acts of stereotyping.

4

Epistemic Innocence and the Ethics of Stereotypes

1. Introduction

There are numerous dimensions along which cognitive states, such as beliefs or implicit attitudes, can be evaluated. One evaluative measure is the extent to which they accurately reflect or make contact with reality. One thought that is likely to be tempting to some is that it can only be poor from the perspective of the goal of forming true beliefs, or gaining knowledge or understanding, if a cognitive state fails to reflect or make contact with reality. The idea is that while it might be pragmatically useful, good for one's wellbeing, or even morally good, to hold an inaccurate belief, e.g. that one's child is innocent of a crime that they really committed, it cannot be good from an epistemic perspective to do so. The reason for adopting this position is clear: having true beliefs, knowledge or understanding involves having accurate beliefs, and, intuitively, having thoughts that reflect reality always increases one's chance of attaining accurate beliefs while having thoughts that fail to reflect reality decreases one's chance of attaining accurate beliefs.[1]

This chapter shows how the multifactorial view of stereotyping challenges the universality of these claims. The multifactorial view shows that the possession of a social attitude that reflects aspects of social reality can bring significant epistemic costs. Correspondingly, the possession of a social attitude that fails to reflect reality can bring significant epistemic benefits,

[1] Notable exceptions to this view are defended by Duncan Pritchard (2016) and by authors who discuss the notion of epistemic innocence (see Section 3.5). Pritchard identifies two cases in which being ignorant can be epistemically valuable: when a subject is ignorant of a misleading defeater, and when a subject is ignorant of a large set of trivial facts (e.g. about the number of grains of sand on a beach) due to focusing their attention on inquiries that yield one substantive true belief that provides a comprehensive grasp of a subject area (e.g. a belief about an area of fundamental physics). Pritchard's position can be distinguished from that defended in the current chapter because his focus is on the epistemic value of a lack of knowledge whereas the focus here is on the epistemic value of false or inaccurate social attitudes.

How Stereotypes Deceive Us. Katherine Puddifoot, Oxford University Press. © Katherine Puddifoot 2021.
DOI: 10.1093/oso/9780192845559.003.0004

facilitating the achievement of various goals relating to the acquisition of epistemic goods like true belief, knowledge, and understanding.

The idea is the following: stereotyping can bring significant epistemic costs, preventing those engaging in stereotyping from achieving various goals relating to the acquisition of epistemic goods like true belief, knowledge, and understanding. Stereotypes also sometimes accurately reflect some aspect of social reality. At times these things coincide: stereotypes that reflect an aspect of social reality bring significant epistemic costs. Under such conditions, the same epistemic costs could be avoided by not stereotyping, where the avoidance of stereotyping involves adopting a social attitude that fails to reflect social reality, or even misrepresents social reality. There can consequently be epistemic benefits to be acquired through failing to reflect social realities that could be reflected by stereotyping.

To establish each of these things it will be first necessary to show that stereotyping can bring substantial epistemic costs while the stereotype that is applied reflects some aspect of reality. Then it will be shown that by avoiding stereotyping it will sometimes be possible to avoid these unfortunate consequences at the same time that the avoidance of stereotyping involves failing to reflect reality in one's social attitudes.

The first part of this argument, which establishes that there can be significant epistemic costs associated with stereotypes that reflect aspects of social reality, has important implications for theories relating to the ethics of stereotyping. Many of the features of stereotypes and stereotyping that are morally objectionable are related to epistemic costs that follow as a result of stereotyping. As a result, we shall see that stereotypes that reflect aspects of social reality can be morally objectionable because of the epistemic costs that they can bring. Towards the end of this chapter the implications of this claim for existing approaches to the ethics of stereotyping, and understandings of the relationship between the ethical and epistemic dimensions of stereotypes and acts of stereotyping, are explored.

A numbers of examples will be used throughout this chapter. At times I will return to the example from Chapter 1 of the career girl, Caroline Bender, depicted in the book, *The Best of Everything*. In the scene that is the focus of our discussion Caroline interacts with a hopeful suitor, Paul Landis, who stereotypes her as a typical career girl. He assumes that she attended one of two colleges, lives in a particular part of the East Side of New York, and has a roommate. Each of these claims turns out to be correct. I take it that the stereotype that is applied to Caroline reflects some aspect of social reality, i.e. the lifestyles of many career girls at the time. Yet, I will show, the application of the stereotype can lead to misperceptions, false beliefs, and misunderstandings.

I will also focus on the stereotype associating scientific expertise more strongly with men than with women (see, e.g. Nosek et al. 2009). At the time of writing far more men than women work in science, technology, engineering, and mathematics (STEM) in the UK. Specifically, only 22 per cent of those working in core STEM careers in 2018 were women (WISE 2018). This means that the stereotype associating scientific expertise more strongly with men than women reflects an aspect of social reality in the UK.[2] I shall show how the application of the stereotype can nonetheless lead to misperceptions, false beliefs, and misunderstandings.

I will return to the example discussed in Chapter 3 of the stereotype of drug crime that associates drug crime more strongly with Black people than White people in the United States. Statistics suggest that Black people are *not* more heavily engaged in drug use than White people but the stereotype reflects the social reality that Black people are more likely to be *arrested* for drug use than White people. Nonetheless, as we shall see, the application of the stereotype can lead to misperceptions, false beliefs and misunderstandings.

Finally, I will consider the stereotype of a barrister. Let us assume that occupying the role of barrister is strongly associated with being White and male. The account given by the Black woman barrister Alexandra Wilson of being repeatedly mistaken for a defendant, which featured in Chapter 1, provides some reason for thinking that at least some people make this association.[3] This stereotype would reflect the social reality in the UK where a disproportionate number of barristers are White and male.[4] However, we shall see the fact that such a stereotype would reflect social reality would not prevent it from leading to misperceptions, false beliefs, and misunderstandings.

[2] There is empirical support for the idea that the stereotype emerged as a result of the social reality of the underrepresentation of women in sciences: it has been found that in nations where there was more participation by women in the sciences people less strongly associate science with men (Miller, Eagly, and Linn 2015).

[3] Alternatively, Wilson's experiences might be due to people having a stereotype associating Black people or Black women with crime.

[4] According to data on the social identity of practising barristers that was gathered in 2018 (Bar Standards Board 2019), only 39.6 per cent of junior barristers in the United Kingdom indicated that they were female while 59.8 per cent indicated that they were male. Of senior barristers (QCs), 15.8 per cent indicated that they were female while 83.8 per cent indicated that they were male. Meanwhile, 13.5 per cent of those who were junior barristers indicated that they were BAME (Black, Asian and Minority Ethnic) while 78.1 per cent were White, and 7.8 per cent of senior barristers indicated that they were BAME while 87.9 per cent indicated that they were White.

2. Epistemic Costs of Stereotyping

Chapter 3 identified numerous features of stereotyping that are epistemically costly, increasing the chance of misperceptions and misunderstandings occurring. The goal of this section is to show that some of these features, and others that have similar effects, are present in some cases where a stereotype reflects an aspect of social reality.

2.1 Reflecting Reality but Not Statistics

In Chapter 3 we saw that a stereotype can reflect an aspect of social reality and yet dispose a person to respond in a way that does not accurately reflect the statistical distribution of traits across social groups. The stereotype can, for example, lead one to overestimate or underestimate the prevalence of a trait within a particular population group.

We found that the stereotype associating Black people with drug crime reflects the reality that there are high arrest rates among the Black population. At the same time, the stereotype leads to an overestimation of the rates of Black involvement in drug crime. In fact, rates of involvement in drug use are similar across the White and Black populations (Substance Abuse and Mental Health Services Administration 2004), and White people are more likely to be users of some drugs than Black people (Office of Applied Studies, Substance Abuse and Mental Health Services Administration, 2007). But there is very little reason to doubt that many people possess stereotypes of Black people and drug usage that associate the two far more strongly than White people are associated with drug use. For example, as we saw in Chapter 3, 90 per cent of experimental participants who were asked to close their eyes and imagine a drug user said that they imagined a Black person (Burston, Jones, and Roberson-Saunders 1995, cited in Alexander 2011). There is already good reason, then, given in Chapter 3, for thinking that a stereotype can reflect some aspect of social reality and yet dispose those who possess the stereotype not to reflect in their judgements the true statistical distribution of traits across a population.

This phenomenon is not unique to the stereotype harboured by many people in the United States relating drugs crimes and race. Take the stereotype associating scientific expertise with men. A person could possess this stereotype and overestimate or underestimate the percentage of people with scientific expertise who are women. Or take the stereotype of the barrister.

Someone could possess the stereotype associating being a barrister with being White and male and underestimate the number of barristers who are Black, Asian, and Minority ethnic (BAME) and women. Or someone (in the 1950s) could overestimate or underestimate the percentage of career women in New York who went to certain colleges or live in the East Side. In each case an association could be made that reflects the fact that certain characteristics (e.g. scientific expertise, being a barrister, attending a certain college, living in certain parts of New York) are more prevalent among certain populations than others, but the association could lead to an overestimation or underestimation of the likelihood that any individual member of the population will possess the characteristic. The stereotype could therefore lead to misperceptions about individuals due to misperceptions about the likelihood that they will possess certain characteristics. They would do this while reflecting social reality.

2.2 Reflecting Reality while Being Irrelevant

There is an interesting feature of the case of drug crime. The aspect of social reality that is reflected by the stereotype is arrest rates but the stereotype associates social group members with crime rather than arrest. Rates of crime and arrests often coincide but what the drug crime case shows is that the two can come apart. Therefore, the drug crime case illustrates another way that the application of a stereotype that reflects some aspect of social reality can lead to misperceptions, false beliefs, and misunderstandings. A stereotype can reflect some aspect of social reality but influence judgements about other aspects of social reality.

We saw in Chapter 3, Section 6, that stereotypes are likely to be triggered when they are irrelevant. The current section therefore emphasizes that stereotypes that reflect some aspect of social reality can be triggered where they are irrelevant. We have seen that the stereotype associating Black people with crime might be triggered where police officers feel that their egos have been threatened but there is no evidence of criminal activity. And politicians might respond by stereotyping to challenges to the social order such as changes to drugs laws to reduce discrimination. Similar results can follow from the application of the stereotype associating scientific expertise more strongly with men than women, the stereotype of the career girl and the stereotype of the barrister.

Consider the following scenario. Campaigners fight for an increase to the number of young women who study STEM subjects at university, with the aim of increasing the numbers of women with scientific expertise. This provides a threat to the existing social order within scientific disciplines at universities and within certain workplaces. This situation provides fertile conditions for stereotyping. Women who enter universities and workplaces to work in STEM subjects are stereotyped as lacking expertise. But the stereotype is not relevant in these cases, in which women have taken the opportunities that have been made available to them, and gained scientific expertise. The fact that the stereotype associating men more strongly than women with scientific expertise reflects some aspect of social reality is not a protective against the stereotype being applied where it is irrelevant.

Consider also a scenario in which a man and woman are competing for promotion and the woman is chosen. The man's ego is threatened because he had believed that he should and would get the promotion. The man applies the stereotype associating career women with a specific set of limited lifestyles to conclude that they lack the qualities of being original and innovative thinkers that is needed to be a successful leader in industry. The stereotype about career women's monolithic lifestyle is applied when irrelevant due to a threat to a person's ego and leads to the misperception of the attributes of an individual career woman to whom the stereotype is applied. Even if the stereotype reflected the social reality that career women tend to share a similar lifestyle this would not prevent the stereotype from being applied when irrelevant and consequently leading to misperception of the qualities of an individual.

2.3 Reflecting Reality while Leading to Misinterpretation of Ambiguous Evidence

We found in Chapter 3, Section 7, that psychological evidence suggests that people tend to misinterpret ambiguous evidence as showing that stereotypical traits are present rather than responding as they should, that the evidence is ambiguous (Duncan 1976; Sagar and Schofield 1980). There is room for stereotypes to have this effect while reflecting some aspect of social reality.

Imagine, for example, that a woman displays errors in her speech when explaining a scientific concept at a conference. The speech errors are ambiguous; they are consistent with her lacking knowledge about the topic about which she is speaking, but also consistent with her lacking confidence speaking in a public arena. Because she is a woman, and many people strongly associate scientific expertise with men, a person applying the scientist stereotype might interpret her ambiguous behaviour as indicative of a lack of knowledge rather than a lack of confidence. On the other hand, a man displaying the same speech errors may be interpreted as knowledgeable but lacking confidence because scientific expertise is associated with men rather than women. Once again, as women are underrepresented in science, most scientific experts are men, so the stereotype reflects something of social reality. Nonetheless, it can lead to inappropriate interpretations of individuals' behaviours. While the behaviours should be interpreted as ambiguous, they are interpreted in ways fitting with a stereotype.

2.4 Reflecting Reality while Distorting Memories

Chapter 3, Section 7, also introduced psychological findings indicating that the application of a stereotype can lead to the formation of distorted memories: features of a situation that fit with the stereotype are sometimes more likely to be remembered than those that are inconsistent with the stereotype (Bodenhausen 1988; Cohen 1981; Signorella and Liben 1984; Stangor 1988; Levinson 2007). At other times, counter-stereotypical features are more likely to be remembered (Dijksterhuis and van Knippenberg 1995; Hastie 1981; Hastie and Kumar 1979; Srull 1981; Srull and Wyer 1989). In each type of case, the outcome will be a biased representation of past events. To see how memories can become distorted in this way even while a stereotype reflects some aspect of reality, we can return to the example discussed in Section 2.3 of the current chapter.

Imagine that after the talk in which the female scientist makes speech errors there is a question and answer session in which she excels. As she is more confident responding to questions, she does not make speech errors, speaking eloquently about her research. However, the stereotype associating men more strongly than women with scientific expertise leads you to remember the speech errors but not the eloquent discussion in the question and answer session. You remember the scientist's performance in a distorted way that leads you to have a false impression that she lacks the good level of expertise that she has displayed.

Imagine further that you are later leading a job search recruiting a scientific researcher to join your lab. The female scientist applies. Psychological findings suggest that you are more likely to remember aspects of her previous performance if you stereotyped when viewing it (see, e.g., Cohen 1981). Therefore, as a result of the application of the stereotype you remember that she made errors in her talk and that you interpreted them as showing that she lacked scientific expertise. Due to the operation of the same stereotype you do not remember that she excelled in the question and answer session. If you did not remember anything about her performance then you would base your judgement about whether to invite her to interview on the details of her achievements that are provided in her CV (resume). The operation of the stereotype leads you to remember more information than you might have otherwise, but the information that you remember is distorted, leading to a false impression of the scientist and her levels of expertise. All of this occurs in spite of the stereotype associating scientific expertise more strongly with men than women reflecting an aspect of reality.

Now imagine a scenario in which counter-stereotypical information is better remembered than stereotypical information. Instead of making speech errors, the female scientist presents extremely well. She is confident and articulate. This challenges your stereotype of women as poor orators. You therefore focus attention on the information about the woman's oratory skills, attempting to reconcile this information with your pre-existing stereotype. Consequently, you remember well the woman's oratory when you are considering her job application for a combined teaching and research position. However, you do not remember how well she interacted with those who asked her questions during the question and answer session. You therefore doubt that she has the interpersonal skills required to succeed as a teacher. You remember the scientist's past performance in a way that is biased, failing to reflect the full breadth of the skills and abilities on display.

2.5 Reflecting Reality and the Failure to Notice Differences

Chapter 3, Section 7, also introduced psychological findings indicating that when people are viewed as part of a minority group as a result of the application of a stereotype, they can be falsely assumed to share characteristics with other members of their group that have previously been encountered (e.g. Bartsch and Judd 1993; Hewstone, Crisp, and Turner 2011). Let us consider how this effect of stereotyping can occur while the stereotype reflects some aspect of social reality.

Consider the career woman stereotype that is applied to Caroline in *The Best of Everything*. As a career woman at that time she would have been a minority in the workplace. Once she is viewed as a career woman rather than an editor (her occupation) as a result of the application of the career woman stereotype, she would be likely to be assumed to be more similar than she really is to other memorable people who are career women. She might be assumed to be more likely than she really is to have an affair with her boss, to leave her job after marriage, and so on. Each of these errors could occur due to the triggering of the stereotype of a career woman that leads her to be perceived in terms of her membership of this social category regardless of the accuracy of the stereotype.

Consider also the case of a Black female barrister. In Chapter 3 we considered how people with multiple subordinate identities—like Black females—are especially likely to be treated as indistinguishable and interchangeable. If a Black female barrister is viewed through the lens of her multiple subordinate social identities, that is, as Black and female, as well as a barrister, then she is likely to be mistaken for other people who share the target subordinate social identities. She is likely to be viewed as more similar to other Black females than she really is. This error could occur due to the triggering of a stereotype that reflects social reality, for example, it might occur due to the triggering of the stereotype of barristers as male and White. The triggering of this stereotype might make her identity as a Black female salient and therefore lead her to be viewed as interchangeable with other Black females.

2.6 Reflecting Reality and the Failure to Notice Similarities

A further finding from psychology discussed in Chapter 3, Section 7, is that the activation of a stereotype, and the way that it leads people to be viewed through the lens of their social group membership, can prevent similarities between members of different social groups being acknowledged (Tajfel 1981). To see how this phenomenon can occur even where a stereotype accurately reflects some aspect of social reality, consider how the activation of the stereotype of a barrister could lead a Black female barrister to be viewed as distinct from her White male colleagues. This could lead similarities between the Black female barrister and her White male colleagues to be missed. If a White male displays certain characteristics, for example, characteristics that are found to reflect a commitment to his career, then the

Black female counterpart may not be attributed with similar characteristics. Significant similarities between the members of the different groups will be missed. Attributes of the Black female barrister will be missed, as a result of the application of a stereotype that reflects some aspect of social reality.

2.7 Reflecting Reality and Poor Explanations

A further psychological finding discussed in Chapter 3, Section 7, is that people can fail to track the truth in their explanations of behaviour if they possess a stereotype related to the person whose behaviour is being explained. If the behaviour is fitting with the stereotype of the actor's social group then it is likely to be explained in terms of their dispositions (Duncan 1976). But if the behaviour does not fit the stereotype then it is likely to be explained by appeal to their situation (Duncan 1976). Stereotypes are often also taken to be a sufficient explanation of a person's behaviour when they are not. In these situations the explanation provided will often fail to track the truth about the real cause of the behaviour. To see how this error can occur when the stereotype that is applied reflects reality, consider the following case.

Jill is a female scientist. She processes some data and the results are later found to contain errors. This outcome fits the stereotype that women lack scientific expertise. The error is therefore attributed to Jill and explained in terms of her lacking relevant expertise. Jill's male colleague, Jonah, also processes some data and the results similarly contain errors. Jonah's error does not fit with the stereotype strongly associating scientific expertise with males. Therefore, in Jonah's case it is assumed that there must have been a problem with the raw data provided to him by his female colleague. Stereotypical explanations like these will often fail to track the truth—for instance, in these cases about the true source of the errors—yet they can occur, as in these cases, due to the operation of a stereotype that reflects an aspect of social reality.

2.8 Reflecting Reality, Testimonial Injustice, and Testimonial Smothering

What about the phenomenon of people suffering testimonial injustice, being given less credibility than they deserve when they provide testimony, due to the operation of stereotypes? (Collins 2000; Fricker 2007) Can this occur when the stereotype that is in operation reflects reality? According to Miranda Fricker, whose book *Epistemic Injustice* introduced the terminology of testimonial injustice, the phenomenon only occurs due to prejudice, where prejudices are defined as 'judgements, which may have a positive or negative valence, and which display some (typically epistemically culpable) resistance to counter-evidence owing to some affective investment on the part of the subject' (p. 35). Given that the stereotypes operational in testimonial injustice are described as occurring due to resistance to counterevidence on the part of the subject, the definition does not sit neatly with the idea that testimonial injustice can occur where a stereotype reflects reality. Or more specifically, it does not seem to be compatible with the definition of testimonial injustice that it could occur in a case where a person acquires a stereotype as a fitting response to facts found in their social environment. It might be insisted, then, that the most interesting types of case relating to the discussion in the current chapter are those where people form stereotypes that reflect reality due to responding to evidence in the environment and that these will not be cases of testimonial injustice due to there being no epistemically culpable failure. However, it suffices for the moment (see more discussion in Section 9.2) to note that a phenomenon that is extremely similar to testimonial injustice, with a similarly distorting effect, can occur due to the application of a stereotype that is formed non-culpably and reflects reality.

Consider the following type of case. Whenever a female scientist, or a Black female barrister, is given less credibility than she deserves for knowing about her area of expertise due to the application of the stereotype associating scientific expertise with males or being a barrister with being White and male, there is a case very similar to one of testimonial injustice as defined by Fricker that is the result of the operation of a stereotype that reflects an aspect of social reality. Testimonial evidence, conveying information about the scientist's or barrister's expertise, is not given due credibility due to the operation of a stereotype.

What about testimonial smothering, which occurs when a person chooses not to provide testimony that they deem to be risky because they believe that it will not be given appropriate uptake due to the operation of a stereotype (Dotson 2011)? Do we have reason to think that people will ever smother their testimony as a result of suspecting that it will not be given appropriate uptake due to a stereotype that reflects reality? Here is an example that illustrates how this could happen. A female scientist decides to withhold a risky opinion or decides not to ask a risky question due to fear that they will be misinterpreted as misunderstanding the material being discussed, due to her awareness of the stereotype associating scientific expertise with men more than women. A case like this would involve the kind of distorting effect described in discussions of testimonial smothering. If people choose not to speak when they have risky information to convey, or are not properly interpreted when they do speak, the information that they could provide will be missed, decreasing the chance of true beliefs being formed and increasing the chance of misunderstanding.

2.9 Reflecting Reality and Inappropriate Associations

A final way that a stereotype that reflects an aspect of social reality may lead to misperceptions or misunderstandings is that it may lead to the triggering of associations that are inaccurate or prevent the activation of associations that are accurate. To understand this point it will be useful to reflect on the nature of a number of popular models of stereotypes and stereotyping[5] that provide good reason to think that when people make associations of this type they consequently either make other associations that fail to reflect the social reality (Kelly and Roedder 2008) or fail to make other associations that would reflect social reality.

On the associative network view, stereotypes are a set of linked attributes (Carlston 1992; Manis, Nelson, and Shedler 1988). The stereotype of a scientist is a set of attributes—for example, lab-coat wearing, bespectacled, male, hardworking, conscientious, expert, attentive to detail, innovative thinker—which are linked together in the mind of the believer. The perception of one of the attributes leads to the activation of associated concepts. Not only are concepts activated, however, feelings of positivity or negativity can also be activated. On this model, stereotyping involves a number of different associations, which are like a tightly-knit cluster of beliefs. When one holds a cluster of beliefs, one belief might be true but it might trigger a number of false beliefs. For example, the association between science and men might trigger a further association between men and attentiveness to

---

[5] There are other accounts of stereotypes and stereotyping, such as the schema view (Fiske and Taylor 1991). This epistemic cost will not necessarily follow on some of these accounts, therefore the claims made in this section are conditional on stereotypes having a certain psychological structure.

detail and high IQs. Individual men might therefore be associated with these positive characteristics even where the positive associations are inappropriate. Men might be associated with attentiveness to detail or a high IQ when they are no more likely to have these traits than women. Meanwhile, the associations might not be made between women and these positive characteristics because the stereotype does not associate them with science.

The prototype model of stereotypes also suggests that inappropriate associations will be made and appropriate associations left unmade. On the prototype model, stereotypes are abstract representations of typical features of members of a group (Cantor and Mischel 1979), for example, the stereotype of a bird might be an abstract representation of a small-winged creature, creature with beak, flying creature, creature that tweets. Whether a stereotype is applied to any individual depends on the similarity between traits of the individual and a set of typical features ordinarily associated with members of the group. But the traits of the individual that determine whether the stereotype is applied are usually superficial features of the individual, such as signs from their face of their gender or race (see, e.g. Ashmore and Del Boca 1979; Bodenhausen and Macrae 1998). These features of human psychology combine to mean that the associations are likely to often be applied inappropriately. A case in which an association would be made when it shouldn't be is the following: a woman displays superficial features that are a part of the abstract representation of a wife and mother, that is, feminine facial and bodily features. Other features of the abstract representation of a wife and mother are triggered. However, the woman has few other characteristics associated with being a wife and mother: most notably, she has no spouse or children. The same case could be one in which associations are not made but they should be. The woman displays superficial features that are not associated with science, that is, the same feminine facial and bodily features. Other features that are a part of the abstract representation of scientists are therefore not associated with her. The perception of the superficial signs that she is a woman inhibits the scientist stereotype. However, the individual possesses many other features associated with the scientist stereotype: she has expertise in science and related positive traits like attentiveness to detail or innovative thinking.

Things seem little better on the exemplar view of stereotypes (see, e.g. Smith and Zarate 1992). According to this view, stereotypes represent groups through particular concrete examples; for instance, the stereotype of a bird is represented through a robin. Whether or not a stereotype is activated in a particular case is determined by the similarity between the target individual and the exemplar. The fact remains that superficial features of an individual determine whether they are judged to be similar to the exemplar. This means that a cluster of features possessed by a particular exemplar will be associated with a target individual only if they possess superficial features that are similar to those of the exemplar. For example, Einstein might be the exemplar of a scientist. Then a cluster of features associated with Einstein (expertise in science, genius, innovative thinking) will be associated with an individual due to stereotyping only if they display superficial features associated with him (being male, looking eccentric, etc.). Individuals who do not display these superficial characteristics will not be stereotyped as a scientist, and will therefore not have Einstein's features associated with them. This is bad news for many women, who are less likely than their male counterparts to possess at least one of the superficial features of exemplars of science like Einstein, that is, having masculine facial features. It is also bad news for those of us who want to make accurate judgements about individual women who are scientists but do not share the superficial features of familiar exemplars of scientists because if the exemplar view is correct we are less likely to associate these individuals than others with features that they actually possess (expertise in science, attentiveness to detail, innovative thinking). In addition to this, individuals who share superficial characteristics with exemplars of scientists are likely to be associated with other characteristics possessed by those exemplars even if the only features that they share are the superficial ones (e.g. their facial features).

Stereotyping claims are also sometimes argued to be generic claims, with a similar structure to claims like 'ducks lay eggs' or 'mosquitoes carry the West Nile virus' (see, e.g. Leslie 2007). They are not universal claims, but they suggest that members of a group typically, characteristically or strikingly possess certain features. Sally Haslanger (2011) presents reason for thinking that if stereotypical thought has the structure of generic claims, it can lead to inappropriate associations, even in a context in which the stereotypes applied reflect something of social reality. Haslanger points out that generic claims that involve associations between members of certain social groups and particular characteristics can imply that there is something essential about the nature of the group members in virtue of which they possess the characteristics associated with them. These essentializing judgements can be inaccurate because it is really the social context in which the group members are located that means that they are more likely than others to possess the traits associated with them. For example, women might not only be associated with being nurturing but also with having a nature in virtue of which they are disposed to be nurturing. While the association between women and nurturing might reflect something of reality, as a result of social constructs that lead women to occupy a nurturing role, it can lead to a further association that fails to reflect reality: the association of women with an essentially nurturing nature.

If any of the accounts of stereotypes discussed in these sections is correct, then, stereotypes may reflect reality and yet nonetheless lead false associations to be made, or prevent accurate associations from being made. A number of negative epistemic consequences can follow from making inappropriate associations or failing to make appropriate associations. We can make poor inferences, assuming that people have characteristics that they lack, or that they do not have characteristics that they do have (Egan 2011). For example, we can assume that women are lacking in scientific expertise but nurturing, because of the superficial characteristics they display. Alternatively, we can notice that we are making erroneous judgements and expend cognitive energy to suppress our stereotyping responses (Egan 2011; Gendler 2011). This can lead to the depletion of our cognitive resources, which can in turn cause errors of judgement. The latter phenomenon has been illustrated through experiments in which White participants are required to interact with Black experimenters before completing a cognitive task (see, e.g. Richeson and Shelton 2007). Those who were found to produce high scores on implicit measures of racial stereotyping, indicating that they make strong negative implicit associations with Black people, performed poorly on the cognitive tasks, seemingly because their cognitive resources were depleted by efforts to suppress their stereotyping.[6]

2.10 Summary

We have now found that stereotypes that reflect aspects of social reality can bring substantial epistemic costs, leading to misperceptions and misunderstandings. They can reflect reality but overestimate or underestimate

---

[6] Gendler (2011) outlines three epistemic costs that can follow from implicit bias. One of these costs is the cognitive depletion that comes with suppressing implicit biases, and the others are stereotype threat and poor cross-racial facial recognition. Cognitive depletion is the only one of Gendler's costs to be included in this discussion because Mugg (2013) has convincingly argued that the other two costs are not epistemic costs for the person engaging in the stereotyping. They are not, therefore, ways that stereotypes can lead people to make epistemic errors when applying a stereotype that reflects reality.

statistical regularities or be applied when they are irrelevant. They may lead (i) ambiguous evidence to be misinterpreted as fitting with a stereotype; (ii) information to be remembered in a distorted manner; (iii) details about individuals to be missed due to assumptions about the similarities within and dissimilarities between groups; (iv) false explanations to be developed; (v) testimonial injustice and testimonial smothering to occur; (vi) inaccurate associations to be made or accurate associations not to be made. Appearances are deceptive if it seems as if stereotypes only bring these costs if they fail to reflect reality.

3. Epistemic Benefits of Avoiding Stereotyping

Where there are epistemic costs associated with social beliefs or other social attitudes like implicit social attitudes that reflect an aspect of reality, there can be epistemic benefits associated with lacking these beliefs or other social attitudes, and even from having false social beliefs or other social attitudes. For instance, there might be epistemic benefits associated with lacking a belief or implicit social attitude that represents the high arrest rates among Black people in comparison to White people in the United States, or lacking a belief or implicit social attitude about the drastically higher number of men compared to women who are employed in roles requiring expertise in science, engineering or maths in the UK. Correspondingly, there might be epistemic benefits associated with having beliefs and other social attitudes that are egalitarian in ways that fail to reflect reality: e.g. associating White people and Black people equally strongly with drug arrests or associating science equally as strongly with women and men. False beliefs or social attitudes of these types can lead one to avoid the epistemic costs associated with stereotyping outlined in Section 2 of this chapter, thereby bringing epistemic benefits.

Take Sara. She does not associate Black people more strongly than White people with crime. As a result, she does not have a stereotype that leads her to treat ambiguous behaviour by a Black person as aggressive. She does not remember the behaviour of Black people that is consistent with them being criminals but not behaviour that is inconsistent with them being criminals. Neither is she susceptible to remembering behaviour that is inconsistent with them being criminals but not behaviour that is consistent with them being criminals. She does not immediately categorize people according to their race when encountered in situations in which a stereotype associating

Black people with crime would be triggered in other people. In such circumstances she avoids falsely assuming that Black people are more similar to each other than they really are and does not miss ways in which individual Black people are similar to people from other racial groups. In many circumstances, where other people's stereotypes associating Black people with crime would be triggered, she would be less likely than these others to explain the behaviour of Black people she encounters in terms of a stereotype if it is stereotypical but in terms of their situation if it is not stereotypical. She would, for example, be less likely to explain the behaviour of a young Black man as being the result of the aggressive nature of Black people if he is displaying actions that seem to be aggressive but explain his behaviour in terms of his situation (e.g. he did gain access to good school x) if he is behaving kindly and thoughtfully. She would be less likely to inappropriately mistrust Black people or indicate to them that she will not give appropriate uptake to their testimony. As a stereotype associating Black people with crimes is not triggered, other inaccurate associations are less likely to be made and features that are inconsistent with the stereotype are more likely to be associated with Black people.

Now take Tim. Tim does not associate science more strongly with men than women. He grew up in a society in which men and women are equally well represented in the sciences before moving to the UK, where men are significantly overrepresented. His social beliefs reflect the state of the country of his origin. He does not treat ambiguous behaviour of women scientists as demonstrating that they lack expertise, instead judging the behaviour as it should be judged, as ambiguous. He does not remember evidence suggesting that any woman scientist lacks expertise more strongly than evidence suggesting that a woman scientist has expertise. Nor does he remember evidence suggesting that woman scientists have expertise better than evidence suggesting that they do not. In circumstances in which the level of expertise of a woman scientist is being evaluated he does not engage in stereotyping, so he does not assume that she is more similar than she really is to other woman scientists, nor does he assume that she is less similar than she really is to other scientists who are men. He does not wrongly explain the errors made by women in terms of the stereotype that women lack scientific expertise and their successes in terms of their situation (e.g. she has an excellent male mentor). He gives women scientists an appropriate level of credibility and reason for thinking that he will give their testimony about scientific matters appropriate uptake even if it is risky. As he does not associate men more strongly with scientific expertise than women, he does not associate men more strongly than he should with having a higher IQ, attentiveness to detail, inquisitiveness. Nor does he fail to associate women with the same features when it is appropriate to do so.

Sara and Tim lack stereotypes that other people possess and which reflect an aspect of social reality. For this reason, prima facie they occupy a poorer position than these other people with regards to the ability to obtain knowledge about whether a person is likely to engage in criminal activity or has scientific expertise. But by avoiding stereotyping, they avoid numerous significant epistemic costs, thereby gaining significant epistemic benefits. There are therefore significant epistemic benefits to lacking stereotypes, even where the stereotypes that one would otherwise possess would reflect some aspect or aspects of social reality.

There are not only significant benefits associated with lacking stereotypes that reflect social reality, there are also significant epistemic benefits to possessing attitudes that inaccurately reflect reality. The possession of the attitude that women and men are equally likely to have scientific expertise will guard against various tendencies that accompany the stereotype associating scientific expertise more strongly with men than women. Tim's case illustrates this point. Not only does he lack the stereotype, he possesses an attitude that inaccurately reflects the reality of the distribution of scientific expertise in the country he currently occupies. It is as a result of possessing the attitude that he avoids the epistemic costs associated with stereotyping. There can therefore be significant epistemic benefits to the possession of false attitudes, particularly false attitudes that represent the world as more egalitarian than it really is. The possession of these attitudes can protect against various epistemic errors, e.g. misinterpreting ambiguous evidence, having distorted memories, and so on.

It is worthwhile stepping back and considering something that is common to most of the epistemic costs associated with stereotyping, and therefore the epistemic benefits associated with cognitions avoiding stereotyping. Most of the epistemic costs involve information about an individual being distorted or made inaccessible. Information about individuals is (a) viewed unambiguously when it should be taken to be ambiguous, (b) remembered selectively, (c) ignored or falsely assumed to exist, (d) inappropriately discredited or left unarticulated, or (e) poorly explained. In the types of cases discussed early in this chapter, stereotypes reflect some aspect of social reality but lead to a distortion of information about individuals and cases to which they are applied.

Because most of the epistemic costs associated with stereotyping involve the distortion of information about individuals, there will be occasions in which the application of a stereotype is unlikely to bring epistemic costs because there is little or no case-specific information to be distorted. Where a stereotype reflects some aspect of social reality, and it does not lead to distortion of case-specific information, there might not be any epistemic costs associated with the application of it. To see this point, consider the following example.

Imagine that you are asked whether a randomly selected woman is more likely to be a scientist or a non-scientist. You harbour a stereotype associating scientific expertise with men, so you respond that the woman is more likely to be a non-scientist. You have access to no other information about the individual that can guide your judgement. In such a situation, there will be epistemic benefits to being influenced by the stereotype: as a result of doing so you will be more likely to make an accurate judgement than if you did not make the association and you will be no less likely to respond appropriately to evidence about the specific individual because there is no such evidence available. As the association tracks something of social reality (say you are in the UK in 2018 and only 22 per cent people working in core STEM workforce are women (WISE 2018)), it will dispose you to respond in certain ways that could, under conditions of this sort, increase your chance of making a correct judgement. On the other hand, there might not be any epistemic costs associated with the application of the stereotype. If you have no specific information about the randomly selected female scientist then the application of the stereotype cannot lead you to respond in a biased and distorting way to evidence about them.

It is crucial to note, however, that in many and probably most cases in which we might engage in stereotyping we have access to, or the potential to access, some case-specific information. We could find out about a person's personal characteristics, their achievements, their interests, whether or not they have scientific training, whether or not they have a history of criminal behaviour, and so on. Therefore, there is case-specific information that can be distorted as a result of the application of a stereotype, bringing epistemic costs. Accordingly, there are potential epistemic benefits associated with avoiding the application of the stereotype: i.e. those associated with avoiding the distortion of case-specific information.

4. Epistemic Innocence of False Social Attitudes

The argument outlined in Sections 1 to 3 of this chapter can be helpfully framed in terms of the notion of epistemic innocence. The notion has been introduced to capture how there can be epistemic benefits to the possession of cognitive states and processes that are epistemically faulty, for example, false or irrational. To say that a cognition is epistemically innocent is not to say that it is flawless, but it is to emphasize that it is not wholly bad from the perspective of achieving epistemic goals.

Lisa Bortolotti (2015a) introduced the notion of epistemic innocence through a comparison with the justification defence in UK and US law. A justification defence is used to establish the innocence of an individual by showing that their act did not constitute an offence under the circumstances in which it was performed. Justification defences can apply where an action prevents serious harms. They apply where an action that would be viewed as a criminal offence under some circumstances is viewed as an emergency response. Bortolotti's claim is that there are some cognitions that can be viewed as poor from an epistemic perspective but are nonetheless valuable because they prevent other serious epistemic harms.[7]

Epistemically innocent cognitions could therefore easily be characterized in terms of their epistemic faults, that is, the way that they are inaccurate or irrational. But they bring substantial epistemic benefits that mitigate, to some extent, the epistemic faults.

The social cognitions that have been discussed in Section 3 of this chapter, where people lack stereotypes and have egalitarian attitudes that fail to reflect social realities, meet these conditions. First, they are epistemically faulty: they fail to reflect aspects of social reality, such as the higher arrest rates among the Black population than the White population in the USA, or the overrepresentation of males in the sciences. When focusing on the epistemic dimension of the attitudes it is tempting to characterize the cognitions in terms of these flaws.

Second, the social cognitions bring substantial epistemic benefits. They do so by avoiding substantial downstream epistemic costs that would follow if an agent engaged in stereotyping. Specifically, agents who fail to reflect social realities like the high arrest rates among the Black population in the USA or the overrepresentation of males in science in the UK avoid the costs of misinterpreting ambiguous evidence, remembering in a biased manner,

---

[7] Examples of beliefs argued to be epistemically innocent are motivated delusions (Bortolotti 2015a), delusions in schizophrenia (Bortolotti 2015b), delusions in depression (Antrobus and Bortolotti 2016), confabulated explanations of actions driven by implicit bias (Sullivan-Bissett 2015), mental states resulting from the use of psychedelic drugs (Lethaby 2016), and distorted memories in the clinical population (Bortolotti and Sullivan-Bissett 2018). See Bortolotti (2020) for an overview of work on epistemic innocence.

ignoring or falsely assuming evidence to exist, discrediting or preventing the articulation of relevant testimony, and poorly explaining information that they do access. These are serious epistemic harms that are prevented as a result of the possession of epistemically faulty social attitudes that fail to reflect some aspects of social reality.

There is a further condition on epistemic innocence: the no alternatives condition. A cognition is epistemically innocent if there is no alternative cognition that would confer the same benefits without the costs. In the current case, an alternative cognition would be one that reflected the social realities that are often encoded in stereotypes without leading to the downstream epistemic costs ordinarily associated with stereotyping. It is difficult to establish whether there are any alternative social cognitions of this type. However, the research on stereotyping strongly suggests that making associations between social groups and characteristics like criminality and scientific expertise will often automatically lead to stereotyping.

Consider the research on the implicit stereotyping involved in implicit bias. Implicit biases are automatically activated mental phenomena that can associate social groups with characteristics such as criminality or expertise (see, e.g. Amodio and Devine 2008; Brownstein 2019; Payne and Gawronski 2010). They can be activated without any intention on the part of the agent within which they operate. Psychological studies suggest that implicit stereotyping of this type can lead to at least some of the epistemic costs outlined in Section 2 of this chapter. For example, implicit stereotypes have been shown to lead ambiguous behaviour to be interpreted in a way fitting with the stereotype (Devine 1989; Gawronski, Geschke, and Banse 2003). Moreover, implicit stereotypes seem to produce memory biases, leading people to remember events in a way that is fitting with the stereotypes that they harbour (see, e.g., Levinson 2007). When stereotypes operate automatically in these types of way, they will often automatically lead to epistemic costs. It could be argued that in such a situation an epistemic agent has two options. They can have: (i) a cognition that fails to reflect the social realities and avoids the epistemic costs associated with stereotyping by avoiding susceptibility to automatically stereotyping, or (ii) a cognition that reflects the social realities but makes the agent highly susceptible to the epistemic costs associated with stereotyping. It might be argued that there is no alternative cognition available to the thinker that reflects the social realities without making them susceptible to automatically making errors such as remembering evidence in a biased way.

But even where it is difficult to establish whether the no alternatives condition applies it is nonetheless useful to adopt parts of the epistemic innocence framework. The notion of epistemic innocence highlights how there can be beliefs and other cognitions that fail to reflect reality but nonetheless bring epistemic benefits by protecting against epistemic harms. This is exactly what we find with social cognitions: there are some that fail to reflect reality but bring substantial epistemic benefits by avoiding epistemic harms.

5. The Lesser of Two Epistemic Evils

Some, but not all, epistemically innocent cognitions are the lesser of two epistemic evils (Bortolotti 2015a). The epistemic benefits that they bring outweigh their epistemic costs. Where a set of cognitions are the lesser of two epistemic evils, people aiming to achieve epistemic goals, such as acquiring knowledge, true belief or understanding, are more likely to achieve those goals if they possess the cognitions rather than some relevant alternatives. It seems clear that some egalitarian social attitudes that fail to reflect social inequities, and thereby avoid stereotyping, are the lesser of two epistemic evils. While they bring the epistemic costs associated with failing to reflect reality they bring such significant epistemic benefits that the costs are outweighed by the benefits.

The following example illustrates the correctness of the claim. Imagine a person making an assessment of the contribution that a female scientist could make to their research team. If they respond by applying the stereotype associating scientific expertise with men (a stereotype that reflects the social reality that women are underrepresented in the sciences), then the disposition that they manifest will be one that would increase the chance of them making an accurate assessment of the probability that a randomly selected individual scientist is a woman or a man, or a randomly selected individual person is a scientist, in the absence of informative case-specific information. However, if they respond in a way that does not involve stereotyping—i.e. the egalitarian response that fails to reflect the social reality—then they will respond in a way that avoids the following numerous pitfalls: (i) memory distortions that would make them selectively remember features of the candidate; (ii) viewing ambiguous behaviours of the candidate as evidence of lack of expertise; (iii) failing to notice differences between the candidate and other, previously encountered female scientists; (iv) failing to notice similarities between the candidate and male scientists who have positive features that suggest that they are experts; (v) the tendency to assume that any behaviours that are stereotypical of non-experts (e.g. lack of confidence speaking about the subject) are indicative of the dispositions of the candidate rather than the situation that she is placed in; and, finally, (vi) the tendency to make associations with the candidate that are inaccurate. The benefits associated with avoiding these pitfalls in this context vastly outweigh the benefits that come from automatically responding in a way that reflects the statistical reality that women are under-represented in the sciences.

It might be tempting to draw the universal conclusion here that the epistemic benefits of failing to reflect social realities by not engaging in stereotyping always outweigh the epistemic costs. This would be too swift. In Chapter 5 we will get a fuller grasp of the complexity of the situation, seeing that frequently a proper understanding of the situation of a person will require an understanding of their position within a social group. For the moment, it is possible to see why the universal conclusion should not be drawn by simply reconsidering how sometimes individuating information about a specific case is sparse and therefore, with information about social group membership as the main guide of one's judgements, one might be more likely to obtain true beliefs if one has an attitude that reflects the social reality.

The main point of this chapter is, however, now well-established: the correctness of our judgements frequently depends on our ability to access and process case-specific information, for example, information about particular individuals who might be scientists, their past experience, their qualifications, their analytic skills, etc. Stereotypes reflecting social realities such as the underrepresentation of women within a particular occupation can lead us to respond in a systematically and predictably distorted way to this case-specific information. Therefore, there can be epistemic benefits associated with failing to reflect these realities in our judgements. On many, and possibly even most, occasions information about specific cases is highly diagnostic, and more diagnostic than stereotypes about their social group. In such cases, allowing one's response to the case specific information to be distorted by reflecting social realities through stereotyping reduces the chance of an accurate judgement being made. The benefits of an egalitarian response, and the way that the response avoids distortion of case-specific information, can outweigh the costs of failing to reflect some social realities.

6. Changing Responses to Stereotyping

In Chapter 3 we found that the multifactorial approach to stereotyping presented a challenge to the thought that is likely to be tempting to many that stereotyping is good from an epistemic perspective as long as the stereotype reflects social reality. We found that the situation is more complex, and there are factors other than the stereotype reflecting reality that determine whether or not it is advantageous to apply it. The argument found in Section 5 of this chapter adds further to this challenge. The argument puts significant pressure on the inference, which people are likely to be tempted to make, from evidence that a stereotype reflects some aspect of social reality to the conclusion that it is best from an epistemic perspective to make the association encoded in the stereotype. If there are some conditions where the best epistemic consequences follow if one does not reflect social realities, evidence that a stereotype reflects some aspect of social reality does not establish that it is best from an epistemic perspective to apply it. Sometimes the search for accurate beliefs about social actors and events is more likely to be successful as a result of avoiding stereotyping, even if the stereotype that one would otherwise apply reflects an aspect of social reality.

7. Embracing Base-Rate Neglect

One implication of the conclusions reached so far in this chapter is that there is a strong case for embracing, in some contexts, a phenomenon that is sometimes taken to be a prime example of irrationality: base-rate neglect.

Base-rate neglect occurs when a person ignores background statistical information when making a calculation of probability. (The phenomenon of base-rate neglect is introduced in Chapter 2, Section 2 in terms of Kahneman and Tversky's (1973) lawyer-engineer experiment.) Base-rate neglect is taken to be a serious epistemic error because it involves ignoring relevant statistical information, and it can lead to highly inaccurate judgements about the probability of certain outcomes. The importance of avoiding base-rate neglect was shown in Chapter 2 to provide one reason for thinking that people ought to stereotype if the stereotype accurately reflects reality. The thought is that accurate stereotypes encode base-rates. Where these stereotypes are applied in judgement, the resulting judgements are properly influenced by base-rates. The failure to apply the accurate stereotypes constitutes base-rate neglect.

Therefore, applying an accurate stereotype is a positive thing because it avoids the serious epistemic error that is base-rate neglect.

This thought is evident in Tamar Szabó Gendler's (2011) influential discussion of implicit bias. Gendler presents what could be viewed as a serious problem for responses to the implicit stereotyping involved in implicit bias that involve preventing people from associating Black people more strongly than White people with certain crimes where the association would reflect higher arrest rates among the Black population. Gendler suggests that not associating Black people more strongly than White people with these crimes would be a serious epistemic error because it would involve base-rate neglect. In societies in which social inequities mean that Black people are more likely to be involved in certain crimes, there are, in Gendler's view, serious epistemic costs involved with being egalitarian because this involves base-rate neglect.

What the arguments in this chapter so far suggest is that sometimes we can put worries about the epistemic costs of base-rate neglect aside because it can be the best thing from an epistemic perspective to ignore base-rate information. The relevant base-rate information relates to the distribution of traits across different social groups. Ignoring this base-rate information by, for example, choosing not to be aware of the social identity of those you are judging, can be the lesser of two epistemic evils.[8]

8. Implications for Ethics of Stereotyping

The point that stereotypes that reflect social reality can lead to epistemic failings, which was established in Section 2 of the current chapter, also has

---

[8] Another way to view this point is as a challenge to the idea that it is useful to use Bayes' theorem as a model of what it is to be rational in social judgement. Bayes' theorem is as follows:

$$C(h|e) = \frac{C(e|h)\, C(h)}{C(e)}$$

Bayes' theorem suggests that when updating the credence one assigns to a hypothesis (e.g. suspect x committed crime C) in response to some new evidence e (suspect x was seen near the scene of the crime), both one's priors, $C(h)$ (e.g. the prior probability one would assign to a hypothesis, such as the hypothesis that the suspect is guilty), and the credence one would assign to the new evidence given the hypothesis ($C(e|h)$) should be factored in. One's priors should be allowed to influence how one updates one's beliefs in response to new evidence. What my argument suggests is that in social judgement, where one's priors are likely to reflect one's social stereotypes (e.g. members of x's social group are highly likely/unlikely/somewhat likely to engage in criminal activities), allowing the priors to influence one's response to new evidence is likely to lead to a distorted response to the evidence. Under such circumstances, violating Bayes' theorem, by not allowing one's responses to new evidence to be influenced by one's priors, might be better than attempting to adhere to the principles of Bayes'.

implications for theories relating to the ethics of stereotyping, and theories linking together the ethics and epistemology of stereotyping. This section outlines these implications, focusing on three accounts in particular: Lawrence Blum's (2004) moral analysis of stereotypes and stereotyping, Miranda Fricker's (2007) analysis of epistemic injustice, and moral encroachment views of epistemic justification, rationality, and knowledge.

8.1 Blum's Moral Analysis

For Blum, the moral objectionability of stereotypes is associated with the cognitive or epistemic distortions involved with stereotypes and stereotyping, 'The cognitive distortions involved in stereotyping lead to various forms of moral distortion' (Blum 2004, p. 251). Some stereotypes are morally objectionable because of the specific explicit content of the stereotype or due to the cultural or historical context of the stereotype formation or use. But all acts of stereotyping are morally objectionable because they lead people not to be viewed as individuals. Being seen as an individual is, for Blum, an important component of being acknowledged as a person. However, when people are stereotyped they are viewed as group members not as individuals so those stereotyping are not alive to the range of characteristics that might be displayed by the individual. Those who are stereotyped can be viewed in terms of a specific stereotypical attribute rather than other attributes. The internal variety within a group is not acknowledged, and the characteristics of subgroup members (e.g. Asians who struggle with maths) are not recognized because they are assumed to be like other group members. Meanwhile, members of different groups are viewed as less alike than they really are, leading to moral distancing, which can intensify social division, and reduce a sense of shared experience and common humanity (see also Blum 2016).

The discussion in Chapter 3 supports some aspects of Blum's account of the moral wrongs of all stereotyping. It supports the claim that stereotypes lead people not to be viewed as individuals. It shows precisely how stereotyping leads information about individuals not to be properly accessed and processed. It shows that we can add the following to Blum's list of ways that people are not treated as individuals when stereotyping: stereotypes that apply to them can overestimate or underestimate the prevalence of a characteristic among their social group; the stereotype can be wholly irrelevant to their specific case but not be recognized as such; their characteristics can be misremembered; their testimony can be given less credit than it deserves, and so on.

In addition to this, it is plausible in light of the arguments presented in Chapter 3 that the moral wrongs of stereotyping are, and perhaps are always, associated with cognitive or epistemic distortions. We have found that when people engage in stereotyping they can respond to information about individuals who are stereotyped in ways that appear to be morally objectionable. The person stereotyping can, for example, fail to recognize the positive attributes of the person being stereotyped, noticing and remembering their negative attributes instead; they can assume that people are more similar than they really are to negative examples of their social group, and fail to recognize their positive contributions to knowledge and society more generally. These are each cognitive or epistemic distortions that can, in some contexts at least, be morally objectionable. It is therefore consistent with the discussion in this book so far that all cases in which an act of stereotyping is morally objectionable involve people failing to respond, or at least the risk of failure to respond, to morally salient information about individuals who are stereotyped.

There are, then, certain aspects of Blum's account of the moral wrongs of stereotyping that find support in the arguments presented in this book so far. However, there is one aspect of Blum's view that is challenged by the arguments found in this chapter. Blum claims that the falsity of a stereotype is a necessary condition on a stereotype being morally objectionable:

> It is false, or at least misleading to say, that Jews are cheap, Blacks lazy, Asians good at math, women emotional, and so on. The falseness of stereotype [sic.] is part of, and is a necessary condition of, what is objectionable about stereotypes in general.   (Blum 2004, p. 256)

This point could be interpreted in various ways. It could be interpreted as what I shall call the *typicality claim*: stereotypes in general are morally objectionable because stereotypes are *typically* false. It could be interpreted as what I shall call the *universality claim*: stereotypes in general are morally objectionable because stereotypes are *always* false. Alternatively, it could be interpreted as what I shall call the *conditional claim*: a stereotype is morally objectionable in any specific case if and only if that specific stereotype is false. In light of the arguments in this chapter, none of these interpretations of Blum's claim are attractive.

Take the typicality claim: stereotypes in general are morally objectionable because stereotypes are typically false. On this view, the moral objectionability of any act of stereotyping is due to the falsity of a large subset of stereotypes. Let us examine the plausibility of this view through the filter of the examples found in Section 2 of this chapter: examples in which people harbour stereotypes that reflect aspects of social reality but nonetheless lead those who engage in stereotyping to fail to access or process relevant information about those who they stereotype. In these examples, people who are stereotyped can suffer in various ways. Their positive attributes can be missed while their negative attributes are overestimated and their positive contributions can be forgotten while their negative behaviours are well remembered. They can be given less credibility than they deserve. They can be falsely accused of crimes. They can be passed over for promotion. Their needs can be poorly assessed. Stereotypes can inflict each of these harms, and many others, without being obviously false. On the current proposal, if any of the stereotypes that inflict these harms are not false then the moral objectionability of the stereotypes in these cases has its source in the falsity of other stereotypes—i.e. the subset of stereotypes that are false. This seems highly implausible. There seems to be little reason to believe that the moral objectionability of the stereotypes involved in such cases has its source in the falsity of other stereotypes, while the stereotypes that cause so many harms are irrelevant to the moral assessment of the stereotype and act of stereotyping. The moral objectionability of the stereotype and stereotyping is linked to the specific stereotype and stereotyping that brings about these harms. Therefore, the typicality claim locates the source of the moral wrong in the incorrect place.

Let us next consider the universality claim. According to this claim, stereotypes in general are morally objectionable because stereotypes are always false. In this book, I have adopted a definition of stereotypes according to which they can be true or false, accurate or inaccurate (see Chapter 2). But Blum adopts a definition of stereotypes according to which they are always false or misleading ('I will use the term stereotype only in regard to false or misleading generalizations' (Blum 2004: p. 256)). Let us therefore concede temporarily, for the sake of argument, that all stereotypes are false, and that the generalizations relating to social groups that have been discussed in this chapter, which reflect an aspect of social reality, are not stereotypes. If this premise were accepted could it be successfully argued that stereotypes are morally objectionable because they are always false?

The problem with adopting this position is that it leaves us requiring different explanations for two very similar phenomena, where it seems as if the phenomena should be explained in the same way. The two phenomena are:

(i) the moral wrongs that can occur when stereotypes influence judgements of individuals, and (ii) the moral wrongs that can occur when true or accurate generalizations about social groups, which reflect social reality, influence judgements of individuals. What the argument in this chapter has shown is that in both types of cases, the same kinds of harms can be inflicted via the same types of cognitive processes. However, the universality claim suggests that the two types of phenomena need separate explanations. While (i) can be explained by the falsity of the social attitudes involved, i.e. the stereotypes (ii) must be explained in another way because the social attitudes involved, which cannot on this view be stereotypes, are not false. It seems plausible that (i) and (ii) can and should be explained in the same way, so there is reason to deny that the moral objectionability of stereotypes or stereotyping is due to stereotypes always being false.

A further problem with tying the moral objectionability of stereotypes and stereotyping to the falseness of a stereotype becomes clear when evaluating the *conditional claim*: that a stereotype is morally objectionable if and only if that specific stereotype is false. This claim would mean that if a stereotype is not false, it simply cannot be morally objectionable to apply it. But we have seen in this chapter that stereotypes that are not false can inflict serious harms on those who are stereotyped. This means that if we accept the conditional claim, we have to be willing to accept that some stereotypes, and acts of stereotyping, that inflict significant harms on those who are stereotyped are not morally objectionable. This is a problematic result. Where stereotypes inflict serious harms on those stereotyped they seem to be morally objectionable regardless of whether the stereotype that is applied is true or false, accurate or inaccurate.

The argument in this chapter presents a challenge, then, to the view that the falseness of a stereotype is a necessary condition on the stereotype being morally objectionable. It presents reason to think that a stereotype and act of stereotyping can be morally objectionable even if the stereotype that is applied is not false.

8.2 Epistemic Injustice

The idea that there can be epistemic costs associated with stereotyping where stereotypes reflect aspects of social reality also has implications for how we should conceptualize the bounds of epistemic injustice. In particular, what has implications for how we should conceptualize epistemic injustice is the observation made in Section 2.8 of this chapter that there is a phenomenon that is extremely similar to testimonial injustice that occurs due to the operation of stereotypes that reflect aspects of social reality. What this observation suggests is that there is a variety of epistemic injustice that occurs in the absence of prejudice but is otherwise similar to testimonial injustice.

We have already seen, in Section 2.8, how the phenomenon can occur: a stereotype can lead a person to be given less credibility that they deserve although the stereotype reflects an aspect of social reality and is not harboured or applied due to prejudice. The main aim of this section is therefore to establish that this phenomenon is a form of epistemic injustice.

Epistemic injustice occurs when a person is wronged in their capacity as a knower (Fricker 2007). Testimonial injustice is a variety of epistemic injustice in which a person is wronged because they are not given the credibility that they deserve as a testifier due to prejudice relating to their social identity. This section shows that people can be similarly wronged in their capacity as a knower when suffering a credibility deficit—i.e. when they are given less credibility than they deserve when testifying—in the absence of prejudice (and therefore the absence of testimonial injustice). To establish this point it will be shown that at least some of the harms associated with testimonial injustice can also be suffered by people who are given less credibility than they deserve due to the operation of a stereotype that reflects an aspect of social reality. To make this point I shall refer once again to the example of a woman scientist who is given less credibility than she deserves as a scientific expert due to the operation of a stereotype that reflects an aspect of social reality. It shall be shown that she could suffer each of the types of harms associated with testimonial injustice by Fricker (2007).

The first harm that is associated by Fricker (2007) with testimonial injustice is the general epistemic harm of being treated as if one is not a knower. Fricker argues that when testimonial injustice occurs the sincerity or competence of the speaker is questioned in a way that can 'cut deep' (Fricker 2007, p. 46) because being a knower is 'a capacity essential to human value' (Fricker 2007, p. 46). It seems clear that if one is treated as lacking credibility as a knower then this could 'cut deep' even if the stereotype that leads one to be denied credibility reflects an aspect of social reality. For example, where a female scientist is given less credibility than she deserves for knowing about her area of expertise it could 'cut deep' to the female scientist that her contributions are undervalued in this way. This remains the case even if the stereotype that is applied to her reflects the social reality that women are underrepresented among scientific experts.

The second harm that Fricker associates with testimonial injustice is that one can come to doubt one's intellectual abilities, and come to doubt what one believes, thereby losing existing knowledge and failing to gain other knowledge due to choosing not to engage in certain epistemic projects (Fricker 2007, p. 47–48). Once again it seems clear that people can suffer these harms even if they are given less credibility than they deserve due to the operation of a stereotype that reflects an aspect of social reality. For instance, the female scientist who is denied credibility due to a stereotype that reflects the underrepresentation of women among scientific experts can suffer these harms. In response to others treating her as if she lacks credibility when speaking about her area of expertise, she might come to doubt her intellectual abilities and expertise, questioning beliefs about her area of expertise that she would otherwise hold with confidence, and choosing not to put herself forward for new projects due to doubting her ability to successfully complete them.

Finally, Fricker (2007) identifies practical harms that can occur due to testimonial injustice. Fricker describes how one can lose out on job opportunities because one's contributions to workplace discussions are undervalued, how one can fail to get justice if denied credibility when testifying in one's defence in a criminal trial, and so forth. There seems to be little reason to insist that practical harms of this type never occur due to the application of a stereotype that reflects an aspect of social reality. On the contrary, it seems clear that people can suffer tangible practical harms of this type if they are denied credibility due to the operation of a stereotype that reflects an aspect of social reality. For instance, the female scientist could be denied job opportunities, such as promotions, if she is not treated as credible when speaking about her area of expertise and her contributions to the workplace are therefore not appreciated.

In sum, then, the types of harms that tend to be associated with testimonial injustice can be present in cases where a person is given less credibility than they deserve due to a stereotype that reflects an aspect of social reality. It is these harms that make it seem plausible that testimonial injustice involves wronging a person in their capacity as a knower. Therefore, there is good reason to think that people can be wronged in their capacities as knowers due to the application of stereotypes that reflect social realities. In other words, there is reason to think that there is a form of epistemic injustice that is extremely similar to testimonial injustice that occurs due to the application of stereotypes that reflect aspects of social reality and in the absence of prejudice.

It might be thought that a different conclusion should be reached: that there can be testimonial injustice in the absence of prejudice. I would resist this move because I believe it is useful to be able to distinguish cases of prejudice-driven credibility deficits from cases of credibility deficits in the absence of prejudice by having a distinct label for the former. Distinguishing prejudice-driven credibility deficits from cases of credibility deficit in the absence of prejudice provides a lens through which to see how those of us who are not driven by prejudice can nonetheless be implicated in harmful credibility deficits. It emphasizes the scale of the problem: even if you are simply responding to social facts as they are found in your environment—and are therefore not committing testimonial injustice—you might nonetheless inflict significant harms on those whose credibility you assess inaccurately.

8.3 Moral Encroachment Views

The arguments presented in Section 2 of this chapter have implications for another set of views relating to the ethics as well as the epistemology of stereotyping: *moral encroachment views* (Basu 2019a, 2019b, 2020; Basu and Schroeder 2018; Bolinger 2020; Moss 2018a, 2018b). According to these views, moral considerations can determine what it is to be rational or justified in believing a certain proposition or what it is to possess knowledge in a particular context. For instance, according to some advocates of moral encroachment theories, where the moral stakes of a situation are high one can be required to have a higher quantity or quality of evidence to be justified in believing than one would otherwise (Basu 2019a, 2019b; Basu and Schroeder 2018; Fritz 2017).

Moral encroachment views present a significant departure from how epistemic rationality, justification and knowledge are traditionally conceived. Ordinarily an epistemic evaluation might involve assessing whether or not a belief has sufficient support from the available evidence, but whether or not there is sufficient evidential support would not be determined by the moral stakes. The radical departure from traditional conceptions of rationality, justification and knowledge that is provided by moral encroachment views is defended in part on the basis of observations about cases of stereotyping like those discussed in this chapter, where stereotypes reflect some aspect of social reality. Defenders of the moral encroachment view claim that there is something epistemically amiss in cases where people apply stereotypes that reflect aspects of social reality, and that this is explicable in terms of moral considerations determining what is epistemically permissible. The aim of this section is to show that the arguments in Section 2 of this chapter provide reason to doubt that the best way to explain how there is something epistemically amiss in these types of case is by accepting that moral considerations determine epistemic standards.

This point can be understood by considering how defences of moral encroachment views often focus on an example of stereotyping presented by Tamar Szabó Gendler (2011). The example is the following:

> *Cosmos Club*: the acclaimed historian John Franklin was hosting a dinner at the swanky Cosmos Club in Washington D.C. A white woman saw Franklin, assumed that he was staff at the club, and presented him with her coat. Franklin was the first Black member of the club and the majority of the staff at the club at the time was Black.   (Franklin and Zabor 2005)

Moral encroachment views purport to be uniquely well placed to explain how the White woman in this scenario has done something epistemically impermissible. Although she has made a judgement that is seemingly well supported by statistical information about the Cosmos Club, its membership, and its staff, the judgement can be criticized on the basis of moral considerations. It is morally risky to make a judgement about whether a person is a staff member at a club on the basis of their race in a cultural and historical context in which members of their racial group are excluded from more prestigious employment due to their race (Basu 2019a). Under such morally risky conditions, according to moral encroachment theorists, the evidentiary standards for believing are high. Basing a judgement on statistical evidence like that used by the woman in the Cosmos club is therefore epistemically impermissible (Basu 2020; Bolinger 2020; Moss 2018b). The statistical evidence does not meet the high evidential standards that are set by the risky, high-stakes moral context.

What we have found in this chapter is an argument that challenges the idea that moral encroachment views are unique in being able to explain how there is something epistemically amiss in cases like *Cosmos Club*, where a judgement is influenced by a stereotype that reflects an aspect of social reality. This is because this chapter has identified various epistemic faults associated with forming judgements on the basis of stereotypes of this type.

When we form beliefs on the basis of stereotypes we are disposed to respond poorly to case-specific information about individual social actors or events, even if the stereotype reflects reality: failing to notice or attend to certain features, misremembering details, failing to track the truth in our explanations, unduly dismissing testimony, etc. We are susceptible to making numerous errors because of the ways stereotypes tend to influence how we perceive and judge information relating to others. In the Cosmos Club example, for instance, the woman might be disposed due to stereotyping to fail to notice the clothes that Franklin is wearing (whether he is wearing a uniform), to fail to remember if she has seen any signs that he is a patron rather than a staff member (e.g. if he has been interacting in a causal manner with other guests), to explain his behaviours in a way that is consistent with him being a staff member (e.g. he must be waiting in the lobby to take the coats of patrons). According to the view presented in this chapter, it is possible to criticize people who apply stereotypes that reflect social reality, including the woman in the Cosmos Club example, on the basis that applying the stereotypes makes them susceptible to these types of errors (see Gardiner 2018 for a similar argument).

Because it is possible to identify errors associated with applying a stereotype that reflects social reality without appeal to moral considerations, moral encroachment views are not unique in providing an explanation of how there can be something epistemically amiss in such cases. In addition to this, moral encroachment views involve a radical revision to our traditional conception of what impacts the epistemic standing of our beliefs, credences, and opinions that only seems to be warranted if traditional epistemic concepts like 'evidence-fittingness' or 'information' cannot be used to provide an alternative explanation of the phenomena that moral encroachment views seek to explain (Begby 2018; Gardiner 2018). However, we have seen that it is possible to explain how there is something epistemically amiss in the target cases by appeal to these traditional epistemic concepts. What happens in such cases is that people are susceptible to responding poorly to evidence, failing to access and properly process information, as a result of harbouring and applying a stereotype that reflects something of social reality. Thus, the case for moral encroachment that is based on examples where people form judgements on the basis of stereotypes that reflect social realities, like the Cosmos Club example, is substantially weakened by the argument found in this chapter.

Simply put, it is not necessary to accept that moral considerations determine epistemic standards—as moral encroachment theorists ask us to—in order to explain how there is something epistemic amiss in cases where people apply stereotypes that reflect aspects of social reality. There is something epistemically amiss in such cases because the application of the stereotype makes the person who is stereotyping susceptible to making errors in their responses to relevant information that they might encounter.

9. Conclusion

This chapter has challenged the intuitive view that there are only epistemic benefits associated with having social attitudes that reflect social realities, and only epistemic costs associated with having social attitudes that fail to reflect social realities. It has been argued that there can be significant epistemic costs associated with having social attitudes that reflect social realities and significant epistemic benefits associated with having social attitudes that do not.

The social attitudes that fail to reflect social realities but bring epistemic benefits have been found to share features with other cognitions that have been labelled as epistemically innocent: they bring epistemic costs but they also bring significant epistemic benefits. Sometimes social attitudes that fail to reflect reality are the lesser of two epistemic evils and it is best from an epistemic perspective to have these inaccurate but egalitarian attitudes. Consequently, it cannot be safely inferred from evidence that a stereotype reflects some aspect of social reality to the conclusion that a person is more likely to achieve their epistemic goals if they possess and apply the stereotype than if they do not. In fact, in some cases, ignoring base-rate information about social realities can be the best thing one can do to achieve epistemic goals such as forming accurate beliefs—an observation that presents a challenge to approaches that suggest that base-rate neglect is always a serious epistemic error.

The observation that stereotypes that reflect aspects of social reality can bring substantial epistemic costs also presents a challenge to, or calls for modification of, existing ideas relating to the ethics as well as the epistemology of stereotyping. The observation suggests that (i) the moral objectionability of stereotypes is not tied to their falsity; (ii) there can be cases of epistemic injustice similar to testimonial injustice in the absence of prejudice; and (iii) it is possible to explain how there is something epistemically amiss when people apply stereotypes that reflect social realities without appeal to moral considerations.

5

Where Ethical and Epistemic Demands Meet

Learning from the Role of Stereotyping in Medicine

1. Introduction

Imagine that you are trying to work out which of two young men from your neighbourhood was recently arrested for a crime. Say that you overhear a discussion about someone called Michael being caught by the police in possession of drugs. You only know two people called Michael, and are confident that the two people who you overhear also only know the same two people called Michael. One Michael is White and the other is Black. You know nothing indicating that one of the people called Michael is more likely than the other to have been involved with drugs, although you could find out such information if you tried. You live in a neighbourhood in which arrest rates for drug possession among Black youths is much higher than arrest rates among White youths.

How should you respond in this situation? Should you assume that the Michael who is White is less likely than the Michael who is Black to have been caught in possession of drugs? If required to act on your belief, should you act as if the Michael who is the member of the racial group more commonly arrested for drug possession was the one who was arrested?

It might seem that if you are aiming to do what is right from an epistemic perspective, responding in a way that maximizes the chance of you forming true beliefs, making a correct judgement, and so forth, then you should associate drug arrests in your area more strongly with Black people than White people and therefore believe it more likely that the Michael who is Black was arrested than that it was Michael who is White. However, it is highly intuitive that it is unethical to assume that the Black person rather than the White person was arrested. On the basis of examples of this sort, Tamar Szabó Gendler (2011) has argued that, in a society rife with

How Stereotypes Deceive Us. Katherine Puddifoot, Oxford University Press. © Katherine Puddifoot 2021.
DOI: 10.1093/oso/9780192845559.003.0005

inequities, people necessarily face an epistemic-ethical dilemma (see also Egan 2011, Mugg 2013, and Section 7 of Chapter 4). If they ignore information about arrest rates across different racial groups, responding in an egalitarian way that fails to reflect the discrepant arrest rates across different racial groups, then they will commit an epistemic error. But if they respond differentially with respect to race and crime, assuming that a crime is more likely to have been committed by a Black person than a White person, or that a particular Black person is more likely than a particular White person to have committed a crime (all else being equal), then they are doing something unethical.

Although discussion of this putative epistemic-ethical dilemma has predominantly focused on stereotypes relating to race and crime, similar arguments could be constructed to deal with any stereotyping that seems to involve the application of a stereotype that reflects some aspect of social reality. For example, the stereotype associating career women in the 1950s with a particular circumscribed set of lifestyle choices (e.g. education, living arrangements), the stereotype associating scientific expertise with men rather than women, and the stereotype associating being a barrister with being White and male could be said to reflect social reality. Ignoring the reality that career women are likely to have had a particular education or made a specific set of life choices might naturally be thought to reduce the chance of true beliefs being formed about those women, but treating all career women as monolithic, with the same education and making the same lifestyle choices, could have poor ethical consequences (e.g. leading to at least short-term harm to a woman's self-esteem and happiness). Ignoring the reality that women are underrepresented in the sciences might naturally be thought to increase the chance of false beliefs being formed, for example, about how many female colleagues you are likely to have in your first job as a scientist. However, associating males more strongly than females with scientific expertise could produce the unethical consequence of, among other things, women not being given the same career opportunities as men (see, e.g. Valian 1999, 2005). Similarly, it is tempting to think that ignoring the reality that Women and BAME persons are underrepresented as barristers in the UK, especially at senior levels, would make one susceptible to making errors when predicting the demographics of those involved in the law. However, associating being a barrister with being White and male could produce the unethical consequence of leading Black women barristers to be treated as if they do not belong, of leading them to be disrespected and treated as if they are invisible or unimportant (see example in Chapter 1).

This chapter addresses this putative epistemic-ethical dilemma; building on the arguments presented in Chapters 3 and 4. It is not denied that we sometimes face competing epistemic and ethical demands. I acknowledge that in some cases like those just described there can be competing epistemic and ethical demands. Instead, my aim is to emphasize that rather than facing the comparatively straightforward dilemma of choosing between prioritizing our ethical or epistemic goals, we frequently face the extremely complex task of discerning whether, in a specific context, epistemic or ethical goals are more likely to be achieved by stereotyping, or by not stereotyping. Sometimes epistemic and ethical goals will be achieved in the same way, and sometimes in different ways.

It shall quickly become clear that the multifactorial approach to stereotyping and the epistemic innocence of some inaccurate social attitudes undermine the claim that epistemic goals always demand reflecting social realities (e.g. crime rates across different racial groups, regularities in the education and lifestyle choices of career women, and the underrepresentation of women in science) in one's judgements. This might seem to suggest an easy solution to the epistemic-ethical dilemma: that both epistemic and ethical goals demand that people avoid stereotyping. However, we shall see that things are far more complex than this, and such a (relatively) simple solution is unavailable. Sometimes ethical and epistemic demands conflict, sometimes they align with both being achieved by stereotyping, and sometimes they align with both being achieved by not stereotyping. People therefore face a complex problem: to identify whether they are in a situation in which either or both of their epistemic or ethical goals can be achieved by stereotyping.

To illustrate the complexity of the situation that we face with regards to our epistemic and ethical goals when it comes to stereotyping, I shall focus on a case study—stereotyping in healthcare—before highlighting the more general implications of the arguments that I present. My aim here is not to underplay the importance of cases where ethical and epistemic goals conflict but instead to emphasize the complex dynamic between ethical and epistemic goals and to stress the deep challenges faced by those aiming to do the right thing when it comes to stereotyping.

2. First Pass at a Solution

A basic assumption of those who argue that people face an epistemic-ethical dilemma with respect to stereotyping, where a stereotype that might be applied reflects some aspect of social reality, is that epistemic principles always demand reflecting these aspects of reality. The arguments of Chapters 3 and 4 challenge this assumption. Chapter 3 shows that there are multiple ways that stereotyping can lead to epistemic errors: stereotypes can lead a person to respond in a way that is not fitting with statistical reality; they can be applied when irrelevant; or the application of the stereotype can lead to a distortion of case-specific information, preventing important and relevant case-specific information from being appropriately accessed and processed. Chapter 4 shows that these epistemic costs can be incurred even if a stereo-type reflects an aspect of social reality. By avoiding the stereotyping that would reflect these social realities it can therefore be possible to avoid suf-fering epistemic costs. Under such conditions, failing to reflect aspects of social reality in one's judgement, by avoiding stereotyping, can facilitate the achievement of epistemic goals, such as the attainment of true beliefs and understanding.

A first pass solution to the epistemic-ethical dilemma could therefore be as follows.

> First pass: Epistemic and ethical principles do not conflict because what is demanded by ethical principles—i.e. the avoidance of stereotyping—is the best thing from an epistemic perspective.

Those who emphasize how ethical and epistemic principles conflict do not adequately acknowledge that case-specific information is overwhelmingly more diagnostic than information encoded in stereotypes. Consequently, avoiding the distortion of case-specific information by avoiding stereotyp-ing—i.e. the seemingly ethical choice—can be best from the perspective of achieving epistemic goals, even if this involves not possessing or applying a stereotype that reflects reality.

3. Resisting the Temptation of a Simple Solution

This first pass at a solution to the epistemic-ethical dilemma applies in very many cases. Stereotyping brings substantial epistemic costs and numerous ethical risks. Under some circumstances, stereotyping leads people to make judgements that reflect relevant information about the society in which they live. However, as we saw in Chapters 3 and 4, in these and other cir-cumstances stereotyping can lead those who engage in the practice to respond in a biased way to information about individuals and cases to which the stereotypes are applied. Individualized information about specific people or cases will often be more diagnostic than generalized information about groups that might be encoded in stereotypes. Therefore, avoiding a biased response to case-specific information will often be a better way of getting to the truth than allowing one's judgements to be influenced by stereotypes, even if they encode generalized information about social groups.

There is also a strong case for the most ethical option often being to avoid stereotyping on the basis that stereotyping can be morally wrongful. As we have seen in Chapter 4, Section 8, there is important ongoing debate about the precise moral wrong(s) of stereotyping but whatever the correct account of the moral wrong(s) of stereotyping, there certainly seems in many cases to be one. Therefore, the first pass solution to the epistemic-ethical dilemma has prima facie appeal: ethical and epistemic principles seem, at face value, to both require avoiding stereotyping. Unfortunately, however, this simple solution to the epistemic-ethical dilemma is incomplete. Although in some cases the best thing from both an ethical and epistemic perspective is to avoid stereotyping, sometimes both ethical and epistemic principles point in the opposite direction. To illustrate this point, let us reflect on a specific case study: the use of stereotypes about social groups in healthcare.

4. Complicating the Epistemic-Ethical Dilemma: The Case of Healthcare

4.1 Implicit Bias in Healthcare

Our focus for the coming sections is stereotyping in healthcare. There are few, if any, domains in which the impact of stereotyping can be more harmful. Healthcare professionals are highly trained individuals, who have been found to mostly harbour egalitarian principles (see, e.g., Dall'Alba 1998; Draper and Louw 2007). However, stereotypes still influence their thoughts and actions, in tangible ways, influencing their diagnoses and treatment decisions. Due to the egalitarian principles harboured by most healthcare professionals, the literature on unintentional and automatic stereotyping involved in implicit bias (see Chapter 1, Section 5 for an introductory discussion of implicit bias) is a good source of information about the stereotyping that they display.

Studies on implicit bias in healthcare indicate that healthcare professionals harbour biases that influence their assessments of pain, the quality of clinician-patient interactions, treatment choices, and diagnostic judgements. It has been found that healthcare professionals primed with White faces are more responsive to the pain described in a study than those primed with Black faces (Mathur et al. 2014) and that healthcare professionals implicitly associated Black people with super-humanization and were less likely to find Black patients than White patients to be in need of medication (Waytz, Hoffman, and Trawalter 2015). Healthcare professionals have been found to associate Black people with non-compliance, and where they did so the dialogue between physician and Black patients was rated as less patient-centred by a third party (Cooper et al. 2012). Another study found healthcare workers to overwhelmingly favour Whites over Blacks and Latinos (two thirds displayed this preference), and the ratings by their Black patients of those who were biased were predicted by the strength of the bias (Blair et al. 2013, see also Penner et al. 2010 and Hagiwara, Kashy, and Penner 2014).

In terms of treatment choice, high levels of negative racial bias towards Black people has been found to correlate with low levels of recommendation for thrombolytic drugs to Black patients (Green et al. 2007). Low levels of cervical cancer screenings and follow-up care for Black women in Massachusetts in the United States were explained by the patients as resulting from the unconscious bias of the healthcare workers, who, they said, did not want to touch them (Nolan et al. 2014). In addition, male healthcare workers were found to be less likely to prescribe opioids to Black patients than White patients under conditions of high cognitive load (Burgess et al. 2014), which are conditions under which implicit biases often manifest (Bertrand, Chug, and Mullainathan 2005; White III, 2014).

Finally, in a study that is of great importance within the context of this chapter, Moskwitz and colleagues (2012) gathered findings suggesting that some diseases are automatically more strongly associated with Black people than White people. Doctors were required to categorize words as either names of diseases, names of treatments or neither. Before doing so, they were primed with either a Black or a White face. When primed with a Black face they were faster at categorizing diseases stereotyped as African American in an earlier study. These results suggest the presence of an automatic association between Black people and certain diseases, that explains why the items are categorized quickly (the diseases have been primed by the recent exposure to the Black face), and would lead certain conditions to be more likely to be considered than others in an encounter with a Black patient.[1]

Taken together, these results provide compelling evidence that healthcare professionals' engagement in automatic and unintentional stereotyping can influence the judgements they make about their patients.[2] Whether a patient is treated well or badly, and whether or not they get treatment appropriate to their needs, can depend upon the associations made by their healthcare provider with the social group(s) to which the patient is perceived as belonging. There is clearly a strong case for saying that this is an unethical outcome, violating principles of justice and fairness in an area of life that is crucial to health, wellbeing, and even survival.[3] Because the stereotypes leading to these negative outcomes operate automatically once a healthcare professional is responsive to the social group status of their patients, there is reason for thinking that it will be ethically costly, that is, it will reduce the chance of healthcare professionals acting fairly and justly, if they are responsive to the social group status of their patients in their clinical judgement and decision-making.

4.2 The Appearance of Epistemic and Ethical Goals Converging Against Stereotyping

Given that there are ethical costs associated with stereotyping in medicine, there is at face value very good reason for thinking that ethical and epistemic principles converge in the case of stereotyping in medicine, at least

---

[1] The Moskowitz study measures automatic associations rather than behavioural manifestations of bias but it nonetheless strongly suggests that healthcare professionals will be biased in their diagnoses because the order in which thoughts about conditions are manifest will determine the order in which they will consider clinical hypotheses.

[2] Doubts have been raised about the effectiveness of one main measure of implicit bias—the implicit association task (IAT)—for example, about whether it measures biases or recognition of attitudes or patterns found in one's society, and about whether high levels of 'bias' as measured by the IAT correlates with real world behaviours. Some of these studies measure implicit biases using the IAT therefore should be treated with caution by those sceptical about this measure. However, the studies discussed in this overview of the literature on implicit bias in medicine use a variety of measures, including measuring patterns of treatment under conditions in which implicit cognition tends to dominate (Burgess et al. 2014) and gathering testimony from Black female patients about their lived experience of bias (Nolan et al. 2014). The latter methodologies have not received the same criticism as the IAT. In fact, there is increased recognition of the importance of the latter source of evidence, i.e. testimony of those who have experienced prejudice and discrimination (Holroyd and Puddifoot 2020a, 2020b).

[3] For further discussion of the psychological research on implicit bias in healthcare see Matthew 2015. For a philosophical discussion, see Fitzgerald 2014.

once one is informed by the multifactorial view of stereotyping. This is because the numerous epistemic costs associated with stereotyping underlined by the multifactorial view can manifest when stereotypes are applied within a healthcare setting.

A first epistemic cost is that where the stereotype that is applied associates a patient with negative characteristics, a healthcare professional can fail to give adequate attention and credibility to the testimony of the patient. Negative stereotypes, like the stereotype that obese people lack will-power, can lead healthcare professionals to communicate less effectively with a patient, giving the patient less time and opportunity to explain their symptoms and generally making the patient less comfortable explaining their condition. Recall the findings discussed in Section 4.1 about the poor quality of interactions between physicians and patients when the physicians are influenced by implicit biases relating to the group(s) to which their patients belong, for example, the findings suggesting that dialogue is less patient-centred when a physician harbours a negative stereotype relating to the patient's social group. These results suggest that where healthcare professionals are influenced by negative stereotypes, they are less likely to enter into productive dialogue with their patients, listening to the details that they can provide about their condition. These findings can be interpreted in two ways. It might be that physicians fail to give the details that the patient provides about their condition appropriate credibility due to a stereotype they associate with the patient's social group, demonstrating what Miranda Fricker (2007) calls testimonial injustice (see also Carel and Kidd 2014). Alternatively, the findings might be explained in terms of testimonial smothering. As we saw in Chapters 3, when people are negatively stereotyped they can also choose to smother their testimony, choosing not to provide information to people who they believe will not engage in appropriate uptake of it (Dotson 2011). Within the healthcare setting, this testimonial smothering can manifest as patients choosing not to disclose information about themselves, their symptoms, and their medical history, because they believe that the information will be either ignored or misinterpreted by their physician who they perceive to be negatively stereotyping them. Each of these phenomena can be costly because many medical practices are fundamentally aimed at soliciting and receiving knowledge via testimony from a patient. Healthcare professionals aim to understand this information, critically evaluate it, and give appropriate weight to it. If they engage in stereotyping, however, they are less likely to access, appropriately evaluate or give appropriate weight to it.

A second epistemic cost of implicit stereotyping is that a healthcare professional can focus on characteristics of a patient (i.e. symptoms and aspects of medical history) that fit stereotypes associated with the patients' social group—e.g. an unhealthy lifestyle in a person with a low socioeconomic status—giving inadequate attention to non-stereotypical characteristics. This is because, as discussed in Chapter 3, people have a general tendency to notice and attend to stereotypical characteristics more than non-stereotypical characteristics (Rothbart, Evans, and Fulero 1979; Srull, Lichtenstein, and Rothbart 1985). People also have a general tendency to build explanations that are consistent with stereotypes when other explanations would fit better with the available information (Duncan 1976; Sanbonmatsu, Akimoto, and Gibson 1994). Healthcare professionals who are responsive to the social group status of their patients are therefore likely to explain some medical symptoms by appeal to stereotypes, e.g. poor lifestyle choices in members of certain social groups, even when more adequate explanations of the information of the symptoms and medical history displayed, e.g. in terms of genetic factors, are available.

It might be thought that errors of the type just described can be avoided if healthcare professionals only focus on *relevant* information about the social group status of their patients—statistical information about the distribution of medical conditions across a population—and are not be influenced by stereotypes associating members of particular social groups with negative characteristics like untrustworthiness or poor lifestyle choices.[4] It might be thought that if healthcare professionals focused only on the relevant information then their responsiveness to the social group status of their patients would only be positive from an epistemic perspective.

There are two problems with this type of response. First of all, psychological results suggest that healthcare professionals who are responsive to the social group status of their patients, perceiving them as members of a social group, e.g. a Black patient, an Obese patient, or a poor patient, will be highly likely to associate those patients with a cluster of characteristics. Conditions of contemporary healthcare mean that healthcare professionals frequently face extremely heavy workloads, which they have to complete under significant time limitations, while undergoing stress and suffering from exhaustion (Byrne and Tanessini 2015; Stone and Moskowitz 2011).

---

[4] Matthew (2015) seems to suggest that it is possible to make a division between being influenced by relevant information about social group status and being influenced by stereotypes.

Under these types of conditions, people tend to depend on implicit forms of cognition, which operate quickly and automatically (Byrne and Tanessini 2015). They can depend on associative patterns of thought rather than thinking in a controlled, deliberate manner (Byrne and Tanessini 2015). In other words, they can automatically depend on stereotyping without having the time and opportunity to engage in other forms of reasoning and decision-making. According to dominant theories about the psychology of stereotypes, any act of stereotyping will associate an individual with a cluster of characteristics and not one (see Chapter 4, Section 2.9). This means that if healthcare professionals rely on stereotypes to associate members of social groups with medical conditions, they are likely to consequently associate those individuals with numerous other characteristics (Blair, Ma, and Lenton 2001, cited in Moskowitz, Stone, and Childs 2012). Some of these associations will be epistemically costly. For example, if the stereotype that an African American patient is more likely than other patients to have sickle cell anaemia is triggered, the general stereotype of an African American patient is likely to be triggered, including an association between African American patients and uncooperativeness (Green et al. 2007). Healthcare professionals influenced by the latter association can, for instance, fail to give appropriate weight to the testimony of African American patients.

The second problem with the suggestion that there could be epistemic benefits without epistemic costs if healthcare professionals only focused on the relevant information about the statistical distribution of medical conditions across a population is that even stereotypes that encode information about the distribution of medical conditions across populations can produce epistemic errors.

Sometimes a medical practitioner will depend on a stereotype associating a social group more strongly than other social groups with a medical condition and the association will fail to reflect reality. For example, the abovementioned study by Moskowitz and colleagues (2012) of medical doctors in the United States found that they named 36 diseases as stereotypical conditions found in African Americans. These included genetically-based conditions, such as hypertension and sickle cell disease, but also behaviour-induced conditions such as drug abuse and obesity. The experimenters found that the conditions that had a genetic basis did tend to be found more frequently in African Americans. However, the conditions induced by behaviour were not found at a higher rate among African Americans. As noted in previous chapters, drug abuse, for example, was found to be equally frequent amongst White people and African Americans in a 2003 report

(Substance Abuse and Mental Health Services Administration 2004). The use of some drugs such as heroin, cocaine, stimulants or methamphetamine was found in a report from 2007 to be higher among the White population than the African American population (Office of Applied Studies, Substance Abuse and Mental Health Services Administration, 2007). This means that only some of the conditions associated with African Americans are more frequently found among the African American population. Whenever stereotypes that falsely associate medical conditions more strongly with some social groups than others are applied, healthcare professionals will give inappropriately high levels of attention to certain conditions that they wrongly associate with a particular social group, reducing the chance that they make the correct diagnosis.

Epistemic costs can follow, however, even if a stereotype associates members of a social group more strongly than others with a particular condition and that condition is more prevalent in that social group than others. First of all, the application of the stereotype can lead to some diagnostic hypotheses being given undue attention and others being given insufficient attention (Moskowitz et al. 2012). When a stereotype is applied in the process of diagnosis, it influences the hypotheses considered by the healthcare professional because certain conditions are more likely than others to be brought to mind as potential explanations of the patient's condition (Moskowitz et al. 2012). This can be beneficial, leading the healthcare professional to focus attention on more rather than less probable explanations of a patient's symptoms. For example, if a patient is Black, they are statistically more likely to have hypertension than members of other racial groups, and in fact highly likely to have the condition (e.g. 41 per cent of the Black population in the USA have hypertension compared to 27 per cent of the White population) so it could be beneficial for a healthcare professional to place hypertension high on the list of conditions that they consider when Black patients present with symptoms consistent with the condition. The stereotype will affect the 'space of theoretical possibilities' that the healthcare professional is primed to consider, which could be a positive thing if the space of possibilities that is considered both reflects the statistical distribution of conditions across different populations and is sufficiently broad. However, the same phenomenon can be costly under other conditions. Given the time pressures that healthcare professionals operate under, the number of potential hypotheses that can be considered is severely limited. This means that they will often be susceptible to failing to formulate the correct clinical hypothesis. The application of a stereotype associating members of certain social groups with particular medical conditions can greatly increase the chance that the healthcare professional will fail to give adequate attention to non-stereotypical clinical hypotheses because many hypotheses will be missed. Under these circumstances healthcare professionals are likely to fail to consider clinical hypotheses that would yield a correct diagnosis.

The application of the stereotype can also have a distorting effect on the way that a healthcare professional perceives the symptoms of a patient. As already noted, stereotypes determine what information people attend to; people sometimes attend to and remember information that confirms their stereotypes but not information that disconfirms them (Rothbart et al. 1979; Srull et al. 1985). In the medical setting, this can manifest as healthcare professionals focusing on symptoms of the patient that are indicative of conditions that they associate with the patient's social group more than other social groups, failing to give adequate attention to symptoms of a patient that do not fit the stereotype. For example, a healthcare professional might attend closely to symptoms that fit hypertension when diagnosing an African American patient but fail to attend to symptoms that do not fit hypertension, or symptoms that better fit an alternative diagnosis. Even where a stereotype reflects the statistical reality, of the high prevalence of a condition within a social group (such as hypertension among the Black population), it can have a distorting influence, reducing the chance of correct judgements being made about some patients (i.e. those with conditions that are not stereotypical).

The healthcare professional is not likely to only attend to symptoms that are consistent with the patient having hypertension, or another stereotypical condition, if they display with symptoms that are clearly unrelated to a stereotypical condition, e.g. a sore elbow. However, there will nonetheless be many cases where symptoms are likely to be missed as a result of stereotyping. Perhaps the patient does not disclose information about a symptom but would provide information that would indicate the presence of the symptom if asked the correct questions, or the presence of the symptom would be revealed if the correct tests were undertaken. Or perhaps a symptom is not easily quantifiable, such as pain, so cannot easily be conveyed to the medical practitioner. Under such circumstances, if the practitioner engages in stereotyping of social groups and conditions, psychological results suggest that they are susceptible to failing to notice or attend appropriately to the symptom if it is not stereotypical, to failing to ask the correct questions or undertake the tests necessary to reveal the presence of the symptom. Even if a stereotype that is applied reflects a genuine correlation between a condition and a social group (e.g. hypertension and the Black population), applying the stereotype can nonetheless provide an impediment to effective clinical diagnosis by preventing the practitioner from noticing and properly attending to what can be more predictive information: about non-stereotypical symptoms that provide a strong indication about which condition is present.

Even if it were the case that a healthcare professional noticed and attended to all relevant symptoms there could still be epistemic costs that follow from applying a stereotype about the types of conditions that members of a social group are likely to have. This is because, as we have seen in Chapter 3, generally when people apply stereotypes (Duncan 1976; Sagar and Schofield 1980), including automatically and unintentionally (Devine 1989), they are disposed to interpret ambiguous behaviour displayed by the target of the stereotyping in a way that is fitting with the stereotype, where the behaviour should be viewed as ambiguous. In the healthcare setting, this phenomenon can manifest as healthcare professionals interpreting ambiguous symptoms in ways that are consistent with stereotypical conditions being present. For example, if a Black person has a symptom that is ambiguous between a number of different conditions, but could be viewed as indicative of hypertension, the healthcare professional might interpret the symptom as providing a higher level of support for hypertension as the correct clinical diagnosis than other conditions that the symptom is compatible with. This is epistemically costly because the correct response to ambiguous evidence is to treat it as ambiguous.

It might initially seem puzzling how it could be harmful from an epistemic perspective for healthcare professionals to interpret symptoms that are ambiguous between different conditions in a way that is consistent with a person having a condition that is prevalent among their social group. And in some cases, a condition might be so highly prevalent in a particular population in contrast to other conditions that the presence of a symptom that might under other circumstances indicate other medical conditions provides a good indication of the presence of the stereotypical condition. For example, in a population with extremely high levels of the Ebola virus, fever-like symptoms might strongly indicate the presence of Ebola, so that it is beneficial for a medical professional to interpret fever, which would otherwise be an ambiguous symptom, as indicative of the virus. Here are two responses that can be made to these objections. First, if a condition is sufficiently prevalent in a population it is not clear that symptoms consistent with the condition should be viewed as ambiguous. If sufficiently many people within a population have Ebola, the presence of a fever might be taken to provide unambiguous, if not conclusive, evidence in support of the conclusion that a particular person has Ebola.

Second, if a symptom S is truly ambiguous between conditions x, y, and z, then each of conditions x, y and z should be weighted as more probable than it would otherwise be due to the presence of S, unless there are some other good reasons for thinking that one of the conditions is not present. To see this point, it will be useful to compare it to a criminal case. There are three suspects of a crime: Johnston, Robertson, and Thompson. Some evidence is found suggesting that the criminal was wearing a red jumper. Each of the three suspects is known to have been wearing a red jumper at the time of the crime. The appropriate response to the evidence about the jumper is to weight as more probable each of the options: that Johnston is guilty, that Robertson is guilty, and Thompson is guilty. There might be independent reasons for thinking that one of the suspects is guilty, but the presence of the red jumper should not be interpreted in a way that that is consistent with that suspect being guilty, if it is truly ambiguous. Instead, the evidence that each of the suspects wore a red jumper should be considered alongside, but independently of, other evidence suggesting that one of the suspects is guilty. Otherwise, the other evidence that supports the conclusion that the suspect is guilty is influential twice over, in a case of 'double book-keeping' because it influences the way that the evidence about the red jumper is interpreted. Similarly, if there are three conditions that are consistent with a particular symptom, evidence that a symptom is present should lead each of the conditions to be taken equally more seriously as potential explanations of the symptoms. If there is some independent reason for thinking that one of the conditions is more likely than the others to be present, because it is prevalent within the patient's social group, then this evidence should be considered independently but alongside the presence of the symptom. Otherwise, the fact that the condition is prevalent within the patient's social group is influential twice over, once again in a case of 'double book-keeping'.

This section has thus identified numerous epistemic costs that are associated with responding to the social group status of a patient even where information about the social group status of the patient is relevant to judgements about their condition. Healthcare professionals who respond to information about their patients' social group status tend to engage in stereotyping, associating the patients with a cluster of characteristics. They can consequently fail to give some patients appropriate opportunity to communicate information about their condition; they can attend closely to stereotypical features while failing to attend to non-stereotypical features; they can fail to give adequate attention to certain medical hypotheses, and so on. Given that each of these features are associated with stereotyping, there initially seems to be good reason to think that the avoidance of stereotyping maximizes the chance of a person achieving their epistemic goals because it prevents them from making these various errors. Epistemic goals appear to converge with the ethical goal of avoiding differential treatment through stereotyping.

4.3 Complicating the Picture: Stereotyping and the Facilitation of Epistemic Goals

Unfortunately, the initial appearance that epistemic and ethical goals converge in an uncomplicated way, and that both can be consistently achieved by avoiding stereotyping, does not withstand closer scrutiny. The fact that some of these epistemic costs can occur as the result of an automatic association between social groups and medical conditions when the association reflects the reality of the distribution of conditions across different social groups points towards a particularly serious problem for those who aim to increase the chance that healthcare professionals achieve their epistemic goals. The problem is this: it will not be possible to prevent healthcare professionals from making all of the stereotypical associations that bring epistemic costs without preventing them from making associations that are extremely valuable for them to make. Information about the social group status of patients can be highly relevant to medical judgement and decision-making and a crucial determinant of whether or not a correct judgement is made. Moreover, for healthcare professionals to gain the information that they require to make accurate clinical judgements and decisions, they will often need to be placed in a situation in which they will inevitably become aware of and respond to the social group status of their patient. Therefore, substantial epistemic costs would be incurred if healthcare professionals were placed in a situation in which they were not likely to be responsive to the social group status of their patients. But due to the automatic way that implicit biases operate, if healthcare professionals are aware of the social group status of their patients they are likely to stereotype. And in fact stereotypes, especially those that operate automatically and unintentionally, provide an effective way for healthcare professionals to be aware of the information that they require.

To see the first of these points, consider how medical conditions are often unevenly distributed across social groups. For instance, hypertension, coronary heart disease, osteoarthritis, diabetes and certain types of cancer are more commonly found among obese people than underweight, normal weight or overweight people (Sturm 2002). People of low socioeconomic status in some countries are more vulnerable than members of other social groups to certain conditions such as tuberculosis, HIV-AIDS and diabetes (Root 2000, cited in Haslanger 2004). Meanwhile, as members of certain ethnic and racial groups, such as Black people in the United States, are statistically more likely to live in poverty, they are more likely than average to have conditions commonly found among those from low socioeconomic backgrounds (Root 2000, cited in Haslanger 2004).

> Blacks are seven times more likely to die of tuberculosis than whites, three times more likely to die of HIV-AIDS and twice as likely to die of diabetes. The diseases are biological but the racial differences are not; How is this possible?... No mystery. Race affects income, housing, and healthcare, and these, in turn, affect health. Stress suppresses the immune system and being Black in the U.S. today is stressful.
>
> (Root 2000, S629, cited in Haslanger 2003–2004, p. 11)

Because medical conditions are not evenly distributed across social groups, if a patient is a member of a particular social group, they can consequently be significantly more likely than non-group members to have a particular condition. Under these circumstances, both information about the social group membership of a patient and information about the prevalence of a medical condition within a patient's social group is relevant background statistical information. If members of social group A are more likely than members of other social groups to have a certain condition C, and patient P is a member of social group A, then P's social group membership is relevant to a judgement about whether they have condition C. As mentioned above, information about the prevalence of a medical condition can, for example, guide judgements about which diagnostic hypotheses are more probable than others. If diseases x, y and z are more common among a patients' social group than other diseases, and a patient displays symptoms consistent with x, y and z, the patient is more likely to have one of these diseases than some other disease, all else being equal. As also mentioned above, healthcare professionals cannot devote equal time and attention to all possible diagnostic hypotheses. This means that they are more likely to identify the correct diagnosis of a patient's disease if they focus on specific, probable, diagnostic hypotheses. If diseases x, y and z are significantly more common among a social group than other diseases, then the diagnostic hypothesis that a patient of the social group has one of the diseases will be probable relative to the probability that the patient has another disease. The healthcare professional who responds to the social group status of her patient by reflecting the information about the distribution of the diseases among the patient's social group in her diagnostic judgements can therefore be more likely to identify the correct diagnosis for the patient than a medical practitioner who does not do so. A healthcare professional who does not reflect information about the distribution of medical conditions across different social groups in her clinical judgements might consider a large and varied range of diagnostic hypotheses. However, without a restriction on the scope of conditions considered to reflect the social group membership of a patient, the healthcare professional is likely to fail to consider some clinical hypotheses that are highly likely given a patient's social group membership because she will be considering very many hypotheses that are less probable.

In some scenarios, information about the social group membership of a patient will be equally if not more diagnostic than information about their symptoms and medical history. Take a patient from a low socioeconomic background in a city in which there has been a high incidence of lead poisoning in areas of high deprivation due to poor housing conditions. Lead poisoning is difficult to diagnose and the symptoms of the condition can also be indicative of a number of other conditions (some key symptoms are high blood pressure, difficulties with memory and concentration, headaches). A healthcare professional could have knowledge of the symptoms and medical history of the patient without considering lead poisoning as a plausible explanation of those things. Meanwhile, knowledge of the social group status of the patient might lead her to quickly consider that the patient has lead poisoning.

What the discussion so far in this section confirms is the first point against the idea that ethical and epistemic principles converge in an uncomplicated way on avoiding stereotyping: the social group status of patients can be highly relevant to medical judgement and decision-making and a crucial determinant of whether or not a correct judgement is made. To see the second point, consider how the process of gaining the information needed to make correct diagnostic and treatment decisions will frequently require direct communication between healthcare professionals and patients and sometimes also a physical examination by the healthcare professional of the patient. If either of these interactions happen then the healthcare professional is likely to discover at least some of the social group statuses of their patients, from their appearance, accent, etc. This means that it will not be possible to do what is required to make correct diagnostic and treatment decisions without occupying a situation in which the social status of the patient is apparent. Mere recognition of a person's social status can lead to an automatic response that involves stereotyping. Therefore, it will often not be possible to get the information required to make correct diagnostic and treatment decisions without automatically responding to the social status of one's patient.

With each of these points in mind it is important to note that automatically stereotyping in a way that associates members of certain social groups more strongly than members of other social groups with certain medical conditions can be an effective way of ensuring that relevant information about the prevalence of medical conditions across social groups influences one's judgements. Recall that healthcare professionals often operate under conditions in which automatic forms of cognition like implicit bias dominate their thinking. If automatic cognition is determining the judgements that healthcare professionals make, and the judgements are more likely to be good ones if they reflect associations between medical conditions and social groups, then it can be a good thing if the automatic cognitions reflect these associations.

What can be concluded on the basis of this discussion is that healthcare professionals who automatically associate members of some social groups more strongly than others with particular medical conditions, where the social group has a higher prevalence of the condition than other social groups, can be more likely to make correct clinical judgements. For this reason, stereotyping should not be characterized as bringing only epistemic costs. It can also be crucial for healthcare professionals to stereotype. In such cases epistemic and ethical goals do not converge on the reduction of stereotyping.

4.4 The Ethical Benefits of Stereotyping

We have now seen the case for stereotyping in healthcare being unethical, and how the same stereotyping can bring significant epistemic costs. We have also seen how stereotyping in healthcare can bring epistemic benefits. For the final piece of the puzzle, let us see how stereotyping can lead to the achievement of ethical goals.

People who adopt the role of medical practitioner take on the responsibility of identifying and responding to patients' clinical needs. Once they take on this responsibility, the ethical goal of treating people fairly demands that they do all that they can within reasonable limits to make accurate judgements about their patients' needs. The ethical goal of treating people fairly can sometimes only be achieved via the fulfilment of the epistemic goal of making a correct judgement. If healthcare professionals are more likely to make correct judgements by being responsive to the social group status of their patients, responding differently in their judgements of members of different social groups, then there can be an ethical demand on them to do so. Where the epistemic goal requires reflecting the social group status of a patient in their judgements, there can be an ethical demand on healthcare professionals to be responsive to social group status. And where reflecting the social group membership of a patient is most likely to be achieved by a person encoding information about the prevalence of medical conditions across social groups in a stereotype that is automatically activated, the application of the stereotype through an act of stereotyping can be demanded on the basis of ethical principles.

To see this point more clearly, consider the inadequacy, in the current context, of the response made by Andy Egan (2011) to the claim that people can face a dilemma with respect to implicit bias. Egan accepts that ethical and epistemic principles clash and responds by arguing that people should be willing to make inaccurate judgements in order to treat people fairly. Egan's suggestion is in a long tradition of arguments to the effect that epistemic goals can be overridden for sake of other goals (Code 1987), but it is unsatisfactory in the current case. A medical practitioner who takes the risk of making an inaccurate clinical judgement in order to be egalitarian could rightly be accused of negligence, failing to meet the responsibilities of her post. She could fail to achieve ethical goals by neglecting epistemic goals.

5. A Dilemma or Something More Complicated?

We are now in a position to see the oversimplification involved with both the idea outlined in Section 1 of this chapter that there is an epistemic-ethical dilemma surrounding stereotyping where a stereotype reflects social realities, and the first pass solution to the epistemic-ethical dilemma outlined in Section 2.

Epistemic and ethical demands can clash. For example, it might be best from an epistemic perspective for a particular healthcare professional, in a specific context, to associate Black people more strongly than others with a particular medical condition. This might lead the healthcare professional to quickly and efficiently identify whether a Black person has the condition. But the stereotype might at the same time lead to poor interactions between the healthcare professional and Black patients. This could occur in the following way. In the process of the stereotype associating Black patients with the condition, the general stereotype of the Black patient might be triggered, associating Black patients with uncooperativeness. If a stereotype associating Black patients with this undesirable feature is triggered the healthcare professional might interact poorly with Black patients. The poor interactions could lead the patients targeted by this stereotyping to be generally distrustful of the health practitioner, and even the medical system more generally, producing significant long-term damage to their health and well-being. Although a quick and efficient correct diagnostic judgement might be made due to the operation of the stereotype associating Black patients with a medical condition that is prevalent among their social group—an epistemic gain for the healthcare professional—there would be significant attendant ethical costs.

It is not, however, consistently the case that epistemic and ethical goals clash in this way. There can also be epistemic costs associated with stereotyping, where a stereotype reflects some aspect of social reality, due to the multiple ways that stereotypes can lead to the distortion of case-specific information. Therefore what initially seems to be the best thing from an ethical perspective—i.e. avoiding stereotyping—can bring epistemic gains. Meanwhile, in those cases in which there are epistemic gains from stereotyping, it can also be best from an ethical perspective. Where a person has a duty or responsibility to form accurate beliefs about social objects, such as other social actors or events, ethical principles can demand that they do all that they can to form accurate beliefs. If stereotyping ensures that they do this, then ethical principles demand stereotyping. Therefore, in some cases ethical and epistemic principles converge, but not as the first pass solution suggested. Rather than converging on stereotyping being worst from both the epistemic and ethical perspective, they can converge on stereotyping being best from both perspectives.

In sum, then, the case study of medicine shows each of these points: stereotyping can lead to poor judgement and decision making in healthcare and unfair differential treatment, but it can also facilitate correct judgements and decision making and the achievement of the ethical goals, when doing the right thing requires forming correct judgements.

6. Broadening the Scope of the Argument

While the focus so far in this chapter has been on stereotyping, and specifically automatic stereotyping, that occurs within a healthcare setting, similar conclusions can be drawn about the broader class of stereotypes and forms of stereotyping. When ethical goals require forming accurate beliefs about a person, and associating members of some social groups more strongly than others with certain characteristics facilitates the formation of accurate beliefs, ethical goals can require stereotyping, where stereotyping is understood as associating some groups more strongly than others with particular features.

Take, for example, the association between heavily pregnant women and physical need. If making this association leads a person to correctly assess the needs of a heavily pregnant woman who is standing on a bus, then it can facilitate ethical treatment of that woman, by leading the person to offer the woman the seat. Or, as Louise Antony (2016) describes, fair assessments of underprivileged students' performances on standardized tests can require associating them with educational disadvantage (see Madva 2016b for a similar view). By associating them with educational disadvantage it is possible to make a correct assessment of the extent to which their performance reflects their true potential—acknowledging that the performance might not accurately reflect their potential—thereby achieving an ethical goal. Proper acknowledgement of how they might have underperformed due to educational disadvantage can ensure that they are given appropriate rewards for what they have managed to achieve in spite of the disadvantages and that they are given further opportunities to reach their full potential. The latter are ethical achievements only possible due to achieving the epistemic goal. More generally, where ethical goals demand that a correct judgement is made, for example, in order to prevent harm to a person to whom a stereotype might be applied, they converge with epistemic goals.

At other times we might forego epistemic goals for the sake of being ethical. We might make efforts not to engage in stereotyping, even when a stereotype reflects some aspect of social reality, because we believe that stereotyping is unethical. However, in many cases where stereotyping is unethical it brings epistemic costs as well as ethical costs. As we have seen in Chapters 3 and 4, there are numerous epistemic costs associated with stereotyping, and therefore many ways that unethical stereotyping can be epistemically costly. Whether a stereotype relates to a group of patients and a medical condition, rates of criminal involvement across different social groups, the lifestyle choices of career women in 1950s New York, scientific expertise and its distribution across the sexes, or legal expertise across racial and gender groups, the application of an unethical stereotype can bring significant epistemic costs. These costs can be incurred even if the stereotype reflects some aspect of social reality (Chapter 4).

The biggest difficulty that we face is consequently not the problem that some have presented, i.e. that ethical and epistemic principles clash where stereotypes reflect some aspect of social reality, such as rates of criminal involvement across racial groups. In some contexts this type of conflict will occur but in many other cases epistemic and ethical goals will be achieved in the same way. The biggest difficulty we face, then, is the following extremely complex problem: ethical and epistemic principles point, together or separately, towards different thoughts and actions in different contexts.

7. A Comparison with the Moral Encroachment Approach

The response presented in this chapter to the suggestion that we can face competing ethical and epistemic demands when it comes to stereotyping is, then, a call to recognize the complexity of the situation that we face. In contrast, some defenders of moral encroachment views suggest that there is a solution to cases of apparent conflict between epistemic and ethical demands when it comes to stereotyping (see Chapter 4, Section 8.3 for an introduction to moral encroachment views). They argue that ethical and epistemic demands do not conflict because moral considerations determine whether it is epistemically permissible to engage in stereotyping (Basu 2019a, 2020; Basu and Schroeder 2018). Where there are high moral stakes in a situation in which a judgement is made, high evidentiary standards need to be met in order for a judgement to be justified or rational or to constitute knowledge. In cases where people might engage in stereotyping, there will often be high moral stakes, and these stakes will raise the evidentiary standards. Those who engage in stereotyping will not meet the high evidentiary standards. Therefore, stereotyping will not be justified or rational. As Basu (2020) puts it, 'if you are going to believe that someone is a valet based on their skin colour, although that might give you a lot of evidence, it's not enough evidence to make the belief justified. Given the high moral stakes, you must look for more evidence' (p. 205).

A complete solution to the epistemic-ethical dilemma of this type, which suggests that epistemic and ethical demands do not ever conflict, might be attractive to some. However, the discussion in this chapter suggests that this type of response to the epistemic-ethical dilemma is overly simplistic, distorting the true nature of the situation we face with regards to stereotypes and stereotyping. There are occasions in which epistemic and ethical demands converge, but there are also cases where they conflict. There are cases where stereotyping is unethical, but there are also cases where stereotyping is ethical. Sometimes the stakes at play in a situation mean that it is unethical to engage in stereotyping, and on some of these occasions it is also best from an epistemic perspective not to engage in stereotyping, because stereotyping would lead to misjudgements. But equally sometimes high-stakes situations demand stereotyping, because stereotyping can be an efficient way to achieve both ethical and epistemic goals, like correct diagnoses and treatment decisions.

What is needed is a fine-grained approach to stereotyping, which reflects how stereotypes can operate in various ways to facilitate or impede the achievement of epistemic and ethical goals, either jointly or separately, in different contexts. Healthcare professionals and others who might reflect on the impact of their stereotyping on others could benefit from being equipped with the means to understand how various epistemic and ethical goals might be achieved, and how they might conflict or converge, in different situations. A broad-brush approach that suggests that ethical and epistemic demands simply do not conflict is misleading given the complexity of the situation that is faced.

8. Practical Upshots

What are the practical implications of the discussion of this chapter? What can be learnt by those who are concerned with improving the epistemic and ethical standing of people who might engage in stereotyping?

The argument presented in this chapter shows is that if some strategies are established to be effective at combating the negative effects of this stereotyping this could facilitate the achievement of both ethical and epistemic goals. (For consideration of the types of strategies that might be adopted see Chapter 6, Section 4). But the argument also highlights a significant and unexpected challenge that is faced by those hoping to ameliorate people's conduct by tackling stereotyping. It suggests that the ideal strategy to use to tackle the negative effects of stereotyping would not eliminate altogether the influence of stereotyping on our thought and action—the strategy that might at face value seem most promising. It would not even eliminate the influence of all of the stereotypes that bring substantial epistemic costs. Instead, it would lead people to control rather than eradicate or completely block the activation of some of these stereotypes, for example, those relating social groups to medical conditions (see, e.g. Madva 2016b; Lassiter and Ballantyne 2017). Why should these stereotypes be controlled rather than eliminated? Because associating social groups with certain features, where the association reflects the distribution of conditions across social groups, can facilitate the quick and efficient formation of a correct judgement. Until control of this sort is taken over people's stereotyping, they are unlikely to consistently achieve either their ethical or epistemic goals with respect to stereotypes. They are unlikely to be able to respond quickly and efficiently to what is important and relevant information without suffering epistemic costs that can reduce the likelihood that they will make correct judgements.

9. Conclusion

There will be cases in which ethical and epistemic demands clash when it comes to stereotypes that reflect aspects of social reality. However, it is not the case that whenever stereotypes reflect reality it is highly likely that there will be an epistemic-ethical conflict. To the contrary, there are numerous ways that ethical and epistemic goals can interact. As well as conflicting, ethical and epistemic goals can converge on either stereotyping (conceived as it is in this book) or on not stereotyping. This is both good news and bad. It means that in many cases we need not compromise either one or the other of our ethical and epistemic goals. But it also means that it is extremely difficult to ascertain for any individual case how to do what is best from the ethical and/or epistemic perspective.

6

Stereotyping and Disclosure of Social Identity

Mental Health and Beyond

1. Introduction

Chapter 5 addressed the position of authors who argue that people face a dilemma with respect to whether to prevent themselves and others from engaging in stereotyping. However, there is another group of people to be considered: those who might be stereotyped. In this chapter we shall see how the multifactorial approach to stereotyping detailed in Chapter 3 reveals the contours of a dilemma that some of these people face if they want to avoid being misperceived. As in Chapter 5, we shall focus first and foremost on a case study: a set of individuals who are often stereotyped, i.e. those with mental health conditions. Then we shall see how the conclusions drawn with regards to this specific group can be generalized.

Many people face a question about whether they should reveal something about themselves that will lead them to be stereotyped. This includes many people who have a mental health condition. People with mental health conditions are often required to address the question of whether they should disclose information about their mental health. Should they inform their employers, colleagues, friends, family, neighbours, etc. that they have a mental health condition? Should they be encouraged by others to do so? There has been a recent move to promote disclosure as a way to increase the empowerment and decrease the self-stigma of people with mental health conditions (see, e.g. Corrigan et al. 2010; Corrigan and Rao 2012). For instance, a three-week intervention, *Coming Out Proud*, has been devised to inform people about the costs and benefits of disclosure, forms of disclosure, and helpful ways to tell others about one's mental health condition (Rüsch et al. 2014).

How Stereotypes Deceive Us. Katherine Puddifoot, Oxford University Press. © Katherine Puddifoot 2021.
DOI: 10.1093/oso/9780192845559.003.0006

However, many people with mental health conditions continue to fear stigma and penalization if they disclose information about their condition. For example, a survey in the UK found that over 50 per cent of the mental health service users surveyed feared disclosing their condition because they anticipated stigma and discrimination (Time to Change 2008). In another survey, almost 50 per cent of female physicians who were surveyed stated that although they thought that they met the criteria for having a mental illness they had not sought treatment, in many cases due to fear of stigma (Gold et al. 2016).

Should people with mental health conditions put these fears aside and respond to the evidence suggesting that disclosure can reduce self-stigma by letting others know about their mental health condition? This chapter shows what the multifactorial approach to stereotyping can contribute to answering this question. It corroborates the view of those who fear stigmatization. As the focus of this book is how stereotyping can lead to misperception, the chapter focuses in particular on the way that people who have mental health conditions can rightly fear that they will be misperceived as a result of others knowing about their mental health condition. In one survey, 51 per cent of service users said that they wanted the message 'We are people—see me, not the illness' to be conveyed because they believed that they were misperceived as a result of their condition. I show that this view of people with mental health conditions is corroborated by the multifactorial view of stereotyping: if they disclose information about their mental health condition they face a substantial risk of being stereotyped and consequently misperceived.

It might seem as if one message of this chapter is therefore that people should not disclose information about their mental health conditions for fear of stigmatization and being misperceived. However, I show that philosophical and psychological research into how people ascribe mental states to each other suggests that the choice not to disclose information about one's mental health condition can also lead to misperception. This chapter will therefore outline the contours of a serious dilemma faced by people with mental health conditions: whether or not they disclose information about their mental health, they risk being misperceived. Then the chapter will show how others, with other social identities that are stereotyped, face a similar dilemma. So whereas we have found that those who might prevent stereotyping of others do not consistently face a dilemma, we shall see that those who might prevent themselves from being stereotyped face a very real one.

2. The Multifactorial View, Disclosure, and Misperception

2.1 The Nature of Mental Health Stereotypes

To see how people can be misperceived due to the operation of stereotypes relating to mental health, it is first necessary to understand the extent and scope of stereotyping of people with mental health conditions.

People with mental health conditions can decide to withhold or disclose information about their condition(s). There is legislation to protect them from discrimination if they disclose information. For example, in the United Kingdom the Equalities Act 2010 disability is a protected characteristic and it is stated that 'A person (A) discriminates against another (B) if, because of a protected characteristic, A treats B less favourably than A treats or would treat others' (13.1). A mental health condition is considered a disability and discrimination is prohibited. However, legislation cannot be expected to prevent all forms of stereotyping relating to mental health conditions.

Studies have repeatedly shown that in spite of equality legislation, and some reduction to negative attitudes (Crisp et al. 2005; Time to Change 2015), stereotypes remain. A recent UK Office of National Statistics opinion survey of attitudes towards people with schizophrenia, depression, and anxiety uncovered stereotypes associating members of these groups with being a 'danger to others', 'unpredictable' and 'hard to talk to' (Wood et al. 2014). These findings replicate earlier studies undertaken by Crisp and colleagues (2000, 2005) and earlier work finding that people with mental health conditions are strongly associated with dangerousness (Link et al. 1999; Phelan et al. 2000). People with mental health conditions have also been found to be associated with incompetence and character weakness (Corrigan and Watson 2002). There is some variety in ways in which different mental health conditions are stereotyped. Schizophrenia is especially strongly associated with dangerousness and unpredictability (Angermeyer and Matschinger, 2003; Crisp et al. 2000, 2005; Wood et al. 2014). Meanwhile, people with anxiety and depression are more likely to be treated as blameworthy for their condition (Wood et al. 2014). People with depression are associated with being lazy and not easy to talk to (Thornicroft, Rose, and Kassam 2007). Further support for the idea that stereotyping frequently occurs comes from the personal experiences of people with mental health conditions. For example, a series of surveys, conducted over the

WPAE! negative Implicit Biases

period 2008–2011 in the UK, found that 87–91 per cent of users of mental health services experienced discrimination in four or five areas of their life (Corker et al. 2013).[1] Discrimination can occur due to stereotyping of individuals being manifest in action.

There is also reason for thinking that many people harbour implicit biases relating to mental illness (see Chapter 1, Section 1.4, for an introduction to the notion of implicit bias). Studies have repeatedly found evidence that people with mental illnesses are implicitly associated more strongly than others with concepts such as dangerous, incompetent, threatening, and unpredictable or helplessness (Rüsch et al. 2011; Teachman, Wilson, and Komarovskaya 2006). The finding that people with mental illnesses are associated with negative or unpleasant concepts has been replicated across various populations: the undergraduate population, the general population, and people with mental illnesses (Teachman et al. 2006); medical students with no direct experience of people with mental illness and mental health care professionals (Kopera et al. 2015); and people of various age groups including young children and adolescents, and older people (O'Driscoll et al. 2012). Various implicit methods have been used to uncover people's implicit biases.[2] Experimental evidence has been gathered suggesting that implicit biases relating to mental illness manifest in behaviour. The degree of negative implicit bias displayed by mental healthcare professionals has been found to predict their certainty that they would help someone with a mental illness (those with high levels of negative bias said that they were less certain to help) (Brener et al. 2013) and the tendency to over-diagnose (those with stronger negative biases were more likely to over-diagnose) (Peris, Teachman, and Nosek 2008).

It is worthwhile recognizing that implicit biases could operate because if they do so they will exacerbate the problems of stereotyping by leading to unintentional stereotyping by people who are explicitly egalitarian. If people are influenced by implicit bias they may associate people with mental health

---

[1] There was some improvement over the period covered by the study (the number of people who had experienced discrimination was 91 per cent in 2008, 87 per cent in 2009 and 2010, and 88 per cent in 2011), during which the Time for Change campaign, which aimed to tackle prejudice and discrimination towards people with mental health issues, was in operation. However, the improvement was not statistically significant, nor did it meet the target of reduction of experiences of discrimination set for the campaign (Corker et al. 2013).

[2] The Implicit Association Task (IAT) (Teachman et al. 2006); a lexical priming task (Rüsch et al. 2011), and the GNAT task (Kopera et al. 2015).

conditions with characteristics due to their social group membership, thereby stereotyping, without intending to do so.[3]

What is important for current purposes, however, is that there exist stereotypes relating to mental illness, which may operate explicitly or implicitly, and people who have mental health conditions often experience being stereotyped. Legislation aimed at preventing people from discriminating cannot be expected to prevent people from applying stereotypes, e.g. associating people with mental illness with dangerousness. When a person is perceived as belonging to the group of people with a mental health condition, or as having a particular mental health condition, a stereotype associated with the group is likely to be triggered. Consequently, any particular individual with a mental health condition is highly likely to be stereotyped.

2.2 Stereotyping and Misperception

This section shows that not only are people with mental health conditions likely to be stereotyped by others who are aware of their condition, they are likely to be misperceived as a result of being stereotyped. We can see this point by applying the insights from the multifactorial view to the case of mental health stereotypes. Recall that this multifactorial approach has revealed that there are multiple ways that stereotyping can lead to the misperception of individuals to whom a stereotype is applied, whether it occurs implicitly or explicitly (Chapter 3).

With respect to mental health, these phenomena can manifest in the following ways. Evidence about the personal traits or characteristics of someone with a mental health condition that is consistent with them fitting a stereotype—e.g. evidence of their incompetence in some domain—can be more likely to be noticed and given attention while evidence that challenges the stereotype—e.g. evidence of their competence—is not noticed or attended to. Meanwhile, ambiguous behaviours displayed by people with mental health conditions, such as lateness or inattention—might be viewed as evidence of stereotypical characteristics like having a weak character or being volatile. When an action of this or a similar sort is best explained by

---

[3] It is especially important to recognize this possibility as research on implicit biases relating to mental illness is well positioned to meet many of the criticisms often levelled at implicit bias research: findings demonstrating implicit biases in this domain have been replicated across different contexts, using various methodologies, and experiments have measured the extent to which implicit bias relating to mental health predicts behaviour.

the personal traits of the individual, or features of their situation, but not by their mental health condition, the actions are likely to nonetheless be explained in terms of the stereotype: e.g. people with mental illness are like that. Meanwhile, people with mental health conditions, because they are viewed through the lens of their membership of the group, *people with a mental illness*, are likely to be assumed to be similar to other previously encountered people with mental health conditions and dissimilar to others who do not have a mental health condition. Judgements based on these assumptions will not reflect their true similarities and dissimilarities to others.

In addition to this, people with mental health conditions can be denied the opportunity to communicate information about themselves and have uptake of this information from people who engage in stereotyping. Where people have mental health conditions, they can be treated as if they are unreliable sources of information about their condition when they are actually providing accurate information (Crichton, Carel, and Kidd 2017). They can be incorrectly assumed to have mental impairments that mean that they lack self-awareness and cannot be trusted to convey information. Where a person believes that their testimony is not likely to receive proper uptake they can choose not to deliver it (Dotson 2011). If this occurs then information about individuals with mental health conditions who are stereotyped, information that they might have otherwise conveyed through their testimony to others, will not be accessible to those who stereotype them. For example, some information about individual people with mental illness, their personal characteristics and abilities, as well as the symptoms of their conditions, is unlikely to be accessed and utilized when making judgements. If important and relevant information of this sort is not accessed, judgements about people with mental illness are less likely to be accurate or fitting with the evidence that is available.

What the multifactorial view shows, then, is that if a person fears being misperceived due to their mental health condition, their fears sadly reflect reality. As things currently stand, they are likely to be stereotyped due to their mental health condition, and are therefore likely to be misperceived by the person engaging in the stereotyping, who will either fail to access or properly respond to relevant information about them. Disclosure of a mental health condition therefore brings the associated risk of being misperceived, e.g. as dangerous, incompetent, and just like other people with mental health conditions.

3. Non-Disclosure and Misperception

3.1 Information and Understanding

A thought that will be tempting to many at this point is that people with mental health conditions should avoid disclosing information about their condition. The philosophical and psychological literatures on which the multifactorial approach to stereotyping is built point in this direction. However, within the philosophy of mind and philosophy of mental disorder, there are other arguments that point in the opposite direction, suggesting that non-disclosure of information about a mental health condition can lead to misperception. This is because someone who lacks information about another person's mental health can consequently fail to properly ascribe mental states and dispositions to that person.

For instance, in the philosophical literature on psychiatric delusions, it has been argued that it is possible to understand, predict and explain the behaviour of people with mental health conditions but only if they are viewed as having unusual thoughts. The following example illustrates this point:

Lizard Man: a 22-year-old Rastafarian man of Jamaican parents was admitted from casualty, having superficially stabbed himself with broken glass. He had become acutely distressed over the past 2–3 days, feeling anxious and depressed and believing that his movements were [being] watched by TV cameras, and signals about him were [being] passed between shopkeepers and that people in shops were talking about him. He was particularly distressed by the scaly appearance of his skin, which he believed was caused by a lizard growing inside his body, the lizard's skin being evident on his arms and legs. He gave the growth of the lizard inside his chest as the reason for stabbing himself. He related this to an incident 10 years before when, in Jamaica, a lizard had run across his face. He believed that the lizard had 'left its mark' and that a curse then had produced his skin lesions.

(Campbell 2009, p. 143, Reimer 2011, p. 662)

Marga Reimer (2011), rightly it seems, claims that it is possible to understand the mental states of the man described in this example. It is even possible to explain why he behaves the way that he does. We could predict related behaviours that he is likely to engage in. However, we are only able to do each of these things because we ascribe to him a bizarre thought: that there is a lizard underneath his skin. We need to focus on an aspect of Lizard Man's thought that is so bizarre that the possession of the thought provides a strong indication of mental illness. Without noticing this aspect of his thought, we would not be able to make sense of his actions or the claims that he makes. We would misperceive and misunderstand his behaviour. But on noticing this aspect of his thought it is natural to ascribe him with a mental health condition, i.e. having a psychiatric delusion. It is therefore not possible to avoid misperceiving him and to instead understand what he is thinking without being aware of his mental health condition.

The Lizard Man example is extreme. Many mental health conditions do not include thoughts with such bizarre content. Take, for example, depression, low mood or borderline personality disorder. None of these conditions commonly involves bizarre thoughts. Nonetheless a brief survey of the dominant philosophical accounts of how mental states and dispositions are ascribed shows that the general point about the Lizard Man case applies to these other mental health conditions. In order for people to properly understand certain aspects of what a person is thinking and how they are disposed to think and behave, and in order to accurately predict and explain certain aspects of their behaviour, it will often be necessary to be aware that they have a mental health condition.

Let us begin by considering *simulation theory*. According to this view, when we ascribe mental states to others we project ourselves into their situation (see, e.g. Goldman 1989; Gordon 1986; Heal 1986). We simulate what we would think and feel if we occupied their situation, making adjustments for any ways that we think that their thoughts are likely to differ from ours. If a person has a mental health condition then they are likely to think and feel in ways that are significantly different to our own. This means that a significant adjustment will need to be made. But the adjustment is only likely to properly reflect the difference between one's own situation and the situation of a person with a mental health condition if one is aware of the condition.

On another account of how mental states and dispositions are ascribed, *theory theory*, mental state ascription involves the application of a tacit theory (e.g. Gopnik et al. 1997; Gopnik, Meltzoff, and Kuhl 1999). The laws of the theory relate to the situation in which an individual is located, their behaviour as it is found in that situation, and the mental states that underwrite the behaviour. People make inferences from the presence of certain behaviours to the presence of particular mental states by applying the theory. In order for the application of a theory to yield accurate judgements about a person's mental states and dispositions when they have a mental health condition it can be necessary to notice that the tacit theory that successfully predicts many people's mental states and dispositions needs to be adjusted. This is because a person with a mental health condition has aspects of their mental life that differ significantly from most other people's. With respect to those aspects of their mental life, their behaviours will relate differently than other people's to their mental states and situation. For example, the belief that a lizard ran over one's arm and the presence of scaly skin would not usually lead to the behaviour displayed by Lizard Man. A tacit theory that ascribes mental states to people who do not have mental health conditions would be unable to account for Lizard Man's behaviour. In order for Lizard Man's thoughts to be properly understood some adjustment needs to be made to the tacit theory about how mental states, behaviours and situations usually interrelate, to reflect his mental health condition.

Another account of how mental states and dispositions are ascribed is *intentional systems theory*. According to this theory, the ascription of mental states and dispositions is achieved by adopting the *intentional stance*, viewing others as having beliefs, desires, intentions, and so on (Dennett 1971, 1987). The intentional stance involves applying a *principle of charity* to others, assuming that they display rational characteristics; that they believe what they should; have largely true beliefs; and are largely correct in the inferences, expectations and the decisions that they make. People who make these assumptions about people with mental health conditions often draw false conclusions about what they think. In order for accurate judgements to be made about people with mental health conditions it will sometimes be necessary to take their condition into consideration, consequently suspending one's commitment to some or all of the principle of charity, the rationality assumption, and the assumption that they are likely to be displaying true beliefs and correct inferences. Therefore, adjustments will need to be made to the principles underlying most mental state ascription to ensure that the mental states and dispositions of people with mental health conditions are properly understood.

According to a final account of how people ascribe mental states and dispositions to others, our capacity for understanding mental states is underwritten by our capacity for creating and applying narratives (Gallagher and Hutto 2008; Hutto 2012). From early childhood, we are exposed to narratives by our caregivers who guide us through the reading of stories such as fairy-tales. In these narratives, characters are introduced within a specific set of circumstances and they act for reasons. Our early exposure to these narratives provides a sense of what is acceptable in certain types of circumstances, what types of activities are interesting and worth noting, what accounts for certain types of action, and what constitutes a good reason for acting. The narratives provide a grasp of cultural norms and likely reasons for action. Then, throughout adulthood, we continue to create and apply narratives to understand the reasons why individuals act in the ways that they do. On this account of the ascription of mental states and dispositions, it will be necessary to take a person's mental health condition into consideration because the pathological mental states and dispositions of people with mental health conditions will often not fit standard narrative structures. They will violate cultural norms and expectations. To properly understand the mental states and dispositions of those with mental health conditions, it will therefore be necessary to factor in how they are likely to deviate from cultural norms and expectations and develop narratives that reflect this.

It is important to note that not all aspects of the mental life of a person with a mental health condition will always be significantly different to the average, deviate from norms of rationality, or violate cultural and social norms and expectations. But there will often be aspects of the mental lives of people with mental health conditions that have these features—the aspects that relate to the mental health conditions. For example, a person with depression might make an unusually negative assessment of their prospects while otherwise having many mental states and dispositions that are like that of the average person who does not have depression. It is the assessment of their prospects that means that they have mental states that deviate significantly from the average and it is the same feature of their mental life that means that they are depressed. It is therefore with respect to the aspects of their mental life that are constitutive of their mental health condition, and those closely related, that people risk being misunderstood if they do not disclose information about their mental health.

In sum, then, proper understanding of the mental states and dispositions of people with mental health conditions often requires knowledge about their conditions. The Lizard Man example illustrates this point. Each of the dominant accounts of the way that mental states and dispositions are ascribed suggests this to be the case. This means that if a person chooses not to disclose information about their mental health condition, they risk being misperceived by people who can consequently lack the information required to develop a proper understanding of their mental states and dispositions.

3.2 What Happens in the Absence of the Information?

Section 3.1 shows how it can be valuable for a person to disclose information about their mental health: disclosure provides other people with the information required for understanding of their mental states, dispositions, and behaviours. This section explores in more depth what happens if they do not disclose the information. What are the specific risks associated with being misperceived due to non-disclosure? This section focuses on two risks, each of which could have a significant impact upon the wellbeing and life outcomes of people with mental health conditions.[4]

First of all, the person who does not disclose information about their mental health condition takes the risk that the needs associated with their mental health condition are not properly understood. Take, for example, a student with anxiety. She dreads public speaking, and therefore misses class when she is aware that she has to orally present her work. If her teacher is not aware of her mental health condition then her absence could be misperceived as indicating that she is lazy, disorganized or lacking commitment to her education. If the teacher misperceives the student in any of these ways then the needs of the student will not be recognized. However, if the teacher has information about the student's mental health condition, special measures could be put in place to support her. For instance, she could be allowed to work as a part of a group, contributing to the research for the presentation without being required to engage in public speaking. There will be many similar cases in which a person has additional needs as a result of their mental health condition. If people are not aware of the condition then their situation will be misperceived and they will not be provided with the necessary support. And it could have a significant negative impact upon their life outcomes, e.g. leading them to underperform in their education or working life.

Second of all, a person with a mental health condition could be misperceived as having a poor character because of a lack of understanding of their condition. A case that illustrates this point is that of personality disorder. The following is the definition of personality disorder provided by the tenth revision of the *International Statistical Classification of Diseases and Related Health Problems (ICD-10)*:

---

[4] This section aims to provide an illustrative rather than a complete list of the misperceptions that can occur.

Specific personality disorders (F60.-), mixed and other personality disorders (F61.-), and enduring personality changes (F62.-) are deeply ingrained and enduring behaviour patterns, manifesting as inflexible responses to a broad range of personal and social situations. They represent extreme or significant deviations from the way in which the average individual in a given culture perceives, thinks, feels and, particularly, relates to others. Such behaviour patterns tend to be stable and to encompass multiple domains of behaviour and psychological functioning. They are frequently, but not always, associated with various degrees of subjective distress and problems of social performance.   (Chapter V, F60-90)

If a person displays ingrained and inflexible responses to personal and social situations, which are extreme or significant deviations from the way that the average person behaves in a culture, their behaviour could easily be misperceived. The behaviour can be viewed as indicative of a poor character or 'badness'. Because a person with personality disorder deviates from social norms it could be tempting to describe them as a troublemaker. If, on the other hand, a person discloses that they have a mental health condition, they provide other people with the opportunity to become informed about their condition, and to understand that they are not bad and instead their behaviour is the result of a mental health issue.

Those who do not disclose information about their mental health condition therefore risk having their needs neglected and being viewed as having a poor character. If they are concerned about being misperceived, then there is good reason for them to be tempted not to disclose information about their condition because doing so reduces the chance of them being misperceived as a result of being stereotyped. However, if they choose not to disclose information about their condition, they risk other forms of misperception. They therefore face a serious dilemma about whether to disclose information about their condition if they want to avoid being misperceived.

4. Responding to the Dilemma

It should now be evident that many people with mental health conditions face a dilemma: whether or not they disclose information about their mental health condition they are likely to be misperceived. Once this dilemma has been acknowledged, it is natural to ask what can and should be done.

A full solution to the dilemma is beyond the scope of the current chapter, but this section argues that any adequate solution will require societal change as well as actions by individuals other than those who have mental health conditions. As it will continue to be the case that people with mental health conditions have aspects of their mental lives that will only be properly understood if their condition is known, the solution to the dilemma will involve ensuring that they can disclose information about their condition without being misperceived due to being stereotyped.

It might seem as if people with mental health issues are equipped to respond to the dilemma themselves. They can use the strategy of *selective disclosure*, only disclosing information about their condition to people who they particularly trust (e.g. close family members and friends) or need to tell (e.g. employers), to reduce the chance that people will stereotype them (Bos et al. 2009). But there are significant shortcomings of selective disclosure. First, even those people who one particularly trusts may harbour stereotypes or implicit biases relating to mental illnesses. Even close family and friends may be influenced by stereotypes due to their pervasiveness in society, leading them to misperceive the person with the mental health condition. Second, those people who are not told about a person's mental health condition will continue to misperceive them due to their ignorance. Selective disclosure is therefore an imperfect and partial solution to the dilemma.

Alternatives to selective disclosure are found in the form of psychological strategies that can be adopted to change the associations that are made with people with mental health conditions. If a person is aware that they are likely to respond in a biased manner towards members of a particular group, they can adopt long-range strategies to try to change their responses (Holroyd 2012). Long-range strategies are adopted prior to a person being in a situation in which they might be biased. For instance, a person might formulate implementation intentions or 'if-then plans', which have been found to be successful in changing the associations that are made with individuals who are encountered (see, e.g. Stewart and Payne 2008). For example, a person might form the plan *if I see a person with a mental health condition then I will think safe*. Alternatively, one might follow the guidance of advocates of contact theory (Corrigan et al. 2012; Kolodziej and Johnson 1996; Pettigrew and Tropp 2005; Pinfold et al. 2003), who argue that it is possible to change one's stereotyping of stigmatized and marginalized groups through contact with members of the group. One might try to change one's responses towards a certain social group by ensuring that one has regular contact with members of the group, perhaps engaging in a joint task. Other similar strategies are available.

However, it is important to note that the long-range strategies that have just been described are first personal; the person whose biases are to be changed must adopt them.[5] This means that, unlike selective disclosure, whether or not they are adopted is beyond the control of the person with the mental health condition(s). For instance, if Ted has a mental health condition, then he might form an implementation intention *if I encounter a person with a mental health condition then I will think safe*. However, Ted's formation of the implementation intention will not prevent other people from stereotyping and consequently misperceiving him. Similarly, Ted cannot decide for other people that they will engage in co-operative activity with people with mental health conditions. Not only do people with mental health conditions face a dilemma with respect to whether or not to disclose information about their mental health, they are severely limited in their ability to resolve the dilemma. They are highly dependent on others to reduce the extent to which they are misperceived by ensuring that strategies are adopted to combat the stereotyping that leads to misperception.

While this might seem like a pessimistic result, things seem more positive once it is recognized that people with mental health conditions are not wholly dependent upon the willingness of other individuals to take action to change the associations that they make. There are changes that can be made to societal structures to reduce the chance of people with mental illnesses being misperceived as a result of stereotyping (see, e.g. Anderson 2010, 2012). It is possible for organizations and institutions to intervene to control how people respond to the information that an individual has a mental health condition, uncoupling mental health conditions from negative associations commonly made with them.

For example, it has been found that although experienced mental health care professionals can display the same amount of negative implicit bias as medical students (Brener et al. 2013; Kopera et al. 2015), the amount of contact time spent directly with patients in a week predicted the nature of the implicit bias displayed (Dabby, Tranulis, and Kirmayer 2015). This suggests

[5] It is also important to note that two recent rigorous studies have called into question the effectiveness of long-range strategies that have been proposed to tackle implicit stereotyping (Lai et al. 2014; Lai et al. 2016). In the first study it was found that many were ineffective in the short term (implementation intentions were effective), and where the strategies were effective the effectiveness was short-lived. These studies provide additional reason for thinking that societal changes will be needed to tackle stereotyping, at least the implicit type.

that employers of mental health workers could change people's biases towards those with mental health conditions, decoupling mental health conditions from negative stereotypes, by enacting a policy that requires mental health workers to meet some minimum requirement for the amount of time that they spend each week with service users. In addition to this, in Japan, the old word for 'schizophrenia' meaning 'split-mind' has been replaced by a new word meaning 'integration-disorder'. Takahashi et al. (2009) found that the old term was strongly associated by participants with 'criminal' versus 'victim', while the new term was less strongly associated with 'criminal'. These results suggest that strategies such as the renaming of mental disorders can be successful at reducing the negative impact of stereotyping. Meanwhile, anti-stigma campaigners can challenge the associations that are made with mental health conditions. It has been found that emphasizing the common group membership (e.g. university attended) between members of different groups (e.g. White vs Blacks) can reduce stereotyping and increase co-operative activity (for a review see Gaertner and Dovidio 2005). By presenting images of people with mental health conditions that emphasize the features that they share with people without mental health conditions, mental health campaigners can therefore reduce the misperception of people with mental health conditions as dangerous, incompetent, etc. Each of these approaches is piecemeal but governments can enact policies to ensure that initiatives that reduce the negative stereotyping of people with mental illnesses are implemented widely.

There has been a great deal of debate in the recent philosophical literature about whether individualistic strategies that focus on human psychology or broader strategies that focus on social structures are likely to be most effective at reducing inequalities (Banks and Ford 2011; Dixon et al. 2012; Haslanger 2015; Huebner 2016, cf. Saul 2013; Madva 2016b). The sensible position seems to be that attempts should be made to change both individuals' psychologies and social structures (see, e.g. Madva 2016c). Where there are strategies that can reduce individuals' stereotyping responses there is little reason not to encourage people to adopt the strategies, but wider structural changes can be necessary to ensure that there is wide-ranging equality. For example, the stereotype that people with mental illnesses are incompetent might only be successfully challenged across society if people with mental illnesses have the opportunity to thrive in the workplace, and the contribution that they make is widely recognized. Meanwhile, changing people's psychologies so that they appreciate the need for structural change can be necessary for structural measures to be successfully adopted (Madva 2016c). I therefore do not mean to commit to the idea that either individual psychologies or social structures should be the sole focus of attention for those aiming to reduce the stereotyping of people with mental health conditions. However, changes to social structures, such as institutions, organizations, and languages, provide a means of adjusting the responses of many people all at once, without depending on the willingness and motivation of each person. Recognition that these can be changed to reduce the negative impacts of stereotyping of people with mental health conditions therefore provides some reason for optimism.

5. How Far Does the Dilemma Extend?

We are now in a position to take a broader look at the dilemma faced by those who have social identities which are commonly stereotyped and that they could choose to divulge or to keep hidden. The claims that were the focus of the previous section related to how mental states are attributed, so it might seem as if the claims have limited application. However, we shall see that there are general lessons that can be learnt about how people can be misperceived whether or not they disclose a social identity that is commonly stereotyped.

The claims based on the multifactorial approach, relating to how stereotyping leads to misperception, apply widely to a variety of stereotypes and social identities. (For more on this point see Chapters 3 and 4.) Therefore, there is no need to establish at this point that people with social identities other than having a mental health condition face being misperceived if they reveal social identities that are commonly stereotyped. The focus of this section will instead be the ways that people with a variety of different social identities can be misperceived if they do not disclose information about their social identity.

We found that, whichever of the dominant theories of mental state attribution are correct, it can be necessary to factor in a person's mental health condition in order to understand their mental states. The mental health condition needs to be factored in to appropriately simulate the mental states; to adjust a tacit theory of mental states so that it applies to people with a specific mental health condition; to ensure that principles of charity, the rationality assumption, and the assumption of correct beliefs and inferences are suspended appropriately; and to ensure that recognition is given to how people's mental states are likely to deviate from narratives of cultural and social norms. We found also that it is the mental states that relate to the mental health conditions—the specific feature that is stereotyped—that are often unlikely to be understood if information is not disclosed. Other mental states, unrelated to the mental health condition, are likely to be understood without factoring in the mental health condition. We can generalize from this point that whenever understanding the mental states of a person requires factoring in their social identity, non-disclosure of social identity will risk misperception.

Let us consider a case outside of the domain of mental health in which understanding a person's mental states requires factoring in their social identity. Imagine that a young, White, working-class student begins to attend a university in which the majority of students are members of the privileged upper classes. The student suffers a crisis in confidence, while being surrounded by confident, privately educated peers, and consequently fails to attend many classes. They do not suffer a mental health condition but do suffer social exclusion and consequently perform poorly in their classes. Let us assume that the student could hide their class membership or divulge the information to a pastoral support tutor. Were the student to divulge the information, the tutor would gain a better understanding of the mental states and dispositions underlying the student's behaviour. However, the student would risk being stereotyped as incompetent (Durante et al. 2017; Lindqvist, Björklund, and Bäckström 2017) and animal-like or dehumanized (Loughnan et al. 2014; Volpato, Andrighetto, and Baldissarri 2017), because these are stereotypes associated with working-class people, and therefore being misperceived in the various ways that the multifactorial approach outlines. (See Durante and Fiske 2017 for an overview of research on how such stereotyping could negatively affect the educational outcomes of the working-class student.)

It is not only people's mental states that are misunderstood as a result of non-disclosure. Consider the situation of a single mother who begins a new job, in a new workplace. She cannot attend evening events due to childcare commitments. She may be stressed and anxious about this, but if she does not divulge information about her status as a single mother it is not only these mental states that will not be properly understood. Some of the things that will not be understood if she does not divulge that she is a single mother are the time restrictions she operates under, her need to be absent from work if the child is ill, why she might be tired some days, and so on.

But if she divulges her status then she risks being misperceived due to the single mother stereotype, for example, as lacking personal responsibility (Dodson 2013). This case shows how easily features other than mental states can be misunderstood where the social identity of a person would need to be known in order for understanding to be facilitated.

Both of the risks that were outlined in Section 3.2 as associated with failing to disclose information about one's mental health condition—the risk of one's needs not being understood and the risk of being viewed as having a bad character—are very real risks for the people who feature in these examples. Both the working-class student suffering a crisis of confidence and the single mother have needs that differ from others around them, specific to them due to their social identity, which will not be met if their social identity is not acknowledged. And they are both at risk of being viewed as having a bad character, for example, due to being perceived as lazy and uncommitted to their work. This is likely to be commonplace: where understanding of a person requires knowledge of their social identity, lack of knowledge of their social identity will risk them being viewed as having a bad character because they will inexplicably deviate from cultural norms and expected behaviour.

Thus, people with a variety of social identities face a dilemma similar to that outlined in Sections 1–4. If they disclose information about their social identity then they are likely to be stereotyped, and misperceived due to the influence of stereotypes. However, if they do not disclose the information, their mental states and dispositions, behaviours, and the broader constraints under which they live due to their social group membership, are likely to be misperceived.

6. Extending the Response

Because there is a dilemma faced by people of numerous social identities that shares the same contours as that faced by people with mental health conditions, similar responses are appropriate (as those outlined in Section 4). Selective disclosure of information about one's social identity is an option available to those who are likely to be stereotyped if they disclose an identity. However, it is only a partial solution because even those selected for disclosure, and chosen because they are trusted, could engage in stereotyping. Meanwhile those to whom the information is not divulged remain susceptible to misperceiving due to lacking information about the person's social identity. These things are true consistently across different social identities. Meanwhile, psychological approaches to combatting stereotyping are first personal, and therefore not available to people who are choosing whether to disclose their social identity, whether the identity relates to a mental health condition, class, status as a single parent, or so forth. However, changes to societal structures can reduce or remove the dilemma faced by people from a variety of different social identities, through, for example, increased intergroup contact, changes to negative labelling, and positive depictions of people in the media, which reduce the negative stereotyping of members of various groups, including working-class students and single mothers.

7. Conclusion

People who have social identities that are commonly stereotyped can face a serious dilemma, if they can choose whether or not to disclose their social identity, and they wish to avoid being misperceived. The case of mental illness illustrates this point. People with mental health conditions are often aware that they will be stereotyped, they are often even aware that they will be misperceived due to stereotyping. The multifactorial approach vindicates this worry by highlighting the numerous ways that stereotyping can lead to the misperception of people with mental health conditions. Yet people with mental health conditions cannot simply decide not to disclose information about their conditions, and thereby ensure that they will not be misperceived. By not disclosing information, they risk having their mental states and dispositions misperceived because other people will lack information that they would need to factor in to make a correct assessment of these things. Members of other social groups, who lack a mental health condition, can face the same dilemma. If they disclose information about a social identity that is commonly stereotyped, their mental states can be consequently misperceived. But the dilemma is broader than this. It is not only mental states that can be misperceived if a person does not disclose their social identity. Any constraints that a person's social situation places on them can also be misperceived. Consequently, there are many ways that people from various different social groups can be misperceived whether they choose to divulge their social group status or decide to withhold that information. Those who are likely to be stereotyped face a serious dilemma. It is a difficult problem for them to address alone because the likelihood of their misperception is due to the attitudes of other people and society more broadly. Therefore changes to other individuals and societal structures provide one of the more promising means for people who are likely to be stereotyped to avoid the dilemma they face.

7

Stereotypes and Epistemic Value

1. Introduction

This book has outlined an account of how stereotyping leads to epistemic faults: the multifactorial view. It has drawn out some implications of the view, for law, medicine and mental health, for theories of the ethics of stereotyping, for people who might engage in stereotyping, and for people who face being stereotyped. This chapter argues that each of the existing accounts of epistemic rationality and epistemic justification found in contemporary Western analytic epistemology fail to capture some of the epistemic faults that have been found to be associated with stereotyping. This means that on these accounts a person can be rational and justified in believing a stereotype even if the act of believing involves significant epistemic faults. I will argue that this means that existing conceptions of epistemic rationality and epistemic justification are inadequate for the task of evaluating the epistemic standing of acts of believing stereotypes. This discussion will provide the foundation for the task of the next chapter, which will present and defend a positive approach to evaluating acts of believing stereotypes that can capture all of the epistemic faults associated with so believing.

2. Rationality and Justification: A Primer

We often assess the epistemic rationality of our beliefs and the beliefs of other people. We also commonly consider whether the beliefs are epistemically justified or epistemically unjustified. Meanwhile, we evaluate acts of believing along the same dimensions, asking: 'is subject S epistemically rational or irrational in believing that p?' or ' is S justified in believing that p'. My concern in this chapter is with the subset of these questions relating to the acts of believing: questions about the epistemic standing of acts of believing, such as whether a subject acts rationally or is justified in believing a proposition.

How Stereotypes Deceive Us. Katherine Puddifoot, Oxford University Press. © Katherine Puddifoot 2021.
DOI: 10.1093/oso/9780192845559.003.0007

The rationality and justification with which I am concerned is epistemic because it is rationality and justification in relation to the goals of attaining truths and avoiding falsehoods. A person is epistemically rational or justified in believing that p only if they are believing in a way that relates positively to the goals of attaining true belief and avoiding falsehoods. There is a great deal of philosophical disagreement about the specific positive feature or features that must be found in an act of believing for it to count as epistemically rational or justified. There are numerous competing accounts of what it is to believe epistemically rationally or justifiedly to reflect these differences. This chapter provides a taxonomy of accounts before highlighting limitations of each of the types of account.[1]

Acts of believing stereotypes are no exception to the rule that people assess acts of believing for their rationality or irrationality, or justification or lack thereof. In fact, the act of believing a stereotype that is wholly unsupported by the evidence and leads to a distorted perception of individual cases to which the stereotype is applied seems to be a prime example of an act of believing that is irrational and unjustified. One might think on the basis of examples of stereotyping of this sort that the epistemic faults associated with acts of stereotyping will easily be captured by at least some existing accounts of rationality or justification. However, we have found in this book that not all stereotypes are unsupported by the evidence available to the believer and not all acts of believing stereotypes lead to distorted perceptions of individuals. We shall see in this chapter why this means that existing accounts of rationality and justification found in the Western analytic tradition do not capture all of the epistemic faults associated with believing stereotypes. It shall be concluded that we should move beyond applying existing conceptions of rationality and justification towards a pluralistic approach when evaluating acts of believing stereotypes.

3. Taxonomy of Existing Views

Traditional views in epistemology can be usefully divided into three types based on the features on which they place emphasis: upstream accounts, static accounts, and downstream accounts (Easwaran 2017). Upstream accounts focus on the causal history of a belief. Static accounts focus on the

---

[1] From this point onwards it can be assumed that the rationality or justification discussed is epistemic rationality and epistemic justification.

state of the belief itself. Downstream accounts focus on the consequences of holding a belief. This section describes the main features and provides some examples of each of these types of account.

3.1 Upstream Accounts

Every belief has a history. It comes from somewhere. It is based on certain evidence, formed through particular cognitive and brain processes, and so on. Upstream accounts of epistemic rationality and justification focus on this history: that is, they focus on the way that the belief was formed. This section illustrates the nature of upstream accounts through a number of examples: evidentialist, process reliabilist, responsibilist, and causal approaches to justification, and deontic approaches to rationality.

According to evidentialism, the justification of a doxastic stance—including an act of believing, disbelieving or suspension of belief—is determined by the quality of the evidence that the believer possesses (Conee and Feldman 2004; Feldman and Conee 1985). The extent to which you are justified in believing, disbelieving or suspending judgement on whether, for example, there is a rainbow in the sky depends on the quality of the evidence that you possess. If you have good quality evidence that there is a rainbow in the sky, your doxastic state is based on that evidence, and there is not competing counter-evidence that undermines this evidential support, then your doxastic stance is justified. Evidentialism is an upstream account of epistemic justification because any assessment of the epistemic standing of an act of believing will involve an examination of the causal history of the belief. It will involve an evaluation of whether the belief is both fitting with and based upon high-quality evidence.

Another upstream account of epistemic justification is process reliabilism. According to process reliabilism, the epistemic standing of a belief is determined by the reliability of the belief-forming process that leads to the production of the belief (Goldman 1979). For example, the perceptual belief that there is a rainbow in the sky is justified if the visual systems that produce the belief produce a high ratio of true beliefs. More specifically, for a belief-forming process (e.g. visual perception) to count as reliable enough for a target belief it produces to be justified it must reliably produce true beliefs when it operates in conditions that are relevantly similar to those in which the target belief was formed (e.g. in similar lighting conditions and at a similar distance). Process reliabilism is an upstream account because the evaluation of a belief or act of believing involves evaluation of the processes that led to the production of the belief.[2]

Elsewhere in epistemology, epistemic justification is tied to epistemic responsibility. It has been argued that being justified in believing that p requires doing what you can to form true beliefs or avoid falsehoods (e.g. Bonjour 1985; Kornblith 1983). This can involve forming new beliefs that are coherent with existing beliefs in one's belief set (or revising the belief set to eliminate conflicts with new beliefs) or forming new beliefs that are fitting with the available evidence. On a responsibilist approach, an assessment of whether an act of believing is justified will focus on whether the agent acted responsibly in the formation of the belief. It will thus focus on the history of the belief. Responsibilist approaches are therefore upstream accounts.[3]

Alvin Goldman's causal theory of knowledge is a prime example of an upstream account from epistemology. In his 1967 paper, Goldman provides the following analysis of knowledge:

> S knows that p if and only if the fact p is causally connected in an 'appropriate' way with S's believing p.   (Goldman, 1967, p. 369)

Knowledge requires an appropriate causal connection between a fact and a belief relating to the fact. For example, one knows via perception that a vase is present if one's belief that there is a vase present is appropriately causally connected to the vase being present. In many cases the belief will be caused by the relevant fact. One can know that the vase is present because of one's visual system being appropriately stimulated by the vase. However, other

---

[2] Virtue reliabilism also focuses on reliability, but argues that positive epistemic standing should be attributed to beliefs produced by virtuous rather than vicious cognitive capacities (see, e.g. Sosa 1991, 2007). The virtue of a cognitive capacity is determined by its reliability, so, for example, visual perception in good lighting from a close distance will count as a virtuous cognitive capacity but wishful thinking is not reliable and therefore vicious. An act of believing evaluated using the virtue reliabilist framework would be assessed for whether it involved a person exercising a virtuous cognitive capacity. Virtue reliabilism also counts as an upstream account because the object of evaluation is the cognitive capacity that produces a belief and whether it is virtuous.

[3] Virtue responsibilist accounts also associate epistemic justification with displaying epistemic responsibility. According to virtue responsibilism, a belief is justified only if it is produced through a display of intellectual virtue, where intellectual virtues are stable character traits like conscientiousness or open-mindedness (see, e.g. Montmarquet 1992; Zagzebski 1996). By displaying intellectual virtues, epistemic agents are forming their beliefs in a responsible way. Virtue responsibilist approaches, by focusing on whether a person has displayed a virtue in forming a belief, are therefore upstream accounts.

appropriate causal connections are possible. It is possible to know that something is going to happen without your belief being caused by the event. For example, it is possible to know about a future event if the event and one's belief about the event have a common cause. Say your brother tells you he intends to travel to Brazil next summer. He follows through on this intention and goes to Brazil. You can know that he is going to Brazil before he does so because your belief that he is going has a common cause with his going: both are caused by his intention to travel. In either case, a belief is knowledge only if there is an appropriate causal connection between the facts known and the beliefs about the facts. The causal history of the belief therefore determines whether or not it counts as knowledge. It is possible to construct a causal account of the justification of beliefs that is analogous to Goldman's causal account of knowledge. In this analogous causal account of justification, the justification of an act of believing would be determined by the causal history of the belief: a person would be justified in believing a particular proposition as long as the belief was appropriately caused by the facts. This would be an example of an upstream account.

There can also be upstream accounts of rationality. Take, for example, the deontic conception of rationality. According to this view, a person rationally believes a proposition, e.g. that there is a rainbow in the sky, as long as they do not, by their own lights, violate any epistemic norm in the formation of the belief (Pritchard 2014). An epistemic norm is a rule that is followed in order to gain true beliefs or avoid false beliefs. If an epistemic agent has done all that they can do to follow epistemic norms, by their own lights, then the agent is rational. On a deontic approach rationality is associated with being blame-free: an act of believing that there is a rainbow in the sky is rational as long as the agent is not to be blamed for their use of certain epistemic norms. The deontic conception of rationality is an upstream account because it involves an evaluation of whether, in forming a belief, an agent has, from their own perspective, followed or violated various epistemic norms.

3.2 Downstream Accounts

Downstream accounts focus on the consequences of holding a belief. It is surprisingly difficult to identify accounts of epistemic value that count as downstream accounts. Consequentialist accounts of epistemic value might seem to be examples. However, existing consequentialist accounts tend not to focus on the consequences of holding a belief, instead focusing on the consequences of forming beliefs using a particular belief-forming process, method or policy. Jeffrey Dunn and Kristoffer Ahlstrom-Vij (2018) explain this point nicely by contrasting consequentialist views in epistemology and ethical consequentialism. There are similarities between the two types of position, for example, both types of account associate rightness with goodness. However, it is important to note that the dominant form of ethical consequentialism is *act consequentialism*, which assesses the rightness of an *act*: an act is right only if there is no other act that would produce greater total value. If a version of epistemic consequentialism were strictly analogous to act consequentialism then it would be a candidate for being a downstream account as described here. It would assess the rightness of an act of believing, considering the consequences of believing. But existing versions of epistemic consequentialism about justification or rationality are analogous to rule consequentialism rather than act consequentialism. Rule consequentialism focuses not on the consequences of an act but on the *rules* that the actions conform to, and the consequences that would tend to follow from the adoption of those rules. Similarly, existing versions of epistemic consequentialism assess the consequences that follow from the application of the rules, processes or policies that produce a belief. In the current framework they should therefore be categorized as upstream accounts. For example, process reliabilism is a form of consequentialism and an upstream account because it assesses the epistemic status of a belief by focusing on the process leading to the belief and whether the process tends to produce good consequences, i.e. true beliefs.[4]

Downstream approaches to epistemic value as discussed here are, then, in contrast to many existing consequentialist theories, accounts that focus on the consequences of the act of believing. While it is difficult to identify representative downstream approaches to epistemic justification

---

[4] Similarly, recent work developing accuracy-first approaches to the norms of rationality influenced by James Joyce (1998) can be viewed as upstream accounts, or alternatively static accounts, on the current framework, although they are also classified as consequentialist. On these approaches, epistemic value is defined as accuracy. Then formal constraints on doxastic states are defended using the methods of decision theory by showing that these constraints produce accurate doxastic states (e.g. maximizing expected accuracy of doxastic states or producing doxastic states that dominate all others in terms of accuracy). Although there is a focus on consequences (i.e. accuracy) it is the consequences of adopting the formal constraints on doxastic states (do the formal constraints produce accurate doxastic states?) rather than the consequences of holding the doxastic states that is the focus of evaluation. Therefore, accuracy-first approaches like this can be classified as upstream accounts because of the focus on the process leading to the doxastic states. Alternatively, they might be classified as static approaches because they focus on the rightness of certain norms that might govern the formation of doxastic states.

and rationality, there is an alternative approach to epistemic value that is partially a downstream account. This is the *epistemic innocence* approach (Bortolotti 2015a, 2015b, 2020; Bortolotti and Antrobus 2016; Bortolotti and Sullivan-Bissett 2018; Letheby 2016; Puddifoot 2017; Sullivan-Bissett 2015), outlined in Chapter 4. A belief is considered to be epistemically innocent if it is both epistemically flawed, for example, inaccurate or irrational, and produces positive epistemic consequences, 'improving the chance of an agent achieving epistemic goals, including acquiring new true beliefs; retaining and using relevant information; increasing the coherence of a set of beliefs; and gaining understanding' (Puddifoot and Bortolotti 2019). When evaluating the potential of downstream approaches we will be assessing the prospects of an approach that focuses, as the epistemic innocence account does, on the consequences of believing.

Some accounts in epistemology focus on the practical gains that follow from holding a belief. For example, Fantl and McGrath (2002) argue that whether a person knows or justifiably believes that p depends on whether it is proper for that person to act on p when deciding what to do. So, for example, whether you know or justifiably believe that the train will stop at a particular destination depends upon whether it is proper for you to act as if the train stops at the destination when deciding what to do. If there are high stakes involved—say, you need to get off at the stop to ensure that you are present for the birth of your child—then you need higher-quality evidence to know or justifiably believe that the train stops there. Merely overhearing someone say that they had been told that the train stops there would not constitute knowing or justifiably believing that the train stops there. To know or justifiably believe in such a case would require, for example, checking with a reliable-seeming train guard. On this view, the consequences of believing p determine the epistemic standing of a person's belief that p, however, it is the practical consequences that determine the epistemic standing of the belief. In contrast, the focus of downstream accounts, as defined in this chapter, is solely on the *epistemic* consequences of holding a particular belief: does believing that p increase the chance of epistemic goals being achieved? As such, consideration of the practical stakes associated with believing shall be put aside.

3.3 Static Accounts

Finally, let us consider static accounts. These accounts focus directly on the state of the belief rather than treating the epistemic status of the belief as dependent upon the causal history of the belief or consequences of believing. Three illustrative static accounts of justification and rationality are outlined here: coherentism, non-deontic accounts of rationality, and Foley's Aristotelian conception of rationality.

Coherentism is a static account because it does not consider what is upstream or downstream from a belief, instead considering the relationship that of a mental state—a belief—to other beliefs. According to coherentism, the justification of a belief is determined by its coherence with other beliefs in the believer's belief set. There is what can be called a positive and a negative version of coherentism (Senor 1993). Positive coherentism states that a belief is justified if it positively coheres with other beliefs in a belief system (Bonjour 2002, p. 183–184). Negative coherentism states that there must not be a conflict between a target belief and other beliefs in a belief system, otherwise the target belief is not justified (Harman 1986).

Non-deontic accounts of rationality could also count as static accounts, depending on the form that they take. According to non-deontic accounts of rationality, there are right and wrong epistemic norms (Pritchard 2014). The rightness and wrongness of the norms is independent of the believer's perspective. Whether or not a belief is rational is fully determined by whether or not the belief adheres to or violates some epistemic norms. A person can violate the norms blamelessly, due to being taught the wrong epistemic norms as a child and even though they are doing their best to form beliefs in the correct way, but their blamelessness does not protect them from being irrational. A non-deontic conception of rationality can take the form of a static account because an act of believing can be evaluated as rational or irrational on the basis of whether it adheres to an epistemic norm regardless of the causal history or consequences of believing. For example, the norms associated with deontic approaches to rationality include the norm that one ought to believe the truth. Whether or not this norm is respected or violated is a feature of the belief itself. It is not dependent on the causal history of the belief, such as how the norm came to be respected or violated, or on the consequences of believing.

Richard Foley's (1987) Aristotelian conception of rationality also fits into the category of static accounts. According to Foley, epistemic rationality involves a person pursuing the goals of believing the truth and not believing falsities in a way (or ways) that she would judge to be effective if she were to reflect carefully on how to achieve these goals. A person S is rational in believing that p if, were she to engage in careful reflection, she would judge that believing p at time t is a good way to achieve the goals of believing the truth and avoiding falsity. So, for example, I am rational in believing that there is a rainbow in the sky if, were I to critically reflect on my believing this proposition, I would judge my believing that there is a rainbow in the sky to be a good way of achieving the goal of believing the truth. On this Aristotelian conception, the rationality of believing that p is not determined by the actual history of the belief. It is not determined by whether the belief was formed in a way that fits the evidence. Instead the nature of the belief itself—whether it is the type of belief that one would judge, on reflection, to be a good belief to believe—that determines the rationality of believing.

4. Stereotyping Beliefs

Approaches within traditional analytic epistemology can therefore be usefully grouped according to whether they are upstream, downstream, or static approaches. We shall proceed for the remainder of the chapter by considering the extent to which upstream, static, and downstream approaches can capture the epistemic faults of acts of believing beliefs that encode stereotypes. For each of the types of approach, we shall see that although they capture some of the epistemic faults associated with believing stereotypes, many faults are not captured.

The focus here is specifically on beliefs that encode generalizations about social groups, associating all group members more strongly than non-group members with some feature. Beliefs of the following type:

Members of group x have trait T

Or

Members of group x are more likely to have trait T than members of group y.

Some examples include *Politicians are untrustworthy, Teenagers are lazy, Scientific experts tend to be men rather than women,* and *Black people are more often criminals than White people.* At times the term *stereotyping beliefs* will be used to identify this type of belief.

The direct target of the current analysis is therefore acts of holding beliefs that encode stereotypes, or acts of believing stereotypes, rather than beliefs that are produced under the influence of the stereotype, e.g. *Pete is untrustworthy because he is a politician.* It is epistemic faults of the former and not the latter which we shall see eluding the grasp of upstream, static and downstream accounts. I focus on the beliefs that encode the stereotypes because this book is primarily concerned with how believing stereotypes can lead us to make errors.

It might be interesting to note, however, that beliefs formed as a result of the application of stereotypes, such as the belief *Pete is untrustworthy because he is a politician*, bring many of the same epistemic faults as the stereotypes themselves. For example, the belief about Pete could lead us to misremember Pete's attributes, to unduly dismiss his testimony, and so on. These faults could occur even if the stereotype is well supported by the evidence. Therefore many of the claims made about stereotyping beliefs also apply to beliefs produced as a result of the application of stereotypes.

5. Upstream Accounts and Stereotyping Beliefs

Let us begin, then, by considering upstream accounts. They show initial promise with regards to capturing the epistemic faults present in acts of believing stereotypes but ultimately fail to capture some.

5.1 Initial Promise of Upstream Accounts

First let us focus on those upstream approaches that associate positive epistemic status with fitting the available evidence and negative epistemic status with not fitting the evidence. These accounts include evidentialism and responsibility-focused approaches to justification and rationality that associate being responsible with forming beliefs fitting with the evidence. As we found in Chapter 2, stereotypes often fail to reflect the available evidence. They can do this by underestimating or overestimating of the prevalence of a trait in a certain population. For example, drug crimes can be more strongly associated with Black people than White people (see, e.g. Burston, Jones, and Roberson-Saunders 1995, cited in Alexander 2011) even though the available evidence suggests that drug use is the same across this racial divide (Substance Abuse and Mental Health Services Administration 2004) and the use of some drugs is higher among the White than the African American population (Office of Applied Studies, Substance Abuse and Mental Health Services Administration, 2007). Stereotypes can also be rigid, failing to update in response to new evidence (Allport 1954; Appiah 1990; Fricker 2016). In such cases, the stereotype does not respond to available evidence. Any account according to which an act of believing is not justified or rational if the belief that is formed does not fit the evidence has the potential to produce the result that acts of believing stereotypes that fail to reflect the evidence in these and similar ways lack the relevant positive epistemic status. These accounts would capture the fact that stereotypes are epistemically faulty where the stereotypes fail to fit with the available evidence.

It seems plausible that where a stereotype does not reflect the evidence it will often not be appropriately causally related to the facts that are available to the believer. For example, if the fact is that Black and White people engage in drug use at the same rate then stereotypes that suggest otherwise are not appropriately caused by the facts. As such, a causal account of justification could also capture the way that some stereotypes fail to fit the evidence, producing the result that a person cannot be justified in believing these stereotypes.

Now let us consider process reliabilism. This view also initially seems to be well positioned to capture the epistemic faults associated with acts of believing stereotypes. Belief-forming processes that produce beliefs that are poorly supported by the evidence, and not based on the facts, are prima facie unlikely to produce a high ratio of true beliefs. We have just seen that the belief-forming processes that produce stereotypes often produce beliefs with these features. Therefore, accounts that associate justification with the reliability of belief-forming processes seem, at least at face value, to be able to capture the epistemic faults associated with believing stereotypes. The accounts seem to imply that people are unjustified in believing stereotypes because the belief-forming process that produces the stereotyping beliefs is unreliable.

Finally, deontic approaches to rationality might be able to capture some epistemic faults associated with stereotyping. In an individual case, a person might violate an epistemic norm, such as the norm to believe the truth and avoid falsehood, when believing a stereotype. They might violate the norm even while being aware that they are in error. They might wilfully resist evidence that contradicts the stereotype, therefore being blameworthy. In such cases, deontic approaches to rationality would imply that the belief in the stereotype is irrational, capturing some epistemic faults that are present.

5.2 Limited Results of Upstream Accounts

Although upstream accounts show initial promise when it comes to capturing the epistemic faults associated with believing stereotypes, the accounts also have significant limitations in this respect. The limitations become apparent once it is acknowledged that some stereotypes are well supported by the evidence, and are formed in a way that is fitting with epistemic norms, but those who believe the stereotypes nonetheless display serious epistemic faults. These epistemic faults are not captured by upstream accounts, which imply that the beliefs are justified or rational.

Nomy Arpaly (2003) and Miranda Fricker (2007) provide the following example that illustrates this point. They encourage us to imagine Solomon, who comes from an isolated farming community in a poor country and believes that women are not nearly as competent at abstract thinking as men are. This stereotype is well supported by the evidence that Solomon has encountered in his life. He has not encountered any women who have displayed aptitude for abstract thinking. His peers and even his educators give him the impression that women are less good at abstract thinking than men. As long as Solomon lives in his isolated community, his belief has a good causal history. It is well supported by the evidence and the facts Solomon has available to him, including the empirical evidence he has derived from experience and the testimony that he has been provided, including by apparently reliable sources.

The stereotype that Solomon holds will not count as unjustified or irrational on upstream accounts of epistemic justification. The belief that women are less good at abstract thinking than men fits with the evidence that Solomon has encountered. The belief is supported by the facts that Solomon is aware of (i.e. facts about his experience and the testimony he has been given). The beliefs on the basis of which Solomon believes the stereotype—beliefs about the people he has encountered and the testimony he has been given—are true. And it could even be argued that Solomon forms his belief on the basis of a reliable belief-forming process. It could be argued that Solomon's belief is formed by a reliable process or processes because it is the result of inductive inference and the exchange of testimony and either or both of these processes tend to produce true beliefs. Solomon's belief therefore plausibly meets the criteria for justification on each of the upstream accounts: fitting and being caused by the available evidence, being supported by the facts, being produced by a reliable belief-forming process. Meanwhile, Solomon does not knowingly violate any epistemic norm so his belief will not count as irrational on the deontic approach to rationality. None of these accounts suggest that Solomon's belief is unjustified or irrational.

Things are not as simple as this initial sketch suggests of course. There are many facts available 'out there' in the world that challenge Solomon's stereotyping beliefs: e.g. facts about women who are excellent at abstract thinking, men who are poor at abstract thinking, and women who are equally as good as or better than relevant counterparts at abstract thinking. An account according to which justification requires fitting beliefs to all of the relevant facts could therefore imply that Solomon's beliefs are unjustified. However, such an account would be unappealing because of its demandingness. People cannot be expected to respond to and fit their beliefs to all of the facts that are 'out there' and are relevant to their beliefs in order for their beliefs to be justified (see, e.g. Cherniak 1981; Stein 1996; Samuels, Stich, and Faucher 2004). Recall that upstream accounts of justification associate a belief's justification with not only fitting with but also being caused by the relevant facts or evidence. It is too much to expect for a believer to respond to and form beliefs that are fitting with and caused by all relevant facts or evidence. An adequate theory of epistemic justification should therefore imply that a belief is justified as long as it is fitting with a subset of the relevant facts. The obvious subset on which to focus is the subset of facts that a believer can reasonably be expected to access within their epistemic environment. Within Solomon's epistemic environment the available facts support his view that men are better than women at abstract thinking. Therefore a satisfactory upstream view focusing on whether the causal history of the belief involves a believer responding to the facts would suggest that Solomon is justified in believing what he does.

Another way to understand this point is to focus on the idea of *normative defeaters*. It might seem plausible that Solomon is not justified in his belief on any upstream accounts that allow that there can be normative defeaters of the justification of a belief. Normative defeaters are propositions that people ought to believe given the evidence that is available to them, and which would undermine the justification for their beliefs if they believed them. It might be argued that there are plenty of propositions establishing women's ability to engage in abstract thinking of which Solomon should be aware. If he were aware of these propositions then he would have reason not to believe the stereotype that women are less good at abstract thinking than men. Therefore, it might be thought, there exist normative defeaters of the justification of Solomon's belief. However, the idea that people ought to believe certain propositions can be cashed out in terms of what it would be epistemically responsible for them to do (Lackey 2005, p. 643). If Solomon ought to believe the aforementioned propositions this is because epistemic responsibility requires that he believe them. However, it is implausible that epistemic responsibility requires that Solomon believes the propositions if they are not well supported by the evidence available in his environment.

It might also be objected that the type of generalization that Solomon makes will not reliably produce true beliefs. Solomon infers on the basis of a limited sample of women that he encounters to a generalization about women and their abilities relative to counterparts who are men. None of the women that he encounters challenge the stereotype but his experience with them does not establish the universal claim that women are poorer at abstract thinking than men. There could be, and indeed are, many women who are very good at abstract thinking whom he has yet to encounter. It might therefore be thought that Solomon is using an unreliable belief-forming process and displaying a cognitive vice of overgeneralizing. However, as Endre Begby (2013) has argued, the stereotype that Solomon holds should not be assumed to be a universal generalization. It could, for example, have the logical form of a generic (Leslie 2007), stating what is typically true of a social group—in this case what is typically true of women with regards to their abstract thinking. Solomon could be understood to be making a generalization from his experiences of women who have displayed no aptitude for abstract thinking and the testimony that he has received suggesting women are less good at abstract thinking than men to the con-clusion that women are typically less good at abstract thinking than men. It is far from clear that a belief-forming process that produces generalizations of this type would tend to produce false beliefs. While it is therefore pos-sible to describe the belief-forming process that produces Solomon's stereo-typing beliefs in such a way that they turn out to be unreliably formed, it is also possible to describe them in such a way that they turn out to be reliably formed. The crucial point, though, is that there are epistemic faults present regardless of whether the belief-forming processes are viewed as reliable or unreliable. There are therefore faults that are not adequately captured by a reliabilist approach to justification.

Upstream accounts of the epistemic standing of beliefs therefore imply that Solomon's belief is justified. More generally, they fail to capture the epistemic faults of beliefs that encode stereotypes and are fitting with the evidence or facts that have been encountered by the believer. However, as we have seen in Chapters 3 and 4, there can be significant epistemic faults associated with believing stereotypes, even where stereotypes reflect evidence or facts.

Where a stereotype is believed a person can apply the stereotype even if it is irrelevant, producing a distorted perception of the person to whom the stereotype is applied. So, for example, Solomon might apply the stereotype that women are not as good at abstract thinking as men to a new person that he encounters who is a female logician. He might allow the stereotype to influence his perception of her expertise. If this female logician is teaching him introductory logic, for example, he might doubt her ability to teach him anything, on the basis that she is a woman and he is a man. In such a case, the stereotype would clearly be irrelevant because of the woman's credentials as a logician. Nonetheless, Solomon might apply the stereotype, perhaps because his ego is threatened by being taught by a woman. Because the stereotype is irrelevant, its application increases the chance of a false judgement being made about the female logician's abilities. Note that if the stereotype is not a universal generalization but rather something akin to a typicality judgement, the stereotype itself would not suddenly be unsupported by the evidence available to Solomon as a result of him meeting the female logician and acknowledging her expertise (Begby 2013). The stereotype that women are typically less good at abstract thinking than men could continue to fit with the evidence that Solomon has available to him as long as the vast majority of the women he has encountered have displayed no ability to engage in abstract thinking and the testimony that he has received continues to support the stereotype. While fitting this evidence, the stereotype nonetheless leads to a distorted perception of the female logician's abilities. Here we see the first way that a stereotyping belief that is justified and rational according to upstream accounts can have a significant epistemic fault: i.e. it can lead to distorted perceptions about individuals when the stereotype is applied but irrelevant.

The same belief, which would be assessed positively on the basis of upstream approaches to the epistemic appraisal of beliefs, would be likely to bring a number of other faults, as we have found in Chapters 3 and 4. Due to possessing the belief, Solomon would be more likely than he would be otherwise to misremember information relating to women's ability to engage in abstract thinking, to misinterpret ambiguous evidence about women's ability as fitting with the stereotype, to falsely assume that individual women are more similar than they really are to each other, and less similar than they really are to individual men, with respect to their abstract thinking abilities. The possession of the stereotyping belief increases the chance that Solomon will fail to give appropriate uptake to the testimony provided by women relating to matters that require abstract thought. It would increase the chance that he would give women less credibility than they deserve when they are providing him with information about abstract matters via testimony. He would therefore be less likely to properly access and process information about and provided by individual women. Each of these epistemic faults is associated with the belief that, on upstream accounts of the epistemic standing of beliefs, would be evaluated positively.

Solomon's belief would be far from alone in being appraised positively on upstream accounts in spite of having these significant epistemic faults. We learnt in Chapter 4 that two things regularly come apart: the extent to which a stereotype reflects the social reality encountered by the believer of the stereotype, and whether or not the stereotype leads to misperceptions of individuals. Although, intuitively, these two things should reliably correlate, we found that commonly a stereotype can reflect the reality encountered by the believer but systematically and predictably lead to the misperception of individuals. In Chapter 4, we considered examples of stereotypes relating to race and drug crime, stereotypes relating to scientific expertise across the genders, stereotypes relating to being a barrister and stereotypes relating to career women. Each of these stereotypes has been found to lead to distorted perceptions of individual members of relevant social groups, although they reflect the social reality in which the believer of the stereotype is located. The conclusion that we can now draw is that in many of these cases there will be substantial epistemic faults associated with believing the stereotypes even when upstream accounts of epistemic rationality and justification will heap only positive epistemic appraisal on the beliefs.[5]

6. Downstream Accounts and Stereotyping Beliefs

Downstream accounts similarly show promise with regards to capturing the epistemic faults associated with stereotyping beliefs, but again fail to capture some of the epistemic faults.

6.1 Initial Promise of Downstream Accounts

The epistemic faults associated with stereotyping beliefs that are not captured by upstream accounts relate to the way that people respond to evidence

---

[5] It is worth noting that Solomon's stereotyping belief will not count as knowledge on any account according to which knowledge requires true belief as long as the stereotype is false. Almost all accounts require true belief for knowledge (an exception being those according to which knowledge does not require belief), therefore almost all accounts of knowledge will imply that Solomon's belief is not knowledge under such conditions. However, the upstream accounts discussed in this section do not in themselves account for the epistemic faultiness of the beliefs. His belief will count as non-knowledge only because of not being true, not because of any feature that is captured by these upstream accounts. It therefore seems to be right to say that the accounts fail to capture the epistemic faults of the belief.

about individuals as a result of possessing and applying a stereotyping belief. It is therefore a virtue of downstream accounts, which focus on the consequences of holding a belief, that they have the potential to capture these epistemic faults.

It is as a consequence of believing that p, where p is a belief that encodes a stereotype, that one becomes likely to apply the stereotype to individuals, and subsequently have a distorted perception of them: misremembering them, failing to give their testimony the credit it deserves, and so forth. Therefore an account that assesses a belief based on the consequences of holding the belief can appraise stereotyping beliefs negatively in virtue of the epistemic faults that follow from stereotyping but which are not captured by upstream accounts.

It is important to note here that it is not necessary to evoke practical concerns to capture the poor consequences that follow from stereotyping. Harm can certainly be done to people's interests by stereotyping—harms to those who are stereotyped and those who engage in stereotyping. However, the poor consequences that have been the focus of the discussion in this book so far are epistemic consequences, relating to the ability of the believer to make correct judgements and perceive individuals and cases accurately. Therefore, a version of epistemic consequentialism that makes no reference to practical concerns could be well placed to capture the faults associated with stereotyping beliefs that fit with the evidence and facts.

6.2 Limited Results of Downstream Accounts

Although downstream accounts have the potential to capture some of the epistemic faults associated with stereotyping, this section outlines reasons for rejecting any account of epistemic value that focuses *solely* on the consequences of holding a belief. An evaluative framework that focused solely on the consequences of holding a belief would not factor in upstream factors when evaluating an act of believing. An account of this type would imply that an act of believing should not be judged to be unjustified or irrational as a result of the belief failing to fit or be caused by the evidence or the facts. This section shows that an approach of this type has a number of unattractive features.

Such an account would, rightly it seems, strike many as deeply implausible. It would imply that a person could be wholly rational for holding a belief that fails to fit with the evidence that they have available to them as long as the belief is in isolation and does not produce further beliefs, or as long as it happens to interact with other beliefs in such a way that it brings only positive epistemic consequences downstream. To the extent that an evaluative framework ought to reflect intuitions, of ordinary people or of philosophical theorists, this account would be deeply problematic because it would not do so.

An evaluative framework that did not associate any negative epistemic appraisal with forming beliefs that fail to fit with the evidence or facts would also lack some of the prescriptive force that notions like justification and rationality ordinarily possess. Typically, appraising an act of believing as irrational or unjustified implies criticism of the belief as poorly supported by the evidence or facts. It implies that the believer could have done better by forming beliefs in a way that is more consistent with the evidence that they had available to them. For example, if a person has formed the stereotyping belief that people of a certain social class are untrustworthy, without the belief being supported by any evidence, then they can be called irrational on the basis of this epistemic failure. The ascription of irrationality has the prescriptive implication that the believer should in future form their beliefs about social groups in a way that is more consistent with the evidence that is available to them. An evaluative framework that lacks this prescriptive force of ordinary judgements about rationality and justification seems to me to be highly problematic.

A further reason for rejecting any account of epistemic value that focuses solely on the consequences of holding a belief is more closely tied to the current project. The reason why it seems so pressing for an evaluative framework to take into consideration the consequences of holding stereotyping beliefs is that these beliefs lead to downstream beliefs that are poorly supported by the evidence that is available to the believer. For the sake of parity, if a belief is to be appraised negatively because it produces beliefs that are poorly supported by the evidence, the same belief should be assessed to see whether it is well or poorly supported by the evidence. Take, once again, the belief that people of a certain social class are untrustworthy. Because this is a stereotyping belief it is likely to lead to a distorted perception of information about individuals to whom the stereotype is applied (e.g. by producing distorted memories or inappropriate responses to testimony). It seems appropriate to appraise the belief poorly from an epistemic perspective because of this distorted response to the evidence. Therefore, consistency demands that the stereotyping belief itself is also appraised poorly due to being formed as a result of a distorted response to the evidence. If this occurs, the stereotyping belief will be evaluated negatively due to its causal history. Therefore parity requires that the causal history of a belief, and not only the consequences of believing, be treated as relevant to the epistemic standing of that belief.

These observations provide reason for rejecting a purely downstream approach to the epistemology of stereotyping. They provide support for the idea that both the causal history of a belief *and* the consequences of holding the belief are relevant to the epistemic standing of an act of believing a stereotype.

The epistemic innocence account discussed in Chapter 4 is an example where both the causal history of a belief and the consequences of holding a belief are taken into account. A belief is epistemically innocent if it has a poor causal history—failing to fit the evidence or facts—but brings positive epistemic consequences. We have seen in Chapter 4 how successfully the notion of epistemic innocence can capture the nature of certain psychological phenomena. But this discussion of stereotyping beliefs suggests that the causal history and consequences of holding a belief can be relevant to their epistemic status regardless of whether the causal history or consequences are bad or good. A stereotyping belief that is well-supported by the evidence but produces poor consequences will not be captured by the notion of epistemic innocence, which focuses on those with a poor causal history but positive consequences. A complete evaluation of this type of stereotyping belief would therefore move beyond the notion of epistemic innocence, allowing *both* positive and negative aspects of *both* the causal history and consequences of believing to be factored in to an evaluation of an act of believing.

7. Static Accounts and Stereotyping Beliefs

Do static accounts of the epistemic standing of beliefs fare any better than either upstream or downstream accounts? Recall that static accounts focus on the state of the belief itself, rather than its causal history or consequences. Coherentism is a static approach: the justificatory status of a belief depends upon the coherence of the belief with other beliefs. Non-deontic approaches to rationality can be static approaches: the rationality of believing can be determined by whether epistemic norms like *believe the truth* are met or violated by the belief, regardless of the causal history of consequences of believing. Foley's Aristotelian account is static: the nature of a belief determines the rationality of believing. Rationality is ascribed if the belief is of a type that the believer would, on critical reflection, judge believing the belief to be a good way to achieve the goals of believing the truth and avoiding falsity. We find, once again, that although these accounts show some initial promise with regards to capturing the epistemic faults associated with stereotyping, some epistemic faults elude them.

7.1 Initial Promise of Static Accounts

A coherentist account of justification could capture some of the epistemic faults associated with some acts of believing stereotypes. For example, if a person endorses general beliefs about racial equality, for example, but also harbours the stereotyping belief that members of a particular race are less kind than others, there is incoherence in their belief set. The coherentist account would capture this incoherence, producing the result that at least one of the beliefs is unjustified.

The non-deontic approach to rationality could also capture something of the epistemic faults of many stereotyping beliefs, for example, where the beliefs are false. Recall that one example of an epistemic norm that might be met or violated is the norm that one ought to believe the truth. Stereotypes can be false. Through the act of believing a stereotype we can therefore violate the epistemic norm that we should believe the truth.

Foley's Aristotelian account of rationality could also capture the epistemic faults associated with some stereotyping beliefs. In some cases, people will believe stereotypes, but they would not endorse the act of believing the stereotypes on critical reflection. If they were to critically reflect on whether believing a target stereotype is a good way to believe the truth and avoid falsity then they would conclude that it is not. Under these conditions, the Aristotelian account of rationality has the potential to capture some epistemic faults of stereotyping beliefs.

7.2 Limited Results of Static Accounts

In spite of being able to capture some of the epistemic faults of some stereotyping beliefs, it is clear that existing static accounts cannot capture all of the epistemic faults because they omit consideration of the consequences that follow from holding a belief. We find in the argument of Chapter 4 very good reason to believe that it is possible to have a stereotyping belief that meets epistemic norms, for example, the norm that one ought to believe the truth, but is nonetheless flawed because it produces poor consequences. The non-deontic account of rationality would not capture the epistemic faults associated with believing these beliefs.

Meanwhile, it is easy to imagine a person harbouring a stereotype that is highly coherent with the other beliefs in their belief set, because they are deeply prejudiced. They might not hold any beliefs that challenge the stereotype. Their prejudice might be stealthy, leading them to reject any evidence that challenges the stereotype (Cassam 2015; Fricker 2016). The stereotyping belief would then be justified on a coherentist approach to justification even if it produces significant epistemic costs downstream. Similarly, a deeply prejudiced person might critically reflect on whether an act of believing a stereotype is a good way to believe the truth and avoid falsity and conclude that it is. Believing the stereotype would therefore be rational on the Aristotelian account of rationality even if so believing brings significant poor epistemic consequences. In such cases there would be epistemic faults that would not be captured by the static approaches, which would suggest that the acts of believing were justified or rational.

More generally, due to the importance highlighted so far in this chapter, and wider book, of evaluative frameworks capturing the consequences of holding a belief, any account that focuses solely on the state of the belief itself is unable to capture at least some of the epistemic faults associated with some acts of believing stereotypes.

8. Summary So Far

We have now seen how upstream, downstream and static approaches to epistemic appraisal all fail to capture some of the epistemic faults associated with believing stereotyping beliefs. A stereotyping belief can be justified on an upstream approach to epistemic justification while nonetheless producing a large number of significant epistemic faults downstream. Due to failing to capture consequences of this type, upstream accounts cannot adequately capture the epistemic faults of stereotyping beliefs. Meanwhile, a stereotyping belief might fail to produce any negative epistemic consequences but the act of believing might nonetheless display significant epistemic faults because the belief is poorly supported by the evidence or facts available to the believer. A purely downstream approach would not capture these facts about the causal history of the belief, so this type of approach would also fail to adequately capture epistemic faults of some acts of believing stereotypes. Static approaches to epistemic appraisal do not capture the negative consequences of holding a belief, and some, such as coherentist approaches, could heap positive epistemic appraisal on a stereotyping belief held by a consistently prejudiced individual, regardless of whether the belief is well-supported by the evidence or has negative consequences. These static approaches are therefore also unable to adequately capture the epistemic faults associated with some acts of believing stereotypes. Given that mainstream theories of epistemic rationality and justification can be classified as either upstream, downstream, and static approaches, the epistemic status of acts of believing stereotypes seems to be inadequately captured by existing mainstream epistemological theories.

9. Upshot

There are two ways that one could respond to the observation that existing theories of epistemic rationality and justification do not capture all of the epistemic faults associated with stereotyping. One option is to defend a new account or accounts of epistemic justification or rationality. Another option is to conclude more modestly that those aiming to gain an adequate understanding of the epistemic faults associated with believing stereotypes will need to move beyond standard conceptions of epistemic justification and rationality.

An argument for the first option would need to go beyond the scope of the current book. It would require identifying the criteria that need to be met for a theory of epistemic justification or rationality to be adequate. It would need to be shown that theories of justification and rationality are inadequate if they fail to capture all epistemic faults associated with believing stereotypes. Alternatively, it would have to be shown that each type of account (upstream, static or downstream), or each specific account, fails to capture some significant epistemic fault that must be captured by any adequate account of rationality or justification. I leave this project to another day.

The argument supplied so far in this chapter does, however, provide strong direct support for the second option. It has been shown that there are significant epistemic faults associated with acts of believing stereotypes that are not given adequate recognition by those limiting their project to considering whether an act of believing is irrational or unjustified on any single standard conception of rationality and justification. This second option is more modest than the first. It does not propose any adjustment to existing theories of epistemic rationality and justification, but it does suggest that the conceptual tools that are provided by existing theories are impoverished. Existing conceptions of rationality and justification supplied within the discipline of Western Analytic Epistemology fail to touch upon significant aspects of our cognitive and epistemic lives that are appropriate objects of criticism. If we want to adequately assess these aspects of our lives, making balanced assessments of acts of believing stereotypes, then we need to move beyond existing conceptions of rationality and justification.

10. A Positive Perspective

There is a more positive angle that can be given to the discussion in this chapter. What we have found is that there are a number of acts of believing—those that involve believing stereotypes—that have interesting and important epistemic features. Upstream, downstream, and static approaches can each capture some of the features. Upstream accounts capture how these acts often involve believing stereotypes that are not supported by the evidence or facts; downstream accounts capture how the acts of believing can produce poor consequences; static accounts capture how the acts of believing can produce beliefs that violate epistemic norms, fail to cohere with other beliefs in a person's belief set, and which would not be endorsed on reflection. So while none of the individual accounts can, on their own, capture all of the epistemic faults of acts of believing stereotypes, all of the accounts have something to contribute: emphasizing important features of the beliefs that should be attended to when making an evaluation of their epistemic standing.

What this positive angle on the discussion suggests is that an adequate understanding of the epistemic faults associated with acts of believing stereotypes will need to be pluralistic. It will need to build on insights provided by various different conceptions of rationality and justification. A pluralistic approach of this kind can better capture the complexity of our cognitive and epistemic lives, as exemplified in cases in which people believe stereotypes. It is this more positive outcome of the discussion in this chapter that will be explored in Chapter 8, as an evaluative framework is proposed that integrates aspects of upstream, downstream, and static accounts.

11. Conclusion

Theories of epistemic rationality and justification can be fitted into the taxonomy of upstream, static, and downstream approaches. None of these types of approach captures all of the epistemic faults present in acts of believing stereotypes. This means that existing accounts of epistemic justification or rationality do not adequately capture all of the significant epistemic faults associated with stereotyping. We might conclude on the basis of this observation that existing accounts of epistemic justification and rationality ought to be revised so that they are able to capture each of the epistemic faults. I believe that this is a promising project but it is beyond the scope of the current book to complete it. However, another conclusion has been provided full support in this chapter: if we are to adequately assess the epistemic standing of acts of believing stereotypes, then we must move beyond the confines of any single evaluative framework provided by existing theories of justification or rationality, or even single type of evaluative framework, i.e. upstream, static or downstream approaches. Each individual framework, and framework type, provides impoverished conceptual resources for the project. Instead, a pluralistic approach needs to be taken, reflecting insights from various types of theory of epistemic justification and rationality.

8

Evaluative Dispositionalism

1. Introduction

This chapter proposes and defends an evaluative framework through which to evaluate acts of believing stereotypes: evaluative dispositionalism. On the evaluative dispositionalist approach, the dispositions of the believer are the focus of epistemic evaluation. Evaluative dispositionalism draws on recent discussions of dispositions in epistemology, some of which have focused on the importance of dispositions that are manifest in believing, and others of which have focused on the importance of dispositions that are possessed due to believing. According to the view defended here, both the dispositions manifested in believing and those that are possessed due to believing should be taken into consideration when evaluating an act of believing a stereotype. We have seen in Chapter 7 that existing approaches to rationality and justification are incapable of capturing all of the significant epistemic faults associated with believing stereotypes. Here we will see that evaluative dispositionalism succeeds where these accounts of rationality and justification fail.

2. What Are Dispositions?

In order to understand evaluative dispositionalism, it is appropriate to begin by asking the question 'what are dispositions?'. Evaluative dispositionalism is closely allied to a position defended within the philosophy of mind: dispositionalism about belief. Dispositions are, on the evaluative dispositionalist approach, the same things that are taken to constitute beliefs by defenders of dispositionalism about belief. To understand the nature of dispositions, as understood by evaluative dispositionalism, it is therefore useful to first consider dispositionalism about belief.

According to dispositionalism about belief, believing that p is having one or more dispositions in relation to the proposition p. Believing is not an

How Stereotypes Deceive Us. Katherine Puddifoot, Oxford University Press. © Katherine Puddifoot 2021.
DOI: 10.1093/oso/9780192845559.003.0008

activity or an occurrence; it does not involve entertaining a proposition, or being in an occurrent state like having a belief in one's belief box.[1] Instead, believing is being disposed to respond in various ways across a range of circumstances.

According to this view, dispositions are counterfactuals (Baker 1995), which might or might not be realized, and dispositional statements are conditional statements, e.g. 'If x were in circumstances c1, an event A would occur in x; if it were in circumstances c2, a different event B would occur in x, etc.' (Price 1969, p. 246). For example, a belief that Manchester City are going to win the English Premier League is a set of counterfactuals or conditionals, such as the following: If asked who will win the English Premier League, the believer will sincerely say 'Manchester City'; if placing a bet on who will win, Manchester City will be the believer's choice, and so on. Most beliefs will involve numerous dispositions, which can interact. Identifying a belief involves recognizing when one or more of the dispositions manifests.

On traditional dispositionalist views, believing that p is being disposed to act as if a certain state of affairs obtains (Braithwaite 1932; Marcus 1990). For example, believing that p might involve the disposition to assent to the truth of p (Quine and Ullian 1970). One can also display a belief by acting in a way that is consistent with the belief being true when pursuing one's wants, desires, and needs (Marcus 1990). I believe, for instance, that Manchester City are going to win the English Premier League if I am disposed to act as if this is true when placing a large bet on who will win. What is important, on traditional dispositional views, is that the focus is on dispositions to act.

In contrast, liberal dispositionalist accounts emphasize the interconnected nature of beliefs and other mental states, such as hope, fear, surprise, doubt, and confidence (Audi 1972; Baker 1995; Price 1969; Schwitzgebel 2002, 2010, 2013). Believing involves dispositions to think as well as act. Price outlines his liberal dispositionalist account in the following way:

> [...] if A believes that p is a dispositional statement about A, the disposition we attribute to him is a multiform disposition, which is manifested or actualized in many different ways: not only in his actions and his inactions, but also in his emotional states such as hope and fear; in feelings of doubt, surprise and confidence; and finally in his inferences. (1969: p. 294)

---

[1] See Schwitzgebel (2013) for a comparison of dispositionalist and belief box approaches to belief, and an endorsement of the former over the latter.

For Lynne Rudder Baker (1995)[2]:

> Whether a person has a particular belief (individuated by the that clause in its attribution) is determined by what S does, says, and thinks and what S would do, say and think in various circumstances, where 'what S would do' may itself be specified intentionally. So whether 'S believes that p' is true depends on there being relevant counterfactuals true of S. The antecedent of the relevant counterfactuals may mention other of S's attitudes, but not, of course, the belief in question.   (p. 155)

By identifying beliefs with dispositions, and stipulating that beliefs are determined by what the subject does, says and thinks and would do and think in various circumstances, Price and Baker, and other liberal dispositionalists, define dispositions as what a person does, says, thinks, and would do and think in various circumstances.

A few further points are worth noting, as they will become more important later. First, people can share the same beliefs without having the same dispositions. What it is to believe that p is different for different people. Consider the belief that Manchester City are going to win the Premier League this season. The gambler might be disposed to place a bet; the Manchester City fan might be motivated to pay big money for a ticket for the last match of the season; and the Manchester United fan might fear the day when the belief becomes true.

Second, a person's behaviour will not always make their beliefs transparent. For example, a person who is a Manchester United fan might not seem to believe that Manchester City are going to win the league because they do not admit in conversation that their rivals are likely to succeed in this way. They might seem to lack the dispositions associated with believing that Manchester City are going to win the league. However, they might not manifest the disposition due to having another belief that you should never admit defeat, which is manifest in their verbal behaviour. Each of these features follows from the complex relationship between different dispositions, actions, and mental states.

As dispositions to have particular mental states (fear, hope, etc.) are a part of what it is to believe on the liberal dispositionalist view, dispositions

---

[2] Baker (1995) labels her position 'Practical Realism' because it aims to capture the explanatory role that beliefs have but is a form of dispositionalism because beliefs are equated with counterfactuals capturing how believers will respond in particular contexts.

to hold further beliefs downstream can determine the nature of a belief. A part of believing that Manchester City are going to win the English Premier League is to be disposed to believe, if one considers Liverpool FC's prospects, that they are not going to win. If, on considering the prospects of Liverpool FC, a person would think that that team is going to win the English Premier League then there would be very good reason for doubting that they really believed that Manchester City are going to win.

Drawing on dispositionalism about belief, then, evaluative dispositionalism defines the dispositions that are the focus of evaluation in the following way: as what a person does, says, thinks, and would do and think in various circumstances, which can be captured by conditionals or counterfactuals true of the individual, where these conditionals might or might not be realized.

3. Evaluative Dispositionalism

With our conception of dispositions to hand it is now possible to provide a formulation of evaluative dispositionalism.

> Evaluative dispositionalism: a complete epistemic evaluation of an act of believing should focus on both (a) the dispositions that are displayed in believing, and (b) the dispositions that are possessed due to believing.

Evaluative dispositionalism is not as metaphysically demanding as dispositionalism about belief. An evaluative dispositionalist need not commit to the idea that beliefs are reducible to dispositions. They could take any view of the metaphysics of belief, as long as that view implies that believers manifest a disposition when they believe, and that believing leads a person to have new dispositions. These might seem to be substantial demands but on brief consideration of the definition of dispositions outlined in Section 2 it becomes clear that they are not.

Once dispositions are defined as what a person does, says, thinks, and would do and think in various circumstances, there is little reason to doubt that believers manifest a disposition when they believe. Believing is a way of thinking. People believe under specified conditions, when eliciting conditions are present, such as evidence in support of the belief, and stimuli that lead them to entertain the thought that the belief might be true. In believing they therefore manifest a disposition to think a certain thought under specified conditions. Prior to believing that p a person is disposed to believe that p if they encounter eliciting conditions for the belief that p, such as evidence or stimuli relating to the belief. Without this disposition, they would not end up believing that p.

On the definition of dispositions used in the evaluative dispositionalist framework it is also clear that there are often, if not always, dispositions associated with believing. If you believe some content, for example that Manchester City are going to win the league, then believing makes some conditional statements true about you. In forming the belief, you may (i) become disposed to agree with people who state the same opinion, (ii) become disposed to attend to the results of games involving Manchester City and games involving their opponents, looking for vindication of your belief, (iii) become disposed to buy those tickets for the final game of the season to watch Manchester City triumph, and so forth. If you were not disposed to think or act in any ways that are consistent with the content, then people would, rightly it seems, doubt whether you truly believe it. This is not to say that believing simply is being disposed to think or act, but rather to say that believing is so closely linked to thinking and acting that in most, if not all, cases of believing people will be disposed to think and act in certain ways due to believing.

Assuming, then, that believing often if not always involves manifesting a disposition and brings with it new dispositions, evaluative dispositionalism claims that a complete epistemic evaluation should consider both dispositions manifested through and possessed due to believing. Take the belief Manchester City are going to win the league. How would this belief be evaluated if the evaluative dispositionalist approach were applied to it? First it would be considered which dispositions are manifest in forming the belief. Say Sally believes this. Was Sally disposed to form the belief that Manchester City are going to win the league even if there are other, equally strong, contenders for the title? For instance, it is easy to imagine an ardent Manchester City fan, or a pessimistic supporter of Manchester City's rivals, being disposed to respond to weak evidence that Manchester City are going to win (say, Manchester City get a couple of good results in a row or their rivals have a couple of poor results) by concluding that it is certain that they are going to win. In doing so, they would manifest a disposition to believe in the absence of good evidential support. Or consider another example. Imagine that you notice a fluttering in your abdomen. You search an online search engine for 'fluttering in abdomen' and the first search result returned is about diaphragm spasms and flutters. You conclude that a diaphragm spasm must explain the fluttering in your abdomen. You do not search any further, and you do not consider any further details, for example, whether the fluttering is located in your lower or upper abdomen. Here, in forming the belief *a diaphragm spasm is the cause of the fluttering in my abdomen,* you once again display a disposition to believe in the absence of good evidential support.

Another thing that would need to be considered if you were applying evaluative dispositionalism to the belief that Manchester City are going to win the league is the dispositions that the believer has due to believing what they do. Does Sally believing that Manchester City are going to win the English Premier League mean that she is disposed to hold further beliefs that are untrue? Is she disposed to ignore evidence of Liverpool's potential to win the league? Or to misperceive the evidence, for example, undervaluing the performance of individual Liverpool players? Or take the belief that a diaphragm spasm is the cause of the fluttering in your abdomen. Does believing this proposition involve dispositions to hold further beliefs that are untrue? Are you, as the believer, disposed to ignore other symptoms related to the fluttering in your abdomen? Or are you disposed to discount the good-quality testimonial evidence provided by a friend with medical training who says that it is unlikely that your diaphragm is in spasm? Dispositions like these, which are associated with holding a belief, also count towards the evaluation of the belief.

Other authors have recently defended claims similar to those found in evaluative dispositionalism. It will be useful to compare and contrast these existing positions to evaluative dispositionalism, to fully understand the contours and commitments of the position proposed here.

Maria Lasonen-Aarnio (2010, 2020) has argued that evaluation of the dispositions of the believer is an ordinary part of many epistemic evaluations of beliefs. She focuses on the dispositions that are manifest in believing and argues that a tendency to evaluate these dispositions can explain the responses people have to some types of cases. For example, she discusses cases in which a belief is safe, that is, it could not easily of been false, but the believer has a defeater for the belief in the form of evidence suggesting that the belief is false (Lasonen-Aarnio 2010). Lasonen-Aarnio's (2010) suggestion is that the beliefs can count as knowledge in such cases, but people are nonetheless critical of the beliefs, rightly deeming them to be unreasonable. The beliefs are unreasonable because in believing that p despite the presence of a defeater of the belief that p one adopts a policy that brings bad dispositions, where bad dispositions are those that fail to produce knowledge across a range of environments. Believing despite the presence of a defeater might be consistent with knowing on a specific occasion, because it is consistent with a belief being safe, but having it as a policy disposes you to fail to know on many occasions. Believing in this way can therefore be viewed poorly because of the dispositions associated with doing so.[3]

Timothy Williamson (forthcoming) also emphasizes the role played by dispositions in evaluative judgements in epistemology. Williamson focuses on sceptical scenarios, such as the New Evil Demon thought experiment. In this thought experiment we are invited to consider two individuals. One has ordinary perceptual experiences, which tend to be reliable. Another has exactly the same perceptual experiences but they are being manipulated by an evil demon so that all of their perceptual beliefs are false. A widely shared intuition is that the individual in the bad case is as justified in believing each of the perceptual beliefs as the individual in the good case because they have identical experiences. Williamson explains this intuition by appeal to dispositions. He argues that the primary epistemic norm of justification is a truth-related norm. This truth-related norm could be *believe the truth*, *believe in line with one's evidence*, or *have beliefs that constitute knowledge* (his favoured example is the latter). One can only comply with the primary norm by meeting the relevant truth-related standard. However, the primary epistemic norm generates derivative norms, and one of these derivative norms focuses on the dispositions of the believer. If you value believing the truth, for example, then you will value being disposed to comply to the truth-related norm of believing the truth across a range of environments. The value placed on the dispositional norm can explain why many philosophers are tempted to think that people are equally justified in the

---

[3] A second type of case that Lasonen-Aarnio (2020) discusses is one in which a person undergoes epistemic akrasia. They believe that p while also believing that it is irrational for them to believe that p. Lasonen-Aarnio (2020) argues that people can be permitted to display akrasia (according to an evidentialist account—see Chapter 7 for a brief introduction to evidentialism), because both the belief that p and the belief that it is irrational to believe that p can be supported by their evidence. This can occur in cases in which a person has misleading evidence about what evidence they have: their evidence supports p, but it is likely that p is not likely on the evidence. In such cases, believing in line with the evidence (both p and that it is irrational to believe that p) violates a structural requirement on rationality. Evidentialist approaches to epistemic norms cannot diagnose what goes wrong in cases of akrasia, because they imply that a person is permitted to violate this structural requirement, but Lasonen-Aarnio argues that a dispositionalist approach to epistemic evaluation can do so. The akratic's epistemic situation is poor because they display bad dispositions, i.e. they respond in ways that in many circumstances would prevent them from successful belief. They display the bad disposition to believe that p while it is irrational for them to believe that there are genuine reasons to believe that p. They display a disposition to fail to respond to a conclusive and conspicuous reason to adopt a particular doxastic stance (non-believing), i.e. the fact that it is irrational for them to believe that there are genuine reasons to believe that p.

good and bad cases proposed by the sceptic. The intuition tracks the fact that in the good and bad cases the same dispositions are manifest.

In discussion of the role of dispositions in epistemology, Lasonen-Aarnio (2020) proposes an approach to evaluating doxastic states (beliefs, disbeliefs, suspension of belief, etc.) that focuses on dispositions. Step one of the approach involves identifying the dispositions manifest in the formation of a doxastic state. Step two involves evaluating these dispositions: how good are they relative to the goal of successfully believing? The second step involves considering how the dispositions manifest in the formation of the doxastic state fare across a number of counterfactual situations: do they tend to fare well relative to the goal of successfully believing?

Williamson's (forthcoming) and, more particularly, Lasonen-Aarnio's (2020) position on the role of dispositions in epistemic evaluation have close affinities to my own. According to the evaluative dispositionalism defended in this chapter, it is valuable when making an epistemic evaluation—specifically of acts of believing stereotypes—to identify the dispositions that are manifested in the formation of a doxastic state. It is important to consider whether these dispositions tend to lead to success in believing, across a range of counterfactual situations. However, my position is distinctive from Lasonen-Aarnio's and Williamson's in the following ways.

First, evaluative dispositionalism as described in this chapter does not first and foremost aim to capture how people already evaluate beliefs, explaining intuitions that epistemologists (or others) have about cases. Instead, evaluative dispositionalism is a prescriptive theory, prescribing how people ought to engage in the evaluation of doxastic states. My suggestion is that people ought to consider the dispositions manifested when believing if they are evaluating acts of believing stereotypes. By focusing on dispositions it is possible to successfully capture each of the epistemic faults associated with stereotyping.

Second, evaluative dispositionalism does not solely focus on the dispositions that are manifest in the formation or retention of a doxastic state. Lasonen-Aarnio (2010) focuses on the dispositions manifested in forming and retaining a belief in the presence of a defeater, and Williamson (forthcoming) focuses on the dispositions manifested in forming beliefs in sceptical scenarios. While dispositions like these are some of the objects of evaluation in evaluative dispositionalism, so too are the dispositions that an agent possesses due to occupying a doxastic state.

Robert Audi's 'Dispositional beliefs and dispositions to believe' also contains a position with similarities to evaluative dispositionalism. Audi argues that:

> It is not just our beliefs, but also our dispositions to believe, that count toward our rationality. Being disposed to believe absurdities would count against my rationality even if I withheld them by reminding myself that I will be thought foolish.   (Audi 1994, p. 430)

For Audi, when a person is disposed to believe that p she would believe p if she entertained the thought that p. Dispositions of this type count towards the rationality of the believer on Audi's account. For example, if our Manchester City fan would believe that Liverpool are going to lose against their team in the season finale match between the two teams if she were to entertain the thought, then this disposition counts towards the fan's rationality.

According to evaluative dispositionalism, a disposition of this type would be taken into consideration in any adequate evaluation of the epistemic standing of an act of believing a stereotype. Evaluative dispositionalism suggests that the evaluation of an act of believing that p should consider the dispositions to believe other beliefs, e.g. q, that a believer has due to believing that p. However, evaluative dispositionalism is distinguishable from Audi's position because as well as claiming that dispositions to believe (e.g. that q) count towards the epistemic standing of an act of believing p, evaluative dispositionalism implies that dispositions manifest in the formation of a belief that p count towards the epistemic standing of the act of believing that p.

Moreover, for Audi, a disposition to believe is something very specific: when a person has a disposition to believe that p she would believe p if she entertained the thought that p. However, on the evaluative dispositionalist account, dispositions that are acquired due to believing that p other than the disposition to form a further belief (e.g. that q) if one entertained the relevant proposition (q) count toward the epistemic standing of the act of believing. Dispositions to discount certain relevant evidence, or to respond in a biased way to the evidence, to fail to trust reliable informants, and other dispositions that increase or decrease the chance of true beliefs being formed downstream, all count towards the evaluation of the act of believing that p. For example, one might be disposed to approach with suspicion the sceptical testimony of a reliable friend due to one's firmly held belief that a diaphragm spasm is the cause of the fluttering in one's abdomen. The disposition to approach trustworthy testimony with suspicion would count towards the evaluation of one's act of believing on the evaluative dispositionalist approach because it is a disposition that reduces the chance of an accurate judgement being made. However, the disposition is not a disposition to believe, as Audi defines them, because one can approach testimony with suspicion without it being guaranteed that one will believe the testimony to be untrustworthy as soon as one has entertained the proposition that it might be.

In the literature on prejudice, a number of authors have characterized prejudice in terms of the possession of poor dispositions. K. Anthony Appiah (1990) argues that racial prejudice is a disposition:

> The disposition was a tendency to assent to false propositions, both moral and theoretical, about races—propositions that support policies or beliefs that are to the disadvantage of some race (or races) as opposed to others, and to do so even in the face of evidence and argument that should appropriately lead to giving those propositions up. This disposition I call 'racial prejudice'. (p. 16)

For Appiah, then, racial prejudice involves being disposed to affirm false propositions about racial groups, which disadvantage members of those racial groups, in the face of counterevidence and argument. The person displaying racial prejudice does not give up their racist attitudes in response to evidence that the attitudes are false. They therefore display poor dispositions that are associated with the content that they believe. Endre Begby (2013) also emphasizes the way that prejudiced attitudes can be resistant to counterevidence, 'it belongs precisely to the insidiousness of prejudice that [prejudiced attitudes] are epistemically robust, in the sense of being highly recalcitrant to apparent counterevidence and therefore often invisible to introspective reflection' (2013: p. 97). Meanwhile, Miranda Fricker (2016) claims, 'an attitude is prejudiced insofar as it is the product of (some significant degree of) motivated maladjustment to the evidence'. Examples of relevant maladjustments include the believer being resistant to counterevidence, or being motivated to generalize from an insufficiently large sample. For Fricker, an attitude is prejudiced if a person holds the attitude due to displaying poor dispositions—dispositions to believe in the face of counterevidence or dispositions to generalize about a social group based on a small sample of that group. Therefore, it is not uncommon to see prejudiced attitudes characterized in terms of dispositions to resist counterevidence.

I am certainly sympathetic to the idea that an important feature of stereotyping attitudes, including those that demonstrate prejudice, is that they are resistant to counterevidence. However, the current discussion focuses on the evaluation of stereotypes, rather than the definition of prejudice. Moreover, the range of dispositions that are the focus of attention in evaluative dispositionalism is more wide-ranging than those that are the focus of these authors. While these authors draw attention to how a person can be disposed to form prejudiced attitudes without the attitudes being properly supported by the evidence, and to retain the attitudes even in light of counterevidence, evaluative dispositionalism focuses attention on a wider range of dispositions possessed as a result of harbouring a stereotype, such as the disposition to misremember or misinterpret evidence about individuals and cases that are stereotyped.

It is worthwhile finally distinguishing evaluative dispositionalism from a further set of approaches to epistemology that focus on dispositions: virtue and vice theories. According to these theories, epistemic evaluation should focus on the dispositions of the believer. When considering whether a belief is justified or counts as knowledge we should ask whether the belief was produced as a result of the manifestation of a virtue or a vice (see, e.g. Sosa 1991, 2007; Zagzebski 1996, for recent overview of literature see Battaly 2008). Virtues are taken to be positive dispositions: either positive character traits, such as conscientiousness, or reliable cognitive capacities like memory. In contrast, vices are negative dispositions: either negative character traits like prejudice, or unreliable cognitive capacities like wishful thinking. It might be thought that evaluative dispositionalism is a species of virtue or vice theory because it emphasizes the importance of focusing on dispositions. However, there are two important differences between evaluative dispositionalism on the one hand and virtue and vice theory on the other.

First, as previously emphasized, evaluative dispositionalism does not focus solely on the dispositions manifest in believing. Instead, there is also a focus on dispositions held due to believing. Virtue and vice theory, in contrast, focus solely on the dispositions manifest in believing. A belief could be formed in a virtuous way, for example, and therefore be judged to be justified on the virtue approach, but nonetheless be criticizable according to evaluative dispositionalism due to bringing poor dispositions. Solomon's belief as described in Chapter 7 could be an example: he could be said to form his belief that women are less good at abstract thinking than men conscientiously, and therefore virtuously, but the belief could nonetheless be criticized on the evaluative dispositionalist framework due to the poor dispositions that it brings.

The second difference between evaluative dispositionalism and virtue or vice theory is that the focus of attention on evaluative dispositionalism is beliefs rather than any character traits or cognitive capacities that might or might not be reflected in the beliefs. For the evaluative dispositionalist, it does not matter if a belief is the product of a stable character trait or cognitive capacity. What matters is whether a person displays positive dispositions in forming the belief and as a result of holding the belief. The belief could be short-lived. It might be more of a reflection of one's society than one's personal character or cognitive capacities. Nonetheless, the belief can be evaluated for the dispositions associated with it.

We are now in a good position to understand the contours and commitments of evaluative dispositionalism. According to this position, a complete epistemic evaluation of an act of believing would consider the dispositions of the believer relating to the belief: the ways that they would think and act under specified circumstances. Put another way, we ought to consider the dispositions of the believer relating to a belief when evaluating acts of believing stereotypes. The relevant dispositions are (a) dispositions that were manifest in the formation of the belief, and (b) dispositions that are possessed as a result of the believer forming the belief. The current project aims to capture the epistemic features displayed by believers, so the relevant dispositions are *epistemic dispositions* that is, dispositions that influence whether the truth or falsities are believed, and, more specifically, dispositions relating to how a person responds to evidence that they encounter. The category of epistemic dispositions includes dispositions to believe (as construed by Audi), dispositions to discount evidence, dispositions to respond in a biased way to evidence that is not immediately discounted, and other dispositions that relate to how people respond to evidence.

4. Applying Dispositionalism to Stereotyping Beliefs

With this exposition of evaluative dispositionalism to hand, it is time to consider what reasons there are for adopting the position when evaluating acts of believing stereotypes. This section outlines the primary reason for adopting evaluative dispositionalism in this context: the account captures the epistemic faults found in a wide range of cases of stereotyping. The types of cases considered include both those where a stereotype succeeds and those where a stereotype fails to reflect the evidence available to a believer, and those where the possession of the stereotype brings positive consequences, negative consequences, and a combination of both.

4.1 Case 1: The Unsupported Belief with Poor Consequences

Take Judy.

> Judy harbours a stereotype, *people who drive white vans are rude*. She has
> never encountered rudeness from any of the people who drive white vans
> in her area, and there are a few. She has, on the other hand, received acts of
> kindness from people who she has later found to be driving white vans.
> She harbours the stereotype because her uncle who she knows to be preju-
> diced used to rant to her about 'white van men' when she was a child. Due
> to possessing the stereotype, she tends to remember when a person in a
> white van seems to her to be driving aggressively but not when they seem
> to be driving carefully. She often interprets the driving as aggressive when
> it is unclear whether it really is. If she is in an unfamiliar area and there is
> someone sitting in a white van drinking a cup of tea then she will not ask
> that person for directions to her destination, preferring to get lost, because
> she believes that they will be rude and unpleasant.

Judy's case is probably what people commonly imagine when thinking
about stereotyping. Judy has come to associate members of a particular
group with a characteristic due to a social interaction with an influential
figure in her life. The stereotype is not well supported by the evidence that
she has encountered, and it leads her to make inaccurate judgements and
miss out on important information (e.g. about the direction to her destination). There seems to be little reason to doubt that Judy is doing badly
(epistemically speaking) in believing that people who drive white vans
are rude.

How does evaluative dispositionalism account for the poor epistemic
standing of Judy's act of believing? There are a variety of ways that it can do
so. When Judy forms the belief that people who drive white vans are rude
she does so on the basis of evidence provided by someone who she knows to
be prejudiced while ignoring evidence from positive personal interactions
with people who drive white vans. She displays a disposition to believe
based on scant, poor-quality evidence; a disposition to trust an untrustworthy informant (whatever else her prejudiced uncle might be a reliable
informant about, he is not trustworthy when it comes to social judgements);
and a disposition to ignore good-quality evidence from personal interactions. These are poor dispositions to manifest, reducing the chance of an

accurate belief being formed. Therefore, evaluative dispositionalism implies that Judy is doing something poor from an epistemic perspective when manifesting the disposition to believe that people who drive white vans are rude. On top of this, Judy acquires other poor dispositions due to believing this stereotype. She acquires the disposition to misinterpret ambiguous evidence, form distorted memories of the driving behaviour of people who drive white vans, and to discount potentially useful testimonial evidence from people who drive white vans. According to evaluative dispositionalism, these dispositions also count towards an assessment of the epistemic status of Judy's act of believing the stereotype. Evaluative dispositionalism can therefore capture each of the epistemic faults associated with Judy's stereotyping belief. Judy turns out to be performing poorly in multiple ways, through the dispositions to believe that she manifests in forming the belief that people who drive white vans are rude, and through the dispositions she comes to possess when forming the belief.

4.2   Case 2: The Weakly Supported Belief with Poor Consequences

Now take Florence.

> Florence is an avid fan of true crime stories. She has read numerous stories in which people who are suffering from mental health issues commit violent crimes. She comes to believe the stereotype *people with mental health conditions tend to be violent.* She thereby becomes disposed to assume that people with mental health conditions have violent tendencies, to misinterpret the behaviours of people with mental health conditions as aggressive when they are ambiguous, and she chooses not to engage with people she knows to have mental health conditions for fear of aggression. As a result she does not know much about certain colleagues who she believes to have had mental health issues.

What does evaluative dispositionalism say about Florence believing that people with mental health conditions tend to be violent? Her situation is similar to Judy's with respect to the dispositions that she acquires through believing the stereotype. These dispositions are poor, increasing the chance of her forming an inaccurate impression of individuals with mental health conditions. The main notable difference between the types of dispositions manifest by Judy and Florence is found in the causal history of the beliefs. While Judy had very poor evidence in support of her belief that white van men are rude, Florence has some slightly better-quality evidence, i.e. the numerous cases described in the true crime stories. While Judy manifested a disposition to believe on the basis of very poor evidence, Florence manifested a disposition to believe on the basis of better evidence. Nonetheless, the disposition that Florence manifests is poor. She has some evidence to support the conclusion that people with mental health conditions tend to be violent, but the evidence is extremely limited, and essentially biased: true crime stories focus on cases of crime, so are likely to depict people (whether they have a mental health condition or not) who are violent. Meanwhile, there are people with whom Florence could interact who have mental health conditions and are not violent, but she chooses not to interact with them so does not gather evidence about them that might prevent her from forming the stereotyping belief. Evaluative dispositionalism therefore produces what seems to be the right result. Florence occupies a slightly better epistemic situation than Judy in the dispositions to believe that are manifest in forming their respective stereotyping beliefs. Nonetheless both people display poor features that are captured by evaluative dispositionalism, via (i) the dispositions that they manifest in forming the beliefs and (ii) the dispositions that they possess as a result.

4.3   Case 3: The Well-Supported Belief with Poor Consequences

Now let us return to Solomon.

> Solomon comes from an isolated farming community. He is not exposed to any women who have displayed an aptitude for abstract thinking and his peers and educators give him the impression that women are less good at abstract thinking than men. All the evidence available to him, including seemingly good-quality testimonial evidence, supports the belief that he forms that women are not nearly as competent at abstract thinking as men. Due to possessing the belief, Solomon is more likely than he would otherwise be to misremember information relating to women's ability to engage in abstract thinking, to misinterpret ambiguous evidence about women's ability as fitting with the stereotype, to falsely assume that individual women are more similar than they really are to each other, and less

similar than they really are to individual men with respect to their abstract thinking abilities. The possession of the stereotyping belief increases the chance that Solomon will fail to give appropriate uptake to the testimony provided by women relating to matters that require abstract thought. It increases the chance that he would give women less credibility than they deserve when they are providing him with information via testimony.

Solomon could be said to manifest good dispositions in the act of believing the stereotype. He manifests the disposition to form beliefs that are fitting with the evidence from his personal experience and evidence that is provided by peers he reasonably believes to be reliable. Evaluative dispositionalism therefore implies that he displays some relevant positive features. But he can nonetheless be identified as displaying significant epistemic faults because of the dispositions that he acquires through holding the belief. In believing that women are not nearly as competent at abstract thinking as men, he is disposed to respond in a number of extremely poor ways to information about, and that could be provided by, women he encounters. These dispositions count towards the epistemic status of Solomon's act of believing, and he will therefore be found to be performing poorly from an epistemic standpoint. By focusing on the dispositions associated with believing, evaluative dispositionalism is thus able to capture both the positive epistemic features and the epistemic faults of this type of example, which has been central to the discussion in this book. That is, evaluative dispositionalism captures how someone can display positive epistemic features while simultaneously displaying negative epistemic features by holding a stereotype that is well-supported by the evidence that they have encountered in their environment. They are doing well in virtue of having manifested dispositions to respond appropriately to the evidence in their environment, but they are doing badly in virtue of being disposed to respond poorly to other evidence that they will encounter.

4.4 Case 4: The Poorly Supported Belief with Positive Consequences

Now let us consider Roger.

Roger is a junior scientist. He is somewhat oblivious to what is going on in his surroundings, so he does not notice that women are significantly underrepresented in science in his society. As a result, he does not form the stereotyping belief that those with scientific expertise in his society are more likely to be men than women. Instead, he believes that women and men are equally likely to have scientific expertise. Because he lacks the stereotyping belief, he is not disposed to apply it when it is irrelevant. He is not disposed to remember indicators of women's expertise in a way that reflects the stereotype. He is not disposed to assume that female scientists are more similar to each other than they are, or to assume that they are less similar to known male scientific experts than they really are. He is not disposed to explain female behaviours in terms of the stereotype. He does not give female scientists less credibility than they deserve or refuse to give their testimony uptake. Each of these is a disposition that he might have had if he had held the stereotype. Sadly, he is also disposed to form false beliefs, such as false beliefs about whether there is a need to implement measures to increase diversity in his workplace, due to not believing that men are more likely to have scientific expertise than women.

What does evaluative dispositionalism say about Roger? It notes that he displays a poor disposition, failing to respond to relevant evidence available in his environment, when he forms the belief that men and women in his society are equally likely to have scientific expertise. He also displays the disposition to form false beliefs downstream, for example, about the need to implement measures to increase diversity. As these dispositions count towards the epistemic status of his act of believing the stereotype, his belief deserves some criticism. But in the absence of the stereotyping belief, he has other positive dispositions that lead him to respond appropriately to evidence. These dispositions also count towards the epistemic status of his act of believing. He therefore deserves some positive epistemic standing in virtue of not believing something that would be fitting with the evidence and instead believing something unsupported by the evidence.

These examples show that evaluative dispositionalism is able to capture the epistemic faults, and the merits, found in a wide range of cases of stereotyping:

(A) Where a stereotype poorly reflects the evidence and brings poor consequences;
(B) Where a stereotype is weakly supported by the evidence but nonetheless brings poor consequences;

(C) Where the stereotype reflects the evidence very well but brings poor consequences;

(D) Where the stereotype poorly reflects the evidence and brings positive consequences.

What these examples show is that whereas upstream, downstream, and static approaches were found in Chapter 7 to be limited in the types of epistemic faults associated with stereotyping beliefs that they could capture, the dispositionalist approach can capture the epistemic faults found in a wide range of stereotyping beliefs. Evaluative dispositionalism is pluralistic in that it integrates aspects from each of these types of approaches—focusing on the nature of the stereotyping belief, factors upstream, and factors downstream—and its pluralism allows it to capture a wide variety of epistemic faults. Evaluative dispositionalism is especially attractive because it captures the epistemic faults found in complex cases such as C and D, where stereotypes are supported by the available evidence but bring poor consequences, or where stereotypes poorly reflect the evidence and yet bring positive consequences. Evaluative dispositionalism is therefore a satisfyingly comprehensive and fruitful pluralistic approach to evaluating the status of acts of believing stereotypes. This is the first point in its favour.

5. Unifying

The second point in favour of evaluative dispositionalism is that the position is satisfyingly simple and unifying. Pluralism is attractive because of its comprehensiveness. It indicates that various different features, each individually important to the epistemic standing of a belief, ought to be taken into consideration when evaluating the belief. However, pluralism can also have the downside of being cognitively and practically demanding. It can be challenging to identify each of the epistemic standards (evidence-fitting, reliability, norm-fitting, and so forth) that need to be evaluated, and then to discover whether each of the standards is met. Evaluative dispositionalism, in contrast, requires relatively little from the evaluator. What it requires is simple: to consider what sorts of dispositions seem to have been manifest by a believer in believing, and what sorts of dispositions they are likely to manifest as a result of believing. The focus on dispositions is therefore unifying and simplifying.

6. Intuitive Response to Cases

As well as comprehensively capturing the epistemic faults involved with believing stereotypes, and being satisfyingly pluralistic, simple, and unifying, I believe evaluative dispositionalism has intuitive appeal. It might seem puzzling how I can claim that dispositionalism is an intuitive view when it goes against the grain of existing theories of epistemic justification and epistemic rationality, which tend to associate rationality and justification with either upstream, static or downstream factors, but not the full set of dispositions associated with believing. To see how this is possible, it will be useful to consider the distinction between pre-theoretical and post-theoretical intuitions. Arguably, most people are not naturally drawn to dispositionalism. Their pre-theoretical intuitions are not dispositionalist. But I believe that there is reason to think that their (and your) post-theoretical intuitions will be dispositionalist.

As the discussion in this book has emphasized, human psychology does not always work in the ways that our pre-theoretical intuitions suggest that it does. Intuitively, believing stereotypes that reflect social reality consistently bolsters our chances of forming true beliefs. Equally intuitively, applying those stereotypes to individual members of the social group to which the stereotype refers only increases the chance of a correct judgement being made about those individuals. However, the discussion in this book (especially Chapter 4) has shown that the application of a stereotype that reflects social reality to a member of a social group to which the stereotype applies can decrease the chance of a correct judgement being made, increasing the chance of an individual being misperceived. Our pre-theoretical intuitions about how stereotypes operate, and the ways that they affect our chances of forming true beliefs, correct judgements and perceptions, and so on, therefore fail to track the psychological reality. This casts doubt upon our pre-theoretical intuitions about the adequacy of various accounts of what constitutes doing well in believing a stereotype.

Pre-theoretically it seems that there are no cases of stereotyping beliefs in which a person forms a stereotyping belief that p that is well supported by the evidence but believing p systematically and predictably produces poor consequences. There are similarly no cases in which a person forms a belief that p which is poorly supported by the evidence but believing p has systematic and predictable positive consequences. Therefore, upstream accounts focusing on the fittingness of a belief to the evidence and downstream accounts focusing on the consequences of believing seem (pre-theoretically) to produce the same satisfying result: that both beliefs that are a poor fit with the evidence and beliefs that bring poor consequences should have a wholly poor epistemic status. What the discussion in this book reveals is that this is not the case. Standard theories of rationality and justification that focus solely on upstream or downstream factors produce one of two counterintuitive results: (i) that a person can be rational or justified due to believing something unsupported by the evidence or (ii) that a person can be rational or justified believing something that systematically and predictably leads to numerous poor epistemic consequences. Once these counterintuitive results are revealed, the intuitive pull of existing approaches to epistemic evaluation is weakened. Therefore, while in the abstract specific upstream or downstream accounts seem intuitively appealing, once we consider how the accounts produce counterintuitive results in relation to concrete cases, their intuitive pull is weakened.

In contrast, a better understanding of concrete cases of stereotyping beliefs provides motivation for accepting evaluative dispositionalism, as we have seen in Section 4 of this chapter. The concrete cases described in this section reflected the psychological realities of how stereotypes operate and evaluative dispositionalism seemed to provide precisely the correct results with respect to them.

The realities of cases like those in Section 4 of this chapter highlight how even if evaluative dispositionalism is not pre-theoretically intuitive when considered in the abstract, it provides intuitive results in important concrete cases, once those cases are properly understood. Post-theoretically, and in light of these concrete cases, evaluative dispositionalism has significant intuitive appeal. It captures intuitions about the genuine psychological phenomena involved with stereotyping.

7. Same Stereotype, Different Evaluation

As well as generally providing the intuitively correct result with regards to cases of stereotyping, evaluative dispositionalism produces the following highly intuitive result: people can hold the same belief but their acts of believing can deserve different levels of criticism.[4] In fact, evaluative

---

[4] Criticism is not meant to equate to blame here. A person might not be blameworthy for believing a stereotype, even if they display significant epistemic faults due to so believing. To

dispositionalism implies that two people can harbour the same belief, as a result of being located in the same society and surrounded by the same social attitudes, but differ in the epistemic standing that they deserve due to so believing. This an extremely intuitive result when it comes to stereotypes.

Consider two people. Nora is a female scientist who has 30 years of experience. She is a feminist and as a result pays close attention to the representation of women in the sciences. She notices over time that a gender gap in the sciences never goes away: there are consistently more men than women in sciences, and therefore consistently more men than women with scientific expertise. Nora therefore harbours a stereotype associating men more strongly than women with scientific expertise. She harbours and endorses the social attitude *men are more likely than women to have scientific expertise*. However, the stereotype does not distort Nora's judgements of individual women scientists and their levels of expertise. The stereotype does not make her assume that women scientists are more similar to each other than they really are, or that they are less similar to men scientific experts than they really are. She does not misremember the features of women scientists due to the operation of the stereotype. And so on. Instead, Nora judges women scientists on the basis of the skills, expertise, and potential that they display in their work, with the stereotype only operating to allow her to understand the challenges that they are likely to have faced as a minority in the profession.

Ned is also a scientist with 30 years of experience. He is not a feminist. He has also registered that women are underrepresented in the sciences and therefore harbours a stereotype associating men more strongly than women with scientific expertise. He endorses the social attitude *men are more likely than women to have scientific expertise* and thereby harbours the same stereotype as Nora. However, the stereotype that he harbours permeates his thought, influencing all of the judgements that he makes about individual women scientists, and about the relative merits of men and women scientists. He makes errors such as misremembering the attributes of his women colleagues, misinterpreting ambiguous behaviours as indicating a lack of expertise, assuming women colleagues are more similar than they really are, and so on.

These two characters harbour the same stereotype: that men are more likely than women to have scientific expertise. Their stereotypes are formed

argue that a person is blameworthy for believing the stereotype would go beyond the scope of the current project.

on the basis of the same evidence: evidence about the underrepresentation of women in the sciences. But on the evaluative dispositionalist account the characters and their act of believing deserve different epistemic evaluations because the characters differ in the dispositions that they have due to possessing the stereotyping belief: Ned has dispositions to respond poorly to the evidence while Nora does not. This seems to be precisely the right result.

Two people can hold the same belief associating members of a social group with particular characteristics but nonetheless differ in the epistemic standing that they deserve due to believing the stereotype. And the difference is not always explained by the evidence that they have available to them. Two people can be brought up in the same society, exposed to the same epistemic environment, and form the same stereotype, but nonetheless differ in the epistemic evaluation that they deserve due to believing the stereotype. For example, when the sexist claims that men are more likely than women to be scientific experts they can be expressing a belief that is epistemically poor, one that will dispose them to respond poorly to evidence, decreasing the chance of that person achieving their epistemic goals. This does not mean that everyone else will be doing similarly poorly if they have the same belief.

Evaluative dispositionalism is explanatorily powerful due to the way that it can distinguish between different examples of people holding the same belief. It can explain the intuition that not all cases of stereotyping are epistemically bad. It can even explain why we do not judge all cases in which a person harbours the same stereotype in the same way. It can explain why we applaud some people for recognizing that there are inequalities, and making generalizations about those inequalities, while we condemn others for making the same generalizations. What might seem at face value to be an unreasonable response to beliefs that encode statistical generalizations is, on the dispositionalist approach, a reasonable response. It is reasonable to accept that some acts of believing statistical generalizations should be criticized while other acts of believing the same generalizations as a result of exposure to the same evidence should not be. It is reasonable to suggest that two instances of believing differ in their epistemic standing if the believers have different dispositions associated with the beliefs.

8. Prescriptive Power

Theories in epistemology are often evaluated for their prescriptive power. It is asked, 'can and should this theory guide action?' (see, e.g. Kornblith 1989;

Bishop and Trout 2005). For some it is an advantage if a theory can have a positive, action-guiding role. For theories of epistemic value, the positive role will usually be guiding a person to achieve epistemic goals, like true belief, knowledge or understanding.

Existing epistemological theories have been shown by the arguments in this book to have less prescriptive power than they might previously have appeared to have. We have found that upstream accounts that associate epistemic justification or epistemic rationality with fitting the evidence or forming beliefs using reliable processes would provide prescriptions that produce beliefs that bring poor epistemic consequences. If one consistently, across different contexts, formed stereotyping beliefs in a way that is fitting with the evidence—which tends to be a responsible and reliable belief-forming process—then one would form some beliefs that reflect information found in society but which lead to distorted perceptions of individual society members.

Meanwhile, downstream accounts that associate epistemic justification and epistemic rationality with beliefs producing good consequences would prescribe that people sometimes form beliefs that are poorly supported by the evidence available to them. It is sometimes theoretically possible for people to follow this advice. For example, when forming a judgement about the merits of job candidates one could ensure that one is unaware of aspects of their social identity, thereby preventing information about their social identity from influencing one's judgements in a way that will produce poor consequences. But it will often be difficult to ignore the evidence that is available. Take a case in which women are underrepresented in the sciences. It will be hard to ignore this information if one is regularly present in staff meetings or conferences where there are only one or two women among a much larger group. Moreover, general advice to ignore the evidence is bad advice. In many cases, ignoring evidence increases the chance of false beliefs being formed. So what would be required for a downstream approach to provide high-quality prescriptions for belief-formation is specific guidance about the conditions under which failing to reflect the evidence produces good consequences. It will not be usefully action guiding to provide the general guidance to ignore the evidence whenever doing so produces good consequences.

In contrast, it is good general advice to tell an epistemic agent to monitor (a) the dispositions that they and other people manifest when coming to believe and (b) the way they and other people are disposed to think due to what they believe. Consider the ardent Manchester City supporter who forms the belief that the team are going to win the English Premier League.

Imagine you are trying to give this person, Sally, advice on how to ensure that she does not make a mistaken judgement about Manchester City's prospects. The following is very good advice: make sure that you are not disposed to believe that Manchester City are going to win the League on the basis of weak evidence, and consider whether believing this makes it likely that you will make further mistakes, for example, when choosing players for your fantasy league team. Or consider the person who forms the belief that a diaphragm spasm is the cause of the fluttering in their abdomen. It is good advice to tell this person to consider whether they were disposed to form this belief when they lacked good evidence, for example, because they wanted a quick answer. It is also good advice to get them to reflect on whether forming this belief disposes them to discount other important evidence, such as other relevant symptoms that they experience or testimony from a knowledgeable friend. On the dispositionalist account, encouraging someone to do the right thing from the epistemic perspective would be equivalent to encouraging him or her to consider each of these things. Dispositionalism therefore has a high degree of prescriptive power.

This book shows that psychological findings can inform one's understanding of the dispositions that one is likely to manifest in, and possess due to forming, certain beliefs. Psychological results have revealed that people can manifest the disposition to form beliefs without a strong evidential basis when forming a stereotyping belief. They have also revealed that stereotyping beliefs dispose people to misremember, misinterpret evidence, make false assumptions about the similarities between different members of a social group, and mistakenly explain people's behaviours in terms of a stereotype (see Chapter 3). Psychological findings can therefore be used when following the prescriptions of the evaluative dispositionalist account to evaluate stereotyping beliefs, because they can contribute to an understanding of how to ensure that one displays good dispositions. But common sense can also reveal how people are disposed to think if they hold a certain belief as is evident in the examples of the Manchester City supporter and the fluttering abdomen.[5]

---

[5] It is important to note that people will not always follow this advice to 'check their dispositions'. It is well known, for example, that people are predisposed to search for evidence in support of their existing views (e.g. Wason 1960; Lord, Ross, and Lepper 1979). This makes it likely that people will frequently find their own dispositions to be wholly satisfactory rather than seeing their flaws. But a similar criticism can be levelled against other theories of epistemic value. People are unlikely to change their beliefs or belief forming processes to follow the advice to fit the evidence, use reliable belief forming processes, form beliefs with good consequences, or any other advice that involves significantly changing their epistemic standpoint

9. Social Role

Although epistemological accounts are not always assessed according to whether they perform an important social role, there is an increasing demand for epistemology not to be detached from society (see, e.g. Code 1987; Goldman 1999; Mills 2007), to articulate the epistemic wrongs found in society, and to facilitate fairer, more just and generally better societies by highlighting ways to right these epistemic wrongs (see, e.g. Collins 2000; Dotson 2011; Fricker 2007; Medina 2013). Evaluative dispositionalism has the capacity to do this. According to this view, a person deserves positive epistemic standing only if their dispositions to respond to evidence are good ones. Many of the injustices that occur due to epistemic wrongs are associated with people having poor dispositions to respond to evidence due to harbouring stereotypes.

When people are misperceived due to stereotypes, receiving unfair or unjust treatment, this can be either because their perceiver has been disposed to form stereotyping beliefs in the absence of evidential support or because the perceiver is disposed, due to possessing the stereotyping belief, to respond inappropriately to information about the individual.

When unfair assessments are made about a person's abilities to contribute to testimonial exchanges (Collins 2000; Fricker 2007) the problem is that the stereotyping beliefs of those making the unfair assessment dispose them to undervalue certain testimonial evidence. Believer B does something wrong in believing that person A lacks credibility because of the dispositions that B manifests in forming the assessment and the dispositions manifest due to making the assessment. In making the assessment that person A lacks credibility B is not guided sufficiently by the evidence about A's credibility but instead driven by a stereotype. Then, the formation of the assessment of person A's credibility leads B to be disposed to discount or undervalue good-quality testimonial evidence.

Sometimes the conceptual resources—e.g. knowledge, concepts, and narratives—of whole social groups are marginalized due to false beliefs about the credibility of group members. For example, Black feminist thinkers have emphasized that the knowledge, concepts, and narratives of Black women

---

for that matter, if they believe that their current epistemic situation is as it should be and reject evidence suggesting that it is not. So while the advice associated with evaluative dispositionalism is unlikely to be perfectly followed, this does not provide reasons for rejecting dispositionalism in favour of other positions.

are often unduly discredited due to stereotypes, for example, about their inferiority (see, e.g. Lorde 1984; Terrell 1995; Collins 2000). For instance, Audre Lorde describes how the thought of Black women is often excluded from curricula:

> The literature of women of color is seldom included in women's literature courses and almost never in other literature courses, nor in women's studies as a whole [...]
>
> This is a very complex question, but I believe one of the main reasons White women have such difficulty reading Black women's work is because of their reluctance to see Black women as women and different from themselves. To examine Black women's literature effectively requires that we be seen as whole people in our actual complexities—as individuals, as women, as humans—rather than as one of those problematic but familiar stereotypes provided in this society in place of genuine images of Black women. (1984, pp. 117–118).

Black women thinkers have often developed unique conceptual resources and understanding due to occupying the perspective of 'outsiders within' (Collins 1986, 2000), being able to access knowledge about societal norms and standards that is unavailable to others within society, including about the injustices that are part of the social and political system (e.g. Cooper 1892; Lorde 1984; Collins 1986, 2000). However, the conceptual resources and understanding have been stigmatized and marginalized, and not permitted to influence mainstream thought. The false stereotyping beliefs that society members hold about the credibility of Black women thinkers involve poor dispositions. People who believe that Black women thinkers cannot contribute to understanding are, in (either implicitly or explicitly) believing this proposition, disposed to lack understanding and fail to gain knowledge. According to evaluative dispositionalism, these believers would be evaluated negatively due to their beliefs producing these dispositions.

Generally, evaluative dispositionalism captures how societal attitudes, once internalized, can dispose people to respond poorly to evidence about and available from other members of their society. If a person can be judged negatively due to the dispositions that they possess due to believing that p then they can be judged negatively due to dispositions to form false beliefs about individuals, including about the contributions that they can make, as individuals or whole social groups, to knowledge and understanding.

Evaluative dispositionalism can therefore fulfil an important social role. It neatly captures and provides the capacity to articulate the problems at the heart of a number of significant epistemic wrongs that can be committed.

10. The Moral Objectionability of Stereotypes

A final advantage of evaluative dispositionalism is that it provides conceptual tools that can be used to distinguish stereotypes that are morally objectionable from others that are not. In Chapter 4, Section 3, it was argued that although stereotypes can be morally objectionable without being false, at least sometimes stereotypes are morally objectionable because they are misleading. Misleading stereotypes can cause harm, and when they do so they are morally objectionable due to the harm that they cause. For example, one person might harm another person who they are stereotyping by failing to recognize their positive attributes, and only noticing their negative attributes. The stereotyped person could suffer tangible practical harms as a result of being misperceived in this way: they might miss out on job opportunities, not be taken seriously when giving testimony in court, have their medical condition misdiagnosed, and so forth. In such cases, the stereotype and act of stereotyping is morally objectionable because it causes harm, and the harm is due to epistemic errors made by the person stereotyping.

Because evaluative dispositionalism provides a framework through which to identify epistemic errors associated with stereotyping, it also provides a way to identify morally objectionable stereotypes of this sort: focus on the epistemic dispositions associated with believing the stereotype. By focusing on the dispositions associated with believing stereotypes, it will be possible to identify cases where stereotypes mislead people in harmful, and therefore morally objectionable, ways.

11. Conclusion

There are numerous epistemic faults associated with believing stereotypes. Evaluative dispositionalism captures each of these faults, providing satisfying responses to a range of cases of stereotyping. It explains how different people can possess the same stereotyping beliefs while deserving different epistemic evaluations. While initially the position might not be intuitive, reflection on the psychological reality of stereotyping highlights its intuitive appeal. The position has prescriptive power: providing simple yet effective advice about how to order our epistemic lives. Furthermore, evaluative dispositionalism can perform an important social and moral role: facilitating the identification and labelling of significant social and moral as well as epistemic wrongs. For each of these reasons, I propose that when we are evaluating cases where people believe stereotypes, we should adopt the evaluative dispositionalist framework, focusing squarely on the dispositions associated with the acts of believing.

9
Conclusion

How do stereotypes deceive us? Sometimes they are wholly false, failing to reflect any aspect of social reality, and it is as a result of their falsity that they deceive us into thinking that the social world and those who occupy it are different to how they really are. But at other times stereotypes reflect aspects of social reality. One might be tempted to think that whenever a stereotype reflects an aspect of social reality stereotyping bolsters the chance that those who apply the stereotype will make correct judgements about social actors and events to which the stereotype is applied. This book has challenged this assumption. It has shown that there are multiple ways that stereotypes can deceive us even if they reflect aspects of social reality. Stereotypes that reflect social realities can be applied when they are irrelevant and they can, in various ways, prevent those who engage in stereotyping from accessing and properly processing diagnostic information about specific individuals and events.

Because stereotypes can deceive us even when they reflect something of social reality, there can be epistemic gains associated with avoiding stereotyping even where one would otherwise apply a stereotype that reflects an aspect of social reality. Possessing social attitudes—beliefs and implicit biases—that are egalitarian but inaccurate because they fail to reflect unequal social relations, such as the underrepresentation in the sciences of women, can bring epistemic benefits. The inaccurate social attitudes can be *epistemically innocent*: although they are epistemically faulty (because they fail to reflect the social reality) they bring epistemic benefits, by avoiding the errors associated with stereotyping.

The observation that stereotypes that reflect aspects of social reality can bring significant epistemic costs reveals a number of shortcomings of or omissions from some existing theories of the ethics of stereotypes and stereotyping. It challenges the idea, articulated by Lawrence Blum (2004), that the moral objectionability of stereotypes and stereotyping is necessarily tied to the falsity of the stereotypes. We have found that significant harms can follow as a result of the application of a stereotype without the stereotype being false, suggesting that the moral objectionability of stereotyping is

How Stereotypes Deceive Us. Katherine Puddifoot, Oxford University Press. © Katherine Puddifoot 2021.
DOI: 10.1093/oso/9780192845559.003.0009

not necessarily tied to the falsity of stereotypes. One of the ways that stereotyping can be morally objectionable, even if it involves the application of a stereotype that reflects an aspect of social reality, is that it can lead to the undue dismissal of the testimony of members of some social groups. When credibility deficits of this type occur, there will at least sometimes be an absence of prejudice, so the effect is not a case testimonial injustice, as defined by Fricker, because this occurs due to the operation of prejudice. This book has therefore identified a set of cases where a person is given less credibility than they deserve, thereby suffering moral harms, due to stereotyping but in the absence of testimonial injustice.

Because stereotypes can deceive us even when they reflect aspects of social reality, there are ways of explaining how there can be something epistemically amiss in cases where a person stereotypes using a stereotype that reflects social reality. What is epistemically amiss is that a person applies a stereotype that makes them susceptible to a catalogue of epistemic errors. This explanation of how there can be something epistemically amiss in these types of cases presents a challenge to some claims made by moral encroachment theorists, who argue that it is possible to explain how there is something epistemic amiss, but that this requires accepting that moral considerations determine what it is to meet epistemic standards.

Due to the observation that stereotypes that reflect social reality can bring significant epistemic costs, there is also reason to think that although we sometimes face a dilemma between achieving our epistemic and ethical goals when it comes to stereotypes that reflect aspects of social reality, as has been suggested by a number of authors, we often face an even more complex situation. When it comes to stereotypes of this type, sometimes our ethical and epistemic goals do conflict. However, sometimes they will align with both types of goal being achieved through stereotyping. Under these conditions the stereotypes facilitate social knowledge that is needed to produce ethical outcomes. Meanwhile, sometimes ethical and epistemic goals will align in the opposite direction, with both being achieved through not stereotyping. This is because stereotyping, if it were to occur, would lead to misperceptions of individuals as well as unethical outcomes. What we face is not simply a relatively straightforward dilemma between achieving our epistemic and ethical goals, then, but instead a serious practical problem of discerning which of these types of situations we occupy.

It is potentially misleading, then, to suggest that we face an epistemic-ethical dilemma with respect to our own acts of stereotyping. We do not always have two straightforward options: achieving our epistemic goals by stereotyping or achieving our ethical goals by not stereotyping. However, people *do* face a dilemma with respect to other people's stereotyping of them. In particular, some people who can choose whether or not to disclose information relating to aspects of their social identity face a dilemma. If they disclose information about their social identity, they are likely to be misperceived due to stereotyping, but if they do not, they are likely to have aspects of their lives misunderstood, i.e. those aspects of their lives that are best understood by considering their social identity. For example, people with mental health conditions could disclose information about their social identity, allowing others to understand how their mental lives and needs deviate from those of other people who lack the same mental health conditions. But this disclosure is likely to lead them to be misperceived due to stereotypes about mental health, and how they deceive us. People who face this type of dilemma have limited options available to use to avoid being misperceived but they can be helped out of the dilemma by actions that challenge the prominence in society of harmful stereotypes about their social group.

Once we recognize that stereotypes can deceive us in multiple and sometimes surprising ways, we might ask, how can we establish, for any act of stereotyping, whether it is likely to lead to misperception or misjudgement? Chapter 3 outlined some specific questions that we can consider when evaluating any act of stereotyping, but what general theoretical approach can be used to identify the epistemic faults associated with stereotyping? It might be thought that at least some existing epistemological frameworks—accounts of what it is to be rational or have justified belief—allow us to identify and to articulate the epistemic faults associated with stereotyping. However, we have seen that these accounts all fail to capture some epistemic faults associated with stereotyping.

Epistemological frameworks tend to focus on either (a) the causal history of a belief or other doxastic attitude, that is, how it is formed; (b) the consequences of holding the belief or other doxastic attitude; or (c) the nature of the attitude itself (e.g. does it conform to epistemic norms?). But we have found that stereotypes can be epistemically faulty either because they are formed in a way that is not fitting with the evidence found in the social environment, or because they dispose us to make erroneous responses to information about specific cases. Put another way, stereotypes can be epistemically faulty because of their causal history or the nature of the stereotypes and the consequences of believing the stereotype, i.e. how the stereotyping belief disposes us to respond to case-specific information. Any account that focuses on only one aspect of stereotypes—causal history, consequences or nature of the stereotype itself—would fail to capture some of the epistemic faults associated with harbouring a stereotyping belief. It is necessary, then, to develop a pluralistic theoretical framework for evaluating stereotypes to capture each of the epistemic faults associated with believing them, taking into consideration the causal history, consequences, and nature of the stereotype itself.

Evaluative dispositionalism—the positive approach to evaluating stereotyping beliefs that is proposed in this book—is suitably pluralistic. According to evaluative dispositionalism, evaluations of stereotyping beliefs ought to focus on the full dispositional profile of the beliefs. This will involve considering the dispositions manifest in the process of coming to harbour the stereotyping belief (did the person display good dispositions in coming to believe stereotype A?) as well as the dispositions that are possessed as a result of harbouring the stereotyping belief. In particular, epistemic evaluations of stereotyping beliefs ought to focus on the *epistemic dispositions* associated with the beliefs; that is, dispositions that influence whether truth or falsities are believed, and, more specifically, dispositions relating to how a person responds to evidence that they encounter. By focusing on the full set of epistemic dispositions, evaluative dispositionalism reflects how we can be disposed due to believing a stereotype, whether it is true or false, to misperceive or misjudge individuals by responding poorly to case-specific information.

There are a number of other pay-offs for adopting evaluative dispositionalism. It captures the epistemic faults found in a range of different cases of stereotyping. It allows us to differentiate satisfactorily between various cases of stereotyping in which people seem to be at fault to varying degrees. It even explains how different people can hold the same stereotype in the same context while being deserving of different levels of criticism: they can manifest different dispositions in coming to harbour the stereotype or possess different dispositions as a result of harbouring the stereotype. While it is pluralistic, evaluative dispositionalism is also relatively simple and unifying, identifying the epistemic faults of stereotyping in a single place—i.e. dispositions—and providing advice that can easily be followed: i.e. *check your dispositions*. Evaluative dispositionalism also has the potential to perform important social and moral roles. It captures how societal attitudes, once internalized, can dispose people to respond poorly to evidence about and available from other members of their society. Finally, evaluative dispositionalism facilitates the identification of morally objectionable stereotypes.

Stereotypes are often morally objectionable due to being epistemically costly. By helping us to identify the epistemic costs associated with believing a stereotype, evaluative dispositionalism can therefore aid us in identifying morally objectionable stereotypes.

How, then, should you respond to a stereotype or act of stereotyping if you are interested in whether the stereotype is likely to deceive you or other people? You should consider whether the stereotype that is in operation is likely to have been formed as a result of poor epistemic dispositions, and whether it is likely to dispose those who apply it to make epistemic errors. Not all stereotypes and acts of stereotyping will be appropriate objects of criticism because some stereotypes will have been formed as the result of a disposition or dispositions to respond appropriately to evidence and will not dispose the person stereotyping to make epistemic errors. However, many stereotypes and acts of stereotyping that might have otherwise been thought to be innocuous—because the stereotypes that are applied reflect aspects of social reality—will turn out to be epistemically faulty because of the poor dispositions associated with believing the stereotypes.

Bibliography

Alexander, Larry, and Kevin Cole (1997). 'Discrimination by proxy.' *Constitutional Commentary* 14: 453–463.

Alexander, Michelle (2011). 'The new Jim Crow.' *Ohio State Journal of Criminal Law* 9: 9–27.

Allport, Gordon (1954). *The Nature of Prejudice*. New York: Perseus Publishing.

Amodio, David, and Patricia G. Devine (2008). 'On the interpersonal functions of implicit stereotyping and evaluative race bias: Insights from social neuroscience.' In *Attitudes*, pp. 213–246. Hove, UK: Psychology Press.

Anderson, Elizabeth (2010). *The Imperative of Integration*. Princeton, NJ: Princeton University Press.

Anderson, Elizabeth (2012). 'Epistemic justice as a virtue of social institutions.' *Social Epistemology* 26, no. 2: 163–173.

Angermeyer, Matthias C., and Herbert Matschinger (2003). 'Public beliefs about schizophrenia and depression: similarities and differences.' *Social Psychiatry and Psychiatric Epidemiology* 38, no. 9: 526–534.

Antony, Louise (2016). 'Bias: Friend or foe? Reflections on Saulish skepticism.' In *Implicit Bias and Philosophy* volume 1, edited by Michael Brownstein and Jennifer Saul, 157–190. Oxford: Oxford University Press.

Appiah, Kwame Anthony (1990). 'Racisms'. In *Anatomy of Racism*, edited by David Theo Goldberg, 3–17. Minneapolis, MN: University of Minnesota Press.

Arpaly, Nomy (2003). *Unprincipled Virtue: An Inquiry into Moral Agency*. Oxford: Oxford University Press.

Ashmore, Richard D., and Frances K. Del Boca (1979). 'Sex stereotypes and implicit personality theory: Toward a cognitive—Social psychological conceptualization.' *Sex Roles* 5, no. 2: 219–248.

Ashmore, Richard D., and Frances K. Del Boca (1981). 'Conceptual approaches to stereotypes and stereotyping.' *Cognitive Processes in Stereotyping and Intergroup Behavior* 1, edited by D.L. Hamilton, 1–35. Hillsdale, NJ: Erlbaum.

Audi, Robert (1972). 'The concept of believing.' *The Personalist* 53, no. 1: 43–62.

Audi, Robert (1994). 'Dispositional beliefs and dispositions to believe.' *Noûs* 28, no. 4: 419–434.

Baker, Lynne Rudder (1995). *Explaining Attitudes: A Practical Approach to the Mind*. Cambridge: Cambridge University Press.

Banks, Ralph R., and Richard T. Ford (2011). 'Does unconscious bias matter?'. *Poverty and Race* 20, no. 5: 1–2.

Bar Standards Board (2019). 'Diversity at the Bar 2019', https://www.barstandards-board.org.uk/uploads/assets/912f7278-48fc-46df-893503eb729598b8/Diversity-at-the-Bar-2019.pdf (last accessed on 26 February 2021).

Bartsch, Robert A., and Charles M. Judd (1993). 'Majority—minority status and perceived ingroup variability revisited.' *European Journal of Social Psychology* 23, no. 5: 471–483.

Basu, Rima (2019a). 'Radical moral encroachment: The moral stakes of racist beliefs.' *Philosophical Issues* 29, no. 1: 9–23.

Basu, Rima (2019b). 'The wrongs of racist beliefs.' *Philosophical Studies* 176, no. 9: 2497–2515.

Basu, Rima (2020). 'The Specter of Normative Conflict: Does Fairness Require Inaccuracy?' In *An Introduction to Implicit Bias: Knowledge, Justice, and the Social Mind*, edited by Erin Beeghly and Madva, A. (Eds.), 191–210. New York: Routledge.

Basu, Rima, and Mark Schroeder (2018). 'Doxastic wronging'. In *Pragmatic Encroachment in Epistemology*, edited by Brian Kim and Matthew McGrath. New York: Routledge.

Battaly, Heather (2008). 'Virtue epistemology.' *Philosophy Compass* 3, no. 4: 639–663.

BBC News (2020), 'Black barrister mistaken for defendant three times gets apology', 24 September 2020, https://www.bbc.co.uk/news/uk-england-essex-54281111 (last accessed on 26 February 2021).

Beale, Frances (1970). 'Double jeopardy: Black and female, A Manifesto.' *The Black Woman: An Anthology*, edited by Toni Cade. New York: Signet.

Beeghly, Erin (2015). 'What is a stereotype? What is stereotyping?' *Hypatia* 30, no. 4: 675–691.

Beeghly, Erin (2018). 'Failing to treat persons as individuals.' *Ergo* 26, no. 5: 687–711.

Begby, Endre (2013). 'The epistemology of prejudice.' *Thought: A Journal of Philosophy* 2, no. 2: 90–99.

Begby, Endre (2018). 'Doxastic morality: A moderately skeptical perspective.' *Philosophical Topics* 46, no. 1: 155–172.

Bertrand, Marianne, Dolly Chugh, and Sendhil Mullainathan (2005). 'Implicit discrimination.' *American Economic Review* 95, no. 2: 94–98.

Bishop, Michael A., and John D. Trout (2005). *Epistemology and the Psychology of Human Judgment*. Oxford: Oxford University Press.

Blair, Irene V., Jennifer E. Ma, and Alison P. Lenton (2001). 'Imagining stereotypes away: The moderation of implicit stereotypes through mental imagery.' *Journal of Personality and Social Psychology* 81, no. 5: 828–841.

Blair, Irene V., John F. Steiner, Diane L. Fairclough, Rebecca Hanratty, David W. Price, Holen K. Hirsh, et al. (2013). 'Clinicians' implicit ethnic/racial bias and perceptions of care among Black and Latino patients.' *The Annals of Family Medicine* 11, no. 1: 43–52

Blum, Lawrence (2016). 'The Too Minimal Political, Moral and Civic Dimension of Claude Steele's 'Stereotype Threat' Paradigm.' In *Implicit Bias and Philosophy, Volume 2: Moral Responsibility, Structural Injustice and Ethics*, edited by Michael Brownstein and Jennifer Saul, 147–172. Oxford: Oxford University Press.

Blum, Lawrence (2004). 'Stereotypes and stereotyping: A moral analysis.' *Philosophical Papers* 33, no. 3: 251–289.

Bodenhausen, Galen V. (1988). 'Stereotypic biases in social decision making and memory: Testing process models of stereotype use.' *Journal of Personality and Social Psychology* 55, no. 5: 726–737.

Bodenhausen, Galen V., and C. Neil Macrae (1998). 'Stereotype activation and inhibition.' *Stereotype Activation and Inhibition: Advances in Social Cognition* 11: 1–52.

Bolinger, Renée Jorgensen (2020). 'The rational impermissibility of accepting (some) racial generalizations.' *Synthese* 197, no. 6: 2415–2431.

BonJour, Laurence (1985). *The Structure of Empirical Knowledge.* Cambridge, MA: Harvard University Press.

BonJour, Laurence (2002) 'Epistemology: Classic Problems and Contemporary Responses.' Langham, MD: Rowman and Littlefield.

Bortolotti, Lisa (2015a). 'Epistemic benefits of elaborated and systematized delusions in schizophrenia.' *The British Journal for the Philosophy of Science* 67, no. 3: 879–900.

Bortolotti, Lisa (2015b). 'The epistemic innocence of motivated delusions.' *Consciousness and Cognition* 33: 490–499.

Bortolotti, Lisa (2020). *The Epistemic Innocence of Irrational Beliefs.* Oxford: Oxford University Press.

Bortolotti, Lisa, and Magdalena Antrobus (2016). 'Depressive delusions.' *Filosofia Unisinos* 17, no. 2: 192–201.

Bortolotti, Lisa, and Ema Sullivan-Bissett (2018). 'The epistemic innocence of clinical memory distortions.' *Mind and Language* 33, no. 3: 263–279.

Bos, Arjan E.R., Daphne Kanner, Peter Muris, Birgit Janssen, and Birgit Mayer (2009). 'Mental illness stigma and disclosure: Consequences of coming out of the closet.' *Issues in Mental Health Nursing* 30, no. 8: 509–513.

Braithwaite, Richard Bevan (1932). 'The nature of believing.' In *Proceedings of the Aristotelian Society*, vol. 33, 129–146. Aristotelian Society, Wiley.

Brener, Loren, Grenville Rose, Courtney von Hippel, and Hannah Wilson (2013). 'Implicit attitudes, emotions, and helping intentions of mental health workers toward their clients.' *The Journal of nervous and Mental Disease* 201, no. 6: 460–463.

Brownstein, Michael (2019). 'Implicit Bias', *The Stanford Encyclopedia of Philosophy* (Fall 2019 Edition), Edward N. Zalta (ed.), https://plato.stanford.edu/entries/implicit-bias/

Burgess, Diana J., Sean Phelan, Michael Workman, Emily Hagel, David B. Nelson, Steven S. Fu, et al. (2014). 'The effect of cognitive load and patient race on physicians' decisions to prescribe opioids for chronic low back pain: a randomized trial.' *Pain Medicine* 15, no. 6: 965–974.

Burston, Betty Watson, Dionne Jones, and Pat Roberson-Saunders (1995). 'Drug use and African Americans: Myth versus reality.' *Journal of Alcohol and Drug Education* 40, no. 2: 19–39.

Byrne, Aidan, and Alessandra Tanesini (2015). 'Instilling new habits: Addressing implicit bias in healthcare professionals.' *Advances in Health Sciences Education* 20, no. 5: 1255–1262.

Campbell, John (2009). 'What does rationality have to do with psychological causation? Propositional attitudes as mechanisms and as control variables.' In *Psychiatry as Cognitive Neuroscience: Philosophical Perspectives*, edited by Matthew Broome and Lisa Bortolotti, 137–149. Oxford: Oxford University Press.

Cantor, Nancy, and Walter Mischel (1979). 'Prototypes in person perception.' In *Advances in Experimental Social Psychology* 12: 3–52.

Carel, Havi, and Ian James Kidd (2014). 'Epistemic injustice in healthcare: A philosophical analysis.' *Medicine, Health Care and Philosophy* 17, no. 4: 529–540.

Carlston, Donal E. (1992). 'Impression formation and the modular mind: The associated systems theory.' In L.L. Martin and A. Tessler (Eds.) *The Construction of Social Judgments*, 301–341. Hillsdale, NJ: Lawrence Erlbaum Associates.

Cassam, Quassim (2015). 'Stealthy Vices.' *Social Epistemology Review and Reply Collective* 4, no. 10: 19–25.

Cherniak, Christopher (1981). 'Minimal rationality.' *Mind* 90, no. 358: 161–183.

Chiricos, Ted, and Sarah Eschholz (2002). 'The racial and ethnic typification of crime and the criminal typification of race and ethnicity in local television news.' *Journal of Research in Crime and Delinquency* 39, no. 4: 400–420.

Chiricos, Ted, Kelly Welch, and Marc Gertz (2004). 'Racial typification of crime and support for punitive measures.' *Criminology* 42, no. 2: 358–390.

Code, Lorraine (1987). *Epistemic Responsibility*. Hanover and London: University Press of New England for Brown University Press.

Cohen, Claudia E. (1981). 'Person categories and social perception: Testing some boundaries of the processing effect of prior knowledge.' *Journal of Personality and Social Psychology* 40, no. 3: 441–452.

Collins, Patricia Hill (1986). 'Learning from the outsider within: The sociological significance of Black feminist thought.' *Social Problems* 33, no. 6: s14-s32.

Collins, Patricia Hill (2000). *Black Feminist Thought: Knowledge, Consciousness, and the Politics of Empowerment*. New York: Routledge.

Conee, Earl, and Richard Feldman (2004). *Evidentialism: Essays in Epistemology*. Oxford: Oxford University Press.

Cooper, Anna Julia (1892). *A Voice from the South by a Woman of the South*. Xenia, OH: Aldine Printing House.

Cooper, Lisa A., Debra L. Roter, Kathryn A. Carson, Mary Catherine Beach, Janice A. Sabin, Anthony G. Greenwald, et al. (2012). 'The associations of clinicians' implicit attitudes about race with medical visit communication and patient ratings of interpersonal care.' *American Journal of Public Health* 102, no. 5: 979–987.

Corker, Elizabeth, Sarah Hamilton, Claire Henderson, Craig Weeks, Vanessa Pinfold, Diana Rose, et al. (2013). 'Experiences of discrimination among people using mental health services in England 2008-2011.' *The British Journal of Psychiatry* 202, no. s55: s58–s63.

Correll, Joshua, Bernadette Park, Charles M. Judd, and Bernd Wittenbrink (2002). 'The police officer's dilemma: Using ethnicity to disambiguate potentially threatening individuals.' *Journal of Personality and Social Psychology* 83, no. 6: 1314–1329.

Corrigan, Patrick W., Scott Morris, Jon Larson, Jennifer Rafacz, Abigail Wassel, Patrick Michaels, et al. (2010). 'Self-stigma and coming out about one's mental illness.' *Journal of Community Psychology* 38, no. 3: 259–275.

Corrigan, Patrick W., Scott B. Morris, Patrick J. Michaels, Jennifer D. Rafacz, and Nicolas Rüsch (2012). 'Challenging the public stigma of mental illness: A meta-analysis of outcome studies.' *Psychiatric Services* 63, no. 10: 963–973.

Corrigan, Patrick W., and Deepa Rao (2012). 'On the self-stigma of mental illness: Stages, disclosure, and strategies for change.' *The Canadian Journal of Psychiatry* 57, no. 8: 464–469.

Corrigan, Patrick W., and Amy C. Watson (2002). 'Understanding the impact of stigma on people with mental illness.' *World Psychiatry* 1, no. 1: 16–20.

Crenshaw, Kimberlé (1989). 'Demarginalizing the intersection of race and sex: A black feminist critique of antidiscrimination doctrine, feminist theory and antiracist politics.' *University of Chicago Legal Forum* 1989, no. 1: 139–167.

Crenshaw, Kimberlé (1991). 'Mapping the margins: Intersectionality, identity politics, and violence against women of color.' *Stanford Law Review* 43: 1241–1299.

Crenshaw, Kimberlé, Andrea J. Richie, Rachel Anspach, Rachel Gilmer, and Luke Harris (2015). 'Say Her Name: Resisting police brutality against Black women', July, http://static1.squarespace.com/static/53f20d90e4b0b80451158d8c/t/560c06 8ee4b0af26f72741df/1443628686535/AAPF_SMN_Brief_Full_singles-min.pdf (last accessed on 26 February 2021).

Crichton, Paul, Havi Carel, and Ian James Kidd (2017). 'Epistemic injustice in psychiatry.' *BJPsych bulletin* 41, no. 2: 65–70.

Crisp, Arthur, Michael Gelder, Eileen Goddard, and Howard Meltzer (2005). 'Stigmatization of people with mental illnesses: a follow-up study within the Changing Minds campaign of the Royal College of Psychiatrists.' *World Psychiatry* 4, no. 2: 106–113.

Crisp, Arthur H., Michael G. Gelder, Susannah Rix, Howard I. Meltzer, and Olwen J. Rowlands (2000). 'Stigmatisation of people with mental illnesses.' *The British Journal of Psychiatry* 177, no. 1: 4–7.

Dabby, Layla, Constantin Tranulis, and Laurence J. Kirmayer (2015). 'Explicit and implicit attitudes of Canadian psychiatrists toward people with mental illness.' *The Canadian Journal of Psychiatry* 60, no. 10: 451–459.

Dall'Alba, Gloria (1998). 'Medical practice as characterised by beginning medical students.' *Advances in Health Sciences Education* 3, no. 2: 101–118.

Davis, Angela (1971). 'Reflections on the Black women's role in the community of slaves', *Black Scholar* 3 (December): 2–15.

Davis, Angela (1981). *Women, Race and Class*. New York: Vintage.

De Houwer, Jan (2014). 'A propositional model of implicit evaluation.' *Social and Personality Psychology Compass* 8, no. 7: 342–353.

Dennett, Daniel C. (1971). 'Intentional systems.' *The Journal of Philosophy* 68, no. 4: 87–106.

Dennett, Daniel C. (1987). *The Intentional Stance*. Cambridge, MA: MIT Press.

Devine, Patricia G. (1989). 'Stereotypes and prejudice: Their automatic and controlled components.' *Journal of Personality and Social Psychology* 56, no. 1: 5–18.

Dijksterhuis, A.P., and A.D. Van Knippenberg (1995). 'Memory for stereotype-consistent and stereotype-inconsistent information as a function of processing pace.' *European Journal of Social Psychology* 25, no. 6: 689–693.

Dixon, Travis L., and Daniel Linz (2000). 'Overrepresentation and underrepresentation of African Americans and Latinos as lawbreakers on television news.' *Journal of Communication* 50, no. 2: 131–154.

Dixon, John, Mark Levine, Steve Reicher, and Kevin Durrheim (2012). 'Beyond prejudice: Are negative evaluations the problem and is getting us to like one another more the solution?.' *Behavioral and Brain Sciences* 35, no. 6: 411–425.

Dodson, Lisa (2013). 'Stereotyping low-wage mothers who have work and family conflicts.' *Journal of Social Issues* 69, no. 2: 257–278.

Dorfman, Lori, and Vincent Schiraldi (2001). *Off balance: Youth, race and crime in the news*. Building Blocks for Youth.

Dotson, Kristie (2011). 'Tracking epistemic violence, tracking practices of silencing.' *Hypatia* 26, no. 2: 236–257.

Dovidio, John F., and Samuel L. Gaertner (2004). 'Aversive racism.' *Advances in Experimental Social Psychology* 36: 4–56.

Draper, Catherine, and Graham Louw (2007). 'What is medicine and what is a doctor? Medical students' perceptions and expectations of their academic and professional career.' *Medical Teacher* 29, no. 5: 100–107.

Duncan, Birt L. (1976) 'Differential social perception and attribution of intergroup violence: Testing the lower limits of stereotyping of blacks.' *Journal of Personality and Social Psychology* 34, no. 4: 590–98.

Dunn, Jeffrey and Kristoffer Ahlstrom-Vij (2018). 'Introduction: Epistemic Consequentialism.' In *Epistemic Consequentialism*, edited by Kristoffer Ahlstom-Vij and Jeffrey Dunn, 1–20. Oxford: Oxford University Press.

Durante, Federica, and Susan T. Fiske (2017). 'How social-class stereotypes maintain inequality.' *Current Opinion in Psychology* 18: 43–48.

Durante, Federica, Courtney Bearns Tablante, and Susan T. Fiske (2017). 'Poor but warm, rich but cold (and competent): Social classes in the stereotype content model.' *Journal of Social Issues* 73, no. 1: 138–157.

Easwaran, Kenny (2017). 'The Tripartite Role of Belief: Evidence, Truth, and Action.' *Res Philosophica* 94, no. 2: 189–206.

Egan, Andy (2011). 'Comments on Gendler's, "The epistemic costs of implicit bias".' *Philosophical Studies* 156, no. 1: 65–79.

Entman, Robert M. (1992) 'Blacks in the news: Television, modern racism and cultural change.' *Journalism Quarterly* 69, no. 2: 341–361.

Fantl, Jeremy, and Matthew McGrath (2002). 'Evidence, pragmatics, and justification.' *The Philosophical Review* 111, no. 1: 67–94.

Fein, Steven, and Steven J. Spencer (1997). 'Prejudice as self-image maintenance: Affirming the self through derogating others.' *Journal of Personality and Social Psychology* 73, no. 1: 31–44.

Feldman, Richard, and Earl Conee (1985). 'Evidentialism.' *Philosophical Studies* 48, no. 1: 15–34.

Fishman, Joshua A. (1956). 'An examination of the process and function of social stereotyping.' *The Journal of Social Psychology* 43, no. 1: 27–64.

Fiske, Susan T., Amy J.C. Cuddy, and Peter Glick (2007). 'Universal dimensions of social cognition: Warmth and competence.' *Trends in Cognitive Sciences* 11, no. 2: 77–83.

Fiske, Susan T., and Shelley E. Taylor (1991). *Social Cognition*. New York: McGraw-Hill Book Company.

Fitzgerald, Chloë (2014). 'A neglected aspect of conscience: awareness of implicit attitudes.' *Bioethics* 28, no. 1: 24–32.

Foley, Richard (1987). *The Theory of Epistemic Rationality*. Cambridge, MA: Harvard University Press.

Franklin, John Hope, and Rafi Zabor (2005). *Mirror to America: The Autobiography of John Hope Franklin*. New York: Farrar, Straus and Giroux.

Fricker, Miranda (2007). *Epistemic injustice: Power and the Ethics of Knowing*. Oxford: Oxford University Press.

Fricker, Miranda (2016). 'Fault and No-fault Responsibility for Implicit Prejudice—A Space for Epistemic Agent-regret.' In *The Epistemic Life of Groups: Essays in the Epistemology of Collectives*, edited by Michael Brady and Miranda Fricker, 33–50. Oxford: Oxford University Press.

Fritz, James (2017). 'Pragmatic encroachment and moral encroachment.' *Pacific Philosophical Quarterly* 98: 643–661.

Fyock, Jack, and Charles Stangor (1994). 'The role of memory biases in stereotype maintenance.' *British Journal of Social Psychology* 33, no. 3: 331–343.

Gaertner, Samuel L., and John F. Dovidio (2005). 'Understanding and addressing contemporary racism: From aversive racism to the common ingroup identity model.' *Journal of Social issues* 61, no. 3: 615–639.

Gallagher, Shaun, and Daniel Hutto (2008). 'Understanding others through primary interaction and narrative practice.' *The Shared Mind: Perspectives on Intersubjectivity* 12: 17–38.

Galinsky, Adam D., Erika V. Hall, and Amy J.C. Cuddy (2013). 'Gendered races: Implications for interracial marriage, leadership selection, and athletic participation.' *Psychological Science* 24, no. 4: 498–506.

Gardiner, Georgi (2018). 'Evidentialism and moral encroachment.' In *Believing in Accordance with the Evidence*, edited by Kevin McCain, 169–195. Cham, Switzerland: Springer.

Gawronski, Bertram, Daniel Geschke, and Rainer Banse (2003). 'Implicit bias in impression formation: Associations influence the construal of individuating information.' *European Journal of Social Psychology* 33, no. 5: 573–589.

Gendler, Tamar Szabó (2008a). 'Alief and belief.' *Journal of Philosophy* 105, no. 10: 634–663.

Gendler, Tamar Szabó (2008b). 'Alief in action (and reaction).' *Mind and Language* 23, no. 5: 552–585.

Gendler, Tamar Szabó (2011). 'On the epistemic costs of implicit bias.' *Philosophical Studies* 156, no. 1: 33–63.

Gilbert, G.M. (1951) 'Stereotype persistence and change among college students.' *The Journal of Abnormal and Social Psychology*, 46, no. 2: 245–254.

Gilliam Jr, Franklin D., and Shanto Iyengar (2000). 'Prime suspects: The influence of local television news on the viewing public.' *American Journal of Political Science* 44, no. 3: 560–573.

Goff, Phillip Atiba, Margaret A. Thomas, and Matthew Christian Jackson (2008). '"Ain't I a woman?": Towards an intersectional approach to person perception and group-based harms.' *Sex Roles* 59, no. 5–6: 392–403.

Gold, Katherine J., Louise B. Andrew, Edward B. Goldman, and Thomas L. Schwenk (2016). '"I would never want to have a mental health diagnosis on my record": a survey of female physicians on mental health diagnosis, treatment, and reporting.' *General Hospital Psychiatry* 43: 51–57.

Goldman, Alvin I. (1967). 'A causal theory of knowing.' *The Journal of Philosophy* 64, no. 12: 357–372.

Goldman, Alvin I. (1979). 'What is justified belief?' In *Justification and knowledge*, 1–23. Dordrecht: Springer.

Goldman, Alvin I. (1989). 'Interpretation psychologized.' *Mind and Language* 4, no. 3: 161–185.

Goldman, Alvin I. (1999). *Knowledge in a Social World*. Oxford: Oxford University Press.

Gopnik, Alison, Andrew N. Meltzoff, and Peter Bryant (1997). *Words, Thoughts, and Theories*. Vol. 1. Cambridge, MA: MIT Press.

Gopnik, Alison, Andrew N. Meltzoff, and Patricia K. Kuhl (1999). *The Scientist in the Crib: Minds, Brains, and How Children Learn*. New York: William Morrow & Co.

Gordon, Randall A., Jennifer L. Michels, and Caroline L. Nelson (1996). 'Majority group perceptions of criminal behavior: The accuracy of race-related crime stereotypes 1.' *Journal of Applied Social Psychology* 26, no. 2: 148–159.

Gordon, Robert M. (1986). 'Folk psychology as simulation.' *Mind and Language* 1, no. 2: 158–171.

Green, Alexander R., Dana R. Carney, Daniel J. Pallin, Long H. Ngo, Kristal L. Raymond, Lisa I. Iezzoni, et al. (2007). 'Implicit bias among physicians and its prediction of thrombolysis decisions for black and white patients.' *Journal of General Internal Medicine* 22, no. 9: 1231–1238.

Greenwald, Anthony G., and Mahzarin R. Banaji (1995). 'Implicit social cognition: attitudes, self-esteem, and stereotypes.' *Psychological Review* 102, no. 1: 4–27.

Greenwald, Anthony G., Debbie E. McGhee, and Jordan L.K. Schwartz (1998). 'Measuring individual differences in implicit cognition: the implicit association test.' *Journal of Personality and Social Psychology* 74, no. 6: 1464–1480.

Haggis, Paul, and Bobby Moresco (2004). *Crash*. Film. Directed by Paul Haggis. Santa Monica, CA: Lions Gate Entertainment.

Hagiwara, Nao, Deborah A. Kashy, and Louis A. Penner (2014). 'A novel analytical strategy for patient–physician communication research: The one-with-many design.' *Patient Education and Counseling* 95, no. 3: 325–331.

Hall, Erika V., Alison V. Hall, Adam D. Galinsky, and Katherine W. Phillips (2019). 'MOSAIC: A model of stereotyping through associated and intersectional categories.' *Academy of Management Review* 44, no. 3: 643–672.

Harman, Gilbert (1986). *Change in View: Principles of Reasoning*. Cambridge, MA: MIT Press.

Haslanger, Sally (2004). 'Future Genders? Future Races?' *Philosophic Exchange* 34: 4–27.

Haslanger, Sally (2011). 'Ideology, generics, and common ground.' In *Feminist Metaphysics*, edited by Charlotte Witt, 179–207. Dordrecht: Springer.

Haslanger, Sally (2015). 'Distinguished lecture: Social structure, narrative and explanation.' *Canadian Journal of Philosophy* 45, no. 1: 1–15.

Hastie, Reid, and Purohit A. Kumar (1979). 'Person memory: Personality traits as organizing principles in memory for behaviors.' *Journal of Personality and Social Psychology* 37, no. 1: 25–38.

Hastie, Reid (1981). 'Schematic principles in human memory.' In *Social Cognition: the Ontario Symposium* vol. 1, edited by E.T. Higgins, C.P. Herman, and M.P. Zanna, 39–88. Hillsdale, NJ: Erlbaum.

Heal, Jane (1986). 'Replication and Functionalism.' In *Language, Mind and Logic*, edited by Jeremy Butterfield, 135–150. Cambridge: Cambridge University Press.

Hewstone, Miles, Richard J. Crisp, and Rhiannon N. Turner (2011). 'Perceptions of gender group variability in majority and minority contexts: Two field students with nurses and police officers.' *Social Psychology* 42, no. 2: 153–179.

Holroyd, Jules (2012). 'Responsibility for Implicit Bias.' *Journal of Social Philosophy* 43: 274–306.

Holroyd, Jules (2016). 'What Do We Want from a Model of Implicit Cognition?.' In *Proceedings of the Aristotelian Society*, vol. 116, no. 2: 153–179.

Holroyd, Jules, and Katherine Puddifoot (2020a). 'Epistemic injustice and implicit bias.' In *An Introduction to Implicit Bias: Knowledge, Justice, and the Social Mind*, edited by Erin Beeghly and Alex Madva, 116–133. New York: Routledge.

Holroyd, Jules, and Katherine Puddifoot (2020b). 'Implicit bias and prejudice.' In *The Routledge Handbook of Social Epistemology*, edited by Miranda Fricker, Nikolaj J.L.L. Pedersen, David K. Henderson, and Peter J. Graham, 313–326. New York: Routledge.

hooks, bell (1982). *Ain't I a Woman?* Bolton, MA: South End Press.

Huebner, Bryce (2016). 'Implicit bias, reinforcement learning, and scaffolded moral cognition.' In *Implicit Bias and Philosophy Volume 1: Metaphysics and Epistemology*, edited by Michael Brownstein and Jennifer Saul, 47–79. Oxford: Oxford University Press.

Hutto, Daniel D. (2012). *Folk Psychological Narratives: The Sociocultural Basis of Understanding Reasons*. Cambridge, MA: MIT Press.

Jaffe, Rona (1958). *The Best of Everything*. New York: Schuster & Schuster.

Johnson, Kerri L., Jonathan B. Freeman, and Kristin Pauker (2012). 'Race is gendered: How covarying phenotypes and stereotypes bias sex categorization.' *Journal of Personality and Social Psychology* 102, no. 1: 116–131.

Johnson, Kerri L., and Negin Ghavami (2011). 'At the crossroads of conspicuous and concealable: What race categories communicate about sexual orientation.' *PLoS One* 6, no. 3: e18025. https://doi.org/10.1371/journal.pone.0018025

Joyce, James M. (1998). 'A nonpragmatic vindication of probabilism.' *Philosophy of Science* 65, no. 4: 575–603.

Jussim, Lee, Thomas R. Cain, Jarret T. Crawford, Kent Harber, and Florette Cohen (2009). 'The unbearable accuracy of stereotypes.' *Handbook of Prejudice, Stereotyping, and Discrimination* 199: 199–227.

Jussim, Lee (2012). *Social Perception and Social Reality: Why Accuracy Dominates Bias and Self-Fulfilling Prophecy*. New York: Oxford University Press.

Kahneman, Daniel (2011). *Thinking, Fast and Slow*. New York: Macmillan.

Kahneman, Daniel, and Amos Tversky (1973). 'On the psychology of prediction.' *Psychological Review* 80, no. 4: 237–251.

Kang, Sonia K., and Alison L. Chasteen (2009). 'Beyond the double-jeopardy hypothesis: Assessing emotion on the faces of multiply-categorizable targets of prejudice.' *Journal of Experimental Social Psychology* 45, no. 6: 1281–1285.

Karlins, Marvin, Thomas L. Coffman, and Gary Walters (1969). 'On the fading of social stereotypes: studies in three generations of college students.' *Journal of Personality and Social Psychology* 13, no. 1: 1–16.

Katz, Daniel, and Kenneth Braly (1933). 'Racial stereotypes of one hundred college students.' *The Journal of Abnormal and Social Psychology* 28, no. 3: 280–290.

Kelly, Daniel, and Erica Roedder (2008). 'Racial cognition and the ethics of implicit bias.' *Philosophy Compass* 3, no. 3: 522–540.

King, Deborah K. (1988). 'Multiple jeopardy, multiple consciousness: The context of a Black feminist ideology.' *Signs: Journal of Women in Culture and Society* 14, no. 1: 42–72.

Kolodziej, Monika E., and Blair T. Johnson (1996). 'Interpersonal contact and acceptance of persons with psychiatric disorders: A research synthesis.' *Journal of Consulting and Clinical Psychology* 64, no. 6: 1387–1396.

Kopera, M., Suszek, H., Bonar, E., Myszka, M., Gmaj, B., Ilgen, M., et al. (2015). Evaluating Explicit and Implicit Stigma of Mental Illness in Mental Health Professionals and Medical Students. *Community Mental Health Journal* 51, 628–634.

Kornblith, Hilary (1983). 'Justified belief and epistemically responsible action.' *The Philosophical Review* 92, no. 1: 33–48.

Kornblith, Hilary (1989). 'Introspection and misdirection.' *Australasian Journal of Philosophy* 67, no. 4: 410–422.

Lackey, Jennifer (2005). 'Memory as a generative epistemic source.' *Philosophy and Phenomenological Research* 70, no. 3: 636–658.

Lai, Calvin K., Maddalena Marini, Steven A. Lehr, Carlo Cerruti, Jiyun-Elizabeth L. Shin, Jennifer A. Joy-Gaba, et al. (2014). 'Reducing implicit racial preferences: I. A comparative investigation of 17 interventions.' *Journal of Experimental Psychology: General* 143, no. 4: 1765–1785.

Lai, Calvin K., Allison L. Skinner, Erin Cooley, Sohad Murrar, Markus Brauer, Thierry Devos, et al. (2016) 'Reducing implicit racial preferences: II. Intervention effectiveness across time.' *Journal of Experimental Psychology: General* 145, no. 8: 1001–1016.

Lasonen-Aarnio, Maria (2010). 'Unreasonable knowledge.' *Philosophical Perspectives* 24: 1–21.

Lasonen-Aarnio, Maria (2020). 'Enkrasia or evidentialism? Learning to love mismatch.' *Philosophical Studies* 177: 597–632.

Lassiter, Charles, and Nathan Ballantyne (2017). 'Implicit racial bias and epistemic pessimism.' *Philosophical Psychology* 30, no. 1–2: 79–101.

Le Rue, Linda (1970). 'The Black movement and women's liberation.' *Black Scholar 1* (May): 36–42.

Leslie, Sarah-Jane (2007). 'Generics and the structure of the mind.' *Philosophical Perspectives* 21: 375–403.

Letheby, Chris (2016). 'The epistemic innocence of psychedelic states.' *Consciousness and Cognition* 39: 28–37.

Levinson, Justin D. (2007). 'Forgotten racial equality: Implicit bias, decision making, and misremembering.' *Duke LJ* 57: 345–424.

Levy, Neil (2015). 'Neither fish nor fowl: Implicit attitudes as patchy endorsements.' *Noûs* 49, no. 4: 800–823.

Lindqvist, Anna, Fredrik Björklund, and Martin Bäckström (2017). 'The perception of the poor: Capturing stereotype content with different measures.' *Nordic Psychology* 69, no. 4: 231–247.

Link, Bruce G., Jo C. Phelan, Michaeline Bresnahan, Ann Stueve, and Bernice A. Pescosolido (1999). 'Public conceptions of mental illness: labels, causes, dangerousness, and social distance.' *American Journal of Public Health* 89, no. 9: 1328–1333.

Lippmann, Walter (1922). *Public Opinion*. New York: Harcourt, Brace and co.

Lord, Charles G., Lee Ross, and Mark R. Lepper (1979). 'Biased assimilation and attitude polarization: The effects of prior theories on subsequently considered evidence.' *Journal of Personality and Social Psychology* 37, no. 11: 2098–2109.

Lorde, Audre (1984). *Sister Outsider*. Trumansburg, NY: Crossing Press.

Los Angeles County Commission on Human Relations (2016). 'Hate Crime Report', https://hrc.lacounty.gov/wp-content/uploads/2019/08/2016-Annual-Report-of-Hate-Crime-in-Los-Angeles-County.pdf (last accessed on 10 May 2021).

Loughnan, Steve, Nick Haslam, Robbie M. Sutton, and Bettina Spencer (2014). 'Dehumanization and social class.' *Social Psychology* 45: 54–61.

Lubiano, Wahneema (1992). '*Black ladies, welfare queens, and state minstrels: Ideological war by narrative means.*' In *Race-ing Justice, En-gendering Power: essays on Anita Hill, Clarence Thomas and the Construction of Social Reality*, edited by Toni Morrison, 323–363. New York: Pantheon Books.

Machery, Edouard (2016). 'De-Freuding implicit attitudes.' In *Implicit Bias and Philosophy Volume 1: Metaphysics and Epistemology*, edited by Michael Brownstein and Jennifer Saul, 104–129. Oxford: Oxford University Press.

Madva, Alex (2016a). 'Why implicit attitudes are (probably) not beliefs.' *Synthese* 193, no. 8: 2659–2684.

Madva, Alex (2016b). 'Virtue, social knowledge, and implicit bias.' In *Implicit Bias and Philosophy, Volume 1: Metaphysics and Epistemology*, edited by Michael Brownstein and Jennifer Saul, 191–215. Oxford: Oxford University Press.

Madva, Alex (2016c). 'A plea for anti-anti-individualism: How oversimple psychology misleads social policy.' *Ergo, an Open Access Journal of Philosophy* 3. https://doi.org/10.3998/ergo.12405314.0003.027

Mandelbaum, Eric (2013). 'Against alief.' *Philosophical Studies* 165, no. 1: 197–211.

Mandelbaum, Eric (2016). 'Attitude, inference, association: On the propositional structure of implicit bias.' *Noûs* 50, no. 3: 629–658.

Manis, Melvin, Thomas E. Nelson, and Jonathan Shedler (1988). 'Stereotypes and social judgment: Extremity, assimilation, and contrast.' *Journal of Personality and Social Psychology* 55, no. 1: 28–36.

Marcus, Ruth Barcan (1990). 'Some revisionary proposals about belief and believing.' *Philosophy and Phenomenological Research* 50, Supp: 133–153.

Mathur, Vani A., Jennifer A. Richeson, Judith A. Paice, Michael Muzyka, and Joan Y. Chiao (2014). 'Racial bias in pain perception and response: Experimental examination of automatic and deliberate processes.' *The Journal of Pain* 15, no. 5: 476–484.

Matthew, Dayna Bowen (2015). *Just Medicine: A Cure for Racial Inequality in American Health Care*. New York: New York University Press.

Medina, José (2013). *The Epistemology of Resistance: Gender and Racial Oppression, Epistemic Injustice, and the Social Imagination*. Oxford: Oxford University Press.

Miller, David I., Alice H. Eagly, and Marcia C. Linn (2015). 'Women's representation in science predicts national gender-science stereotypes: Evidence from 66 nations.' *Journal of Educational Psychology* 107, no. 3: 631–644.

Mills, Charles (2007). 'White ignorance.' In *Race and Epistemologies of Ignorance* edited by Shannon Sullivan and Nancy Tuana, 11–38. New York: Suny Press.

Montmarquet, James (1992). 'Epistemic virtue and doxastic responsibility.' *American Philosophical Quarterly* 29, no. 4: 331–341.

Moskowitz, Gordon B., Jeff Stone, and Amanda Childs (2012). 'Implicit stereotyping and medical decisions: unconscious stereotype activation in practitioners' thoughts about African Americans.' *American Journal of Public Health* 102, no. 5: 996–1001.

Moss, Sarah (2018a). *Probabilistic Knowledge*. Oxford: Oxford University Press.

Moss, Sarah (2018b). 'IX—Moral Encroachment.' In *Proceedings of the Aristotelian Society*, vol. 118, no. 2: 177–205.

Mugg, Joshua (2013). 'What are the cognitive costs of racism? A reply to Gendler.' *Philosophical studies* 166, no. 2: 217–229.

Nolan, Jacqueline, Tajan Braithwaite Renderos, Jane Hynson, Xue Dai, Wendy Chow, Anita Christie, et al. (2014). 'Barriers to cervical cancer screening and follow-up care among black women in Massachusetts.' *Journal of Obstetric, Gynecologic and Neonatal Nursing* 43, no. 5: 580–588.

Nosek, Brian A., Frederick L. Smyth, Natarajan Sriram, Nicole M. Lindner, Thierry Devos, Alfonso Ayala, et al. (2009). 'National differences in gender–science stereotypes predict national sex differences in science and math achievement.' *Proceedings of the National Academy of Sciences* 106, no. 26: 10593–10597.

O'Driscoll, Claire, Caroline Heary, Eilis Hennessy, and Lynn McKeague (2012). 'Explicit and implicit stigma towards peers with mental health problems in childhood and adolescence.' *Journal of Child Psychology and Psychiatry* 53, no. 10: 1054–1062.

Office of Applied Studies, Substance Abuse and Mental Health Services Administration (2007). *National Survey on Drug Use and Health: Demographic and Geographic Variations in Injection Drug Use*. Washington, DC: US Department of Health and Human Services.

Payne, B. Keith, and Bertram Gawronski (2010). 'A history of implicit social cognition: Where is it coming from? Where is it now? Where is it going.' *Handbook of Implicit Social Cognition: Measurement, Theory, and Applications* 1: 1–15.

Penner, Louis A., John F. Dovidio, Tessa V. West, Samuel L. Gaertner, Terrance L. Albrecht, Rhonda K. Dailey, et al. (2010). 'Aversive racism and medical interactions with Black patients: A field study.' *Journal of Experimental Social Psychology* 46, no. 2: 436–440.

Peris, Tara S., Bethany A. Teachman, and Brian A. Nosek (2008). 'Implicit and explicit stigma of mental illness: Links to clinical care.' *The Journal of Nervous and Mental Disease* 196, no. 10: 752–760.

Pettigrew, Thomas F., and Linda R. Tropp (2005). 'Allport's intergroup contact hypothesis: Its history and influence.' In *On the Nature of Prejudice: Fifty Years after Allport*, edited by J. F. Dovidio, P. Glick, and L. A. Rudman, 262–277. Malden, MA: Blackwell Publishing.

Phelan, Jo C., Bruce G. Link, Ann Stueve, and Bernice A. Pescosolido (2000). 'Public conceptions of mental illness in 1950 and 1996: What is mental illness and is it to be feared?.' *Journal of Health and Social Behavior* 41, no. 2: 188–207.

Pickett, Justin T., Ted Chiricos, Kristin M. Golden, and Marc Gertz (2012). 'Reconsidering the relationship between perceived neighborhood racial composition and whites' perceptions of victimization risk: do racial stereotypes matter?.' *Criminology* 50, no. 1: 145–186.

Pinfold, Vanessa, Hilary Toulmin, Graham Thornicroft, Peter Huxley, Paul Farmer, and Tanya Graham (2003). 'Reducing psychiatric stigma and discrimination: evaluation of educational interventions in UK secondary schools.' *The British Journal of Psychiatry* 182, no. 4: 342–346.

Price, H.H. (1969) *Belief*. London: Allen and Unwin.

Pritchard, Duncan (2014). *What is this Thing Called Knowledge?*. Abingdon: Routledge,.

Pritchard, Duncan (2016). 'Ignorance and epistemic value.' In *The Epistemic Dimensions of Ignorance*, edited by Rik Peels and Martijn Blaauw, 132–143. Cambridge: Cambridge University Press.

Puddifoot, Katherine (2017). 'Dissolving the epistemic/ethical dilemma over implicit bias.' *Philosophical Explorations* 20, no. sup1: 73–93.

Puddifoot, Katherine, and Lisa Bortolotti (2019). 'Epistemic innocence and the production of false memory beliefs.' *Philosophical Studies* 176, no. 3: 755–780.

Quillian, Lincoln, and Devah Pager (2010). 'Estimating risk: Stereotype amplification and the perceived risk of criminal victimization.' *Social Psychology Quarterly* 73, no. 1: 79–104.

Quine, W.V., and Joseph S. Ullian (1970). *The Web of Belief*. New York: Random House.

Reimer, Marga (2011). 'A Davidsonian perspective on psychiatric delusions.' *Philosophical Psychology* 24, no. 5: 659–677.

Richeson, Jennifer A., and J. Nicole Shelton (2007). 'Negotiating interracial interactions: Costs, consequences, and possibilities.' *Current Directions in Psychological Science* 16, no. 6: 316–320.

Richie, Beth (1985). 'Battered Black women: A challenge for the black community.' *Black Scholar* 16 (March/April): 40–44.

Rojahn, Krystyna, and Thomas F. Pettigrew (1992). 'Memory for schema-relevant information: A meta-analytic resolution.' *British Journal of Social Psychology* 31, no. 2: 81–109.

Root, Michael (2000). 'How we divide the world.' *Philosophy of Science* 67: S628–S639.

Rothbart, Myron, Mark Evans, and Solomon Fulero (1979). 'Recall for confirming events: Memory processes and the maintenance of social stereotypes.' *Journal of Experimental Social Psychology* 15, no. 4: 343–355.

Rothbart, Myron, Solomon Fulero, Christine Jensen, John Howard, and Pamela Birrell (1978). 'From individual to group impressions: Availability heuristics in stereotype formation.' *Journal of Experimental Social Psychology* 14, no. 3: 237–255.

Rüsch, Nicolas, Elvira Abbruzzese, Eva Hagedorn, Daniel Hartenhauer, Ilias Kaufmann, Jan Curschellas, et al. (2014) 'Efficacy of Coming Out Proud to reduce stigma's impact among people with mental illness: pilot randomised controlled trial.' *The British Journal of Psychiatry* 204, no. 5: 391–397.

Rüsch, Nicolas, Patrick W. Corrigan, Andrew R. Todd, and Galen V. Bodenhausen (2011). 'Automatic stereotyping against people with schizophrenia, schizoaffective and affective disorders.' *Psychiatry Research* 186, no. 1: 34–39.

Sagar, H. Andrew, and Janet W. Schofield (1980). 'Racial and behavioral cues in Black and White children's perceptions of ambiguously aggressive acts.' *Journal of Personality and Social Psychology* 39, no. 4: 590–98.

Samuels, Richard, Stephen Stich, and Luc Faucher (2004). 'Reason and rationality.' In *Handbook of Epistemology*, 131–179. Dordrecht: Springer.

Sanbonmatsu, David M., Sharon A. Akimoto, and Bryan D. Gibson (1994). 'Stereotype-based blocking in social explanation.' *Personality and Social Psychology Bulletin* 20, no. 1: 71–81.

Sanford, R. Nevitt, Theodor W. Adorno, Else Frenkel-Brunswik, and Daniel J. Levinson (1950). *The Authoritarian Personality*. New York: Harper and Row.

Saul, Jennifer (2013). 'Scepticism and implicit bias.' *Disputatio* 5, no. 37: 243–263.

Schauer, Frederick (2017). 'Statistical (and non-statistical) discrimination.' In *The Routledge Handbook of the Ethics of Discrimination*, edited by Kasper Lippert-Rasmussen, 42–53. Abingdon: Routledge.

Schwitzgebel, Eric (2002). 'A phenomenal, dispositional account of belief.' *Noûs* 36, no. 2: 249–275.

Schwitzgebel, Eric (2010). 'Acting contrary to our professed beliefs or the gulf between occurrent judgment and dispositional belief.' *Pacific Philosophical Quarterly* 91, no. 4: 531–553.

Schwitzgebel, Eric (2017). 'A dispositional approach to attitudes: Thinking outside of the belief box.' In *New Essays on Belief*, edited by Nikolaj Nottlemann, 75–99. London: Palgrave Macmillan.

Senor, Thomas D. (1993). 'Internalistic foundationalism and the justification of memory belief.' *Synthese* 94, no. 3: 453–476.

Sesko, Amanda K., and Monica Biernat (2010). 'Prototypes of race and gender: The invisibility of Black women.' *Journal of Experimental Social Psychology* 46, no. 2: 356–360.

Sesko, Amanda K., and Monica Biernat (2018). 'Invisibility of Black women: Drawing attention to individuality.' *Group Processes and Intergroup Relations* 21, no. 1: 141–158.

Shalby, Colleen (2017). 'What's the difference between "looting" and "finding"? 12 years after Katrina, Harvey sparks a new debate', *Los Angeles Times*, 29 August 2017, https://www.latimes.com/nation/la-na-harvey-20170829-story.html (last accessed on 26 February 2021).

Signorella, Margaret L., and Lynn S. Liben (1984). 'Recall and reconstruction of gender-related pictures: Effects of attitude, task difficulty, and age.' *Child Development* 55, no. 2: 393–405.

Sinclair, Lisa, and Ziva Kunda (1999). 'Reactions to a black professional: motivated inhibition and activation of conflicting stereotypes.' *Journal of Personality and Social Psychology* 77, no. 5: 885–904.

Smith, Eliot R., and Michael A. Zarate (1992). 'Exemplar-based model of social judgment.' *Psychological Review* 99, no. 1: 3–21.

Sosa, Ernest (1991). *Knowledge in Perspective: Selected Essays in Epistemology.* Cambridge: Cambridge University Press.

Sosa, Ernest (2007). *A Virtue Epistemology: Apt Belief and Reflective Knowledge Vol. 1.* Oxford: Oxford University Press.

Spencer, Steven J., Steven Fein, Connie T. Wolfe, Christina Fong, and Meghan A. Duinn (1998). 'Automatic activation of stereotypes: The role of self-image threat.' *Personality and Social Psychology Bulletin* 24, no. 11: 1139–1152.

Spillers, Hortense J. (1987). 'Mama's baby, papa's maybe: An American grammar book.' *Diacritics* 17, no. 2: 65–81.

Srull, Thomas K. (1981). 'Person memory: Some tests of associative storage and retrieval models.' *Journal of Experimental Psychology: Human Learning and Memory* 7, no. 6: 440–63.

Srull, Thomas K., Meryl Lichtenstein, and Myron Rothbart (1985). 'Associative storage and retrieval processes in person memory.' *Journal of Experimental Psychology: Learning, Memory, and Cognition* 11, no. 2: 316–345.

Srull, Thomas K., and Robert S. Wyer (1989). 'Person memory and judgment.' *Psychological Review* 96, no. 1: 58–83.

Stangor, Charles, and David McMillan (1992). 'Memory for expectancy-congruent and expectancy-incongruent information: A review of the social and social developmental literatures.' *Psychological Bulletin* 111, no. 1: 42–61.

Stangor, Charles (1988). 'Stereotype accessibility and information processing.' *Personality and Social Psychology Bulletin* 14, no. 4: 694–708.

Stein, Edward (1996). *Without Good Reason: The Rationality Debate in Philosophy and Cognitive Science.* Oxford: Oxford University Press.

Stewart, Brandon D., and B. Keith Payne (2008). 'Bringing automatic stereotyping under control: Implementation intentions as efficient means of thought control.' *Personality and Social Psychology Bulletin* 34, no. 10: 1332–1345.

Stone, Jeff, and Gordon B. Moskowitz (2011). 'Non-conscious bias in medical decision making: what can be done to reduce it?.' *Medical Education* 45, no. 8: 768–776.

Sturm, Roland (2002). 'The effects of obesity, smoking, and drinking on medical problems and costs.' *Health Affairs* 21, no. 2: 245–253.

Substance Abuse and Mental Health Services Administration (2004). 'Results from the 2003 National Survey on Drug Use and Health (NSDUH): National Findings', 2004, https://www.datafiles.samhsa.gov/study/national-survey-drug-use-and-health-nsduh-2003-nid13569 (last accessed 10 May 2021).

Sullivan-Bissett, Ema (2015). 'Implicit bias, confabulation, and epistemic innocence.' *Consciousness and Cognition* 33: 548–560.

Sullivan-Bissett, Ema (2018). 'Biased by our imaginings.' *Mind and Language* 34, 5: 627–647.

Tajfel, Henri (1981). *Human Groups and Social Categories: Studies in Social Psychology.* Cambridge: Cambridge University Press.

Takahashi, Hidehiko, Takashi Ideno, Shigetaka Okubo, Hiroshi Matsui, Kazuhisa Takemura, Masato Matsuura, et al. (2009). 'Impact of changing the Japanese term for "schizophrenia" for reasons of stereotypical beliefs of schizophrenia in Japanese youth.' *Schizophrenia Research* 112, no. 1–3: 149–152.

Teachman, Bethany A., Joel G. Wilson, and Irina Komarovskaya (2006). 'Implicit and explicit stigma of mental illness in diagnosed and healthy samples.' *Journal of Social and Clinical Psychology* 25, no. 1: 75–95.

Terrell, Mary Church (1995). 'The progress of colored women.' In *Words of Fire: An Anthology of African-American Feminist Thought*, edited by Beverly Guy-Sheftall, 64–68. New York: The New Press.

Thornicroft, Graham, Diana Rose, and Aliya Kassam (2007). 'Discrimination in health care against people with mental illness.' *International Review of Psychiatry* 19, no. 2: 113–122.

Time to Change (2008), 'Stigma Shout Service user and carer experiences of stigma and discrimination', https://www.time-to-change.org.uk/sites/default/files/Stigma%20Shout.pdf (last accessed on 26 February 2021).

Time to Change (2015), 'Attitudes to Mental Illness 2014 Research Report', https://www.time-to-change.org.uk/sites/default/files/Attitudes_to_mental_illness_2014_report_final_0.pdf (last accessed on 26 February 2021).

Todd, Andrew R., Kelsey C. Thiem, and Rebecca Neel (2016). 'Does seeing faces of young black boys facilitate the identification of threatening stimuli?' *Psychological Science* 27, no. 3: 384–393.

Uhlmann, Eric Luis, Victoria L. Brescoll, and Edouard Machery (2010). 'The motives underlying stereotype-based discrimination against members of stigmatized groups.' *Social Justice Research* 23, no. 1: 1–16.

Valian, Virginia (1999). *Why So Slow? The Advancement of Women*. Cambridge, MA: MIT Press.

Valian, Virginia (2005). 'Beyond gender schemas: Improving the advancement of women in academia.' *Hypatia* 20, no. 3: 198–213.

Vasquez, Tina (2015). 'I've experienced a new level of racism since Donald Trump went after Latinos', *Guardian*, 9 September 2015, https://www.theguardian.com/commentisfree/2015/sep/09/donald-trump-racism-increase-latinos (last accessed on 26 February 2021).

Volpato, Chiara, Luca Andrighetto, and Cristina Baldissarri (2017). 'Perceptions of low-status workers and the maintenance of the social class status quo.' *Journal of Social Issues* 73, no. 1: 192–210.

Wade, Lisa (2013). 'Two 7-year-old boys, two dramatically different news stories', Huffpost, 24 July 2013, https://tinyurl.com/pbfattr4 (last accessed on 10 May 2021).

Walker, Alice (1988). 'In the closet of the soul.' In *Living by the word: Selected writings, 1973–1987*. Houghton Mifflin Harcourt.

Wason, Peter C. (1960) 'On the failure to eliminate hypotheses in a conceptual task.' *Quarterly Journal of Experimental Psychology* 12, no. 3: 129–140.

Waytz, Adam, Kelly Marie Hoffman, and Sophie Trawalter (2015). 'A superhumanization bias in Whites' perceptions of Blacks.' *Social Psychological and Personality Science* 6, no. 3: 352–359.

Weisbuch, Max, Kristin Pauker, and Nalini Ambady (2009). "The subtle transmission of race bias via televised nonverbal behavior." *Science* 326, no. 5960: 1711–1714.

White III, Augustus (2014). "Some advice for minorities and women on the receiving end of health-care disparities." *Journal of Racial and Ethnic Health Disparities* 1: 61–66.

Williamson, Timothy (forthcoming). "Justification, excuses and sceptical scenarios". In *The New Evil Demon*, edited by Julien Dutant and Fabian Dorsch. Oxford: Oxford University Press, forthcoming.

WISE (2018). "Workforce Statistics", https://www.wisecampaign.org.uk/statistics/2018-workforce-statistics/ (last accessed on 26 February 2021).

Wood, Lisa, Michele Birtel, Sarah Alsawy, Melissa Pyle, and Anthony Morrison (2014). "Public perceptions of stigma towards people with schizophrenia, depression, and anxiety." *Psychiatry Research* 220, no. 1–2: 604–608.

Zagzebski, Linda Trinkau (1996). *Virtues of the Mind: An Inquiry into the Nature of Virtue and the Ethical Foundations of Knowledge*. Cambridge: Cambridge University Press.

Index

For the benefit of digital users, indexed terms that span two pages (e.g., 52–53) may, on occasion, appear on only one of those pages.

The issue is not so much
fighting against one's own and
others' stereotypes — they
are inevitable. Rather, realizing
the moral & ethical implications
of repeatedly them publicly.

It's impossible not to categorize;
~~are too~~ evolution has hard
wired us to do this. Categorization
requires stereotypes, when

The link between
epistemic injustice (p 53-4)
+ stereotypes is
good reason to tackle
autoe! Susan Gray in
Tracking Tolerance
+ Grear er. al.
Restorying Narrative
identity

(p 53 this book

Caution for autoethnographers:
implicit biases can act both
ways — leads to epistemic
injustices via stereotypes — + leading Lessons on
to autoethnographer unable to see is blocked
the whole humanity. Humans traduces
so some people empiricity (or surveilpes
ert plurally) stereotyped: Babes, Lovers,
Freeman (boom I have too)
— Epistemic gains can be made pro
watchdog stereotypes: stereotypes can
obscure knowledge above the other ad events;
can act as a substitute for accurate
+ empathic under